JOURNEY TO
SERVICE-LEARNING

EXPERIENCES FROM INDEPENDENT LIBERAL ARTS COLLEGES AND UNIVERSITIES

BY ROBERT L. SIGMON AND COLLEAGUES

This book was produced with funding from Special Friends of CIC.

CIC

THE COUNCIL OF INDEPENDENT COLLEGES

Stephen G. Pelletier

General Editor

ISBN: 0-937012-12-2

Printed in the United States of America

The members of the Council of Independent Colleges work together to support college leadership, advance institutional excellence, and enhance private higher education's contributions to society. CIC provides ideas, resources, and services that assist institutions to improve leadership expertise, educational programs, administrative and financial performance, and institutional visibility. The Council was founded in 1956. In 1993, CIC expanded its programs through the acquisition of CAPHE, the Consortium for the Advancement of Private Higher Education. CIC's membership includes more than 400 colleges and universities, 20 state, regional and national associations as affiliate members, and 60 corporations and foundations as sponsoring members.

Copies of this publication can be purchased from the Council of Independent Colleges. Call or write CIC for a list of other publications.

Council of Independent Colleges
One Dupont Circle, Suite 320
Washington, DC 20036
(202) 466-7230   Fax (202) 466-7238   cic@cic.nche.edu

On the cover: Photo by Frank Miller, courtesy of Alverno College.

DEDICATION AND ACKNOWLEDGEMENTS

This book is dedicated to the community residents throughout the country who have been increasingly educating students at independent liberal arts colleges; to those students and faculty who have joined with these citizens in forging creative service and learning programs in recent years; and to the next generations of college students who will benefit from the experiences reported here from the journey to Service-Learning.

At one point in the early 1970s, I heard a speaker say that the "young of this country need to be surprised by some tremendous thing." Service-Learning is "some tremendous thing" when it is working for the benefit of citizens and students in mutual pacts of endeavor. You will find in this book a series of snapshots of a "tremendous thing" as voiced by citizens, students, faculty, and community service practitioners.

A great number of people, not listed here as authors, contributed ideas and thoughts to this book, along with the staff and faculty members of the 30 colleges and universities in the Council of Independent Colleges Alliance for Service-Learning, who contributed much in the course of three lively working seminars in 1994 and 1995.

Robert L. Sigmon

TABLE OF CONTENTS

APPENDICES

PREFACE

In late 1993, when I announced what was then the largest externally funded program in CIC's history—on Service-Learning—I wrote that the independent liberal arts colleges in our network will make an important contribution to society by developing and sharing a next generation of Service-Learning programs. We wanted to demonstrate our commitment to linking service and learning as an important goal of higher education; offer ideas to the nationwide community of Service-Learning practitioners; and demonstrate how independent colleges, working together, contribute to society.

This book is a result of that effort. It draws on the work of 30 colleges and universities that collaborated in a CIC-sponsored Learning and Service Alliance, and another 145 institutions that joined them in CIC's highly successful National Institute on Learning and Service in June 1995. In engaging with and listening to their stories, CIC Senior Associate Robert Sigmon and his colleagues have identified a powerful set of ideas that can guide developing Service-Learning initiatives, and help existing programs find new ways to partner with communities. I congratulate them on these contributions.

With this collection, we want to capture ideas emerging from recent work and set a continuing agenda. This volume, particularly in the last section, takes seriously CIC's own ambitious rhetoric about advancing toward a "next generation" of Service-Learning. We articulate that goal knowing that the spirit which undergirds the framework of such relationships—between faculty and community organization leaders, between students and citizens—is in many cases more vision than practice. There is clearly much more work to be done. Importantly, however, the kind of progress outlined in this book strengthens our original conviction that the nation's independent colleges and universities are uniquely suited—by virtue of their missions, histories, and connections with communities—to lead higher education to a next generation of Service-Learning.

Hence we suggest that we are on a journey—one in which we are interested in where we have been, where we are now, and where we might go in the future. Our journey to Service-Learning is an ongoing trip, an evolving experience. To continue the metaphor, we do not intend this book so much as a road map for our journey than as a guidebook. These chapters report on what we have found to work, and what we expect might work in the future. These are suggestions here, not dictates. They are ideas for our continuing journey as educators.

Each of the participants—

student, community

resident, faculty, and

community agency

representative—is seen as

contributor and beneficiary,

each a teacher and a learner.

he first section of *Journey* refreshingly opens a conversation on some possible definitions of Service-Learning and why it is important for each community and college to work out its own meanings and processes. An important contribution here is Robert Sigmon's two chapters, one titled "Design Considerations" and the other titled "The Reflective Arts." The "Design" chapter suggests an approach to involving multiple participants in the planning, implementation, and evaluation of Service-Learning programs. A distinctive feature in this design approach is that each of the participants—student, community resident, faculty, and community agency representative—is seen as contributor *and* beneficiary, each a teacher *and* a learner. This design lifts up and celebrates the key principle of mutuality among the participants. The chapter on reflective arts highlights subtle approaches for each of the Service-Learning participants to reflect on their experience through open conversations, and "contesting common sense cultural meanings."

In Section Two, *Journey* lifts up the distinctive voices of residents in communities who assist in teaching students and who in turn are sometimes served by students and faculty, the voices of community groups, the voices of students, and the voices of independent college faculty. As I listened to these voices, I was aware of the importance of relationships among the participants in a Service-Learning enterprise. These stories from the direct experience of participants in well-designed Service-Learning programs offer a potpourri of examples for others to draw upon for their own program design.

Five points of view from independent liberal arts higher education are shared in Section Three. Here is some creative and imaginative thinking about rationales and practices for linking service and learning within our network of colleges. John Eby makes a passionate plea for linking service with scholarship. Richard Slimbach outlines a detailed and elegant design for a departmental focus on outcomes for Service-Learning students. Yoram Lubling describes how a college set in motion a new course for pedagogy and how the department of philosophy took hold of it, and in detail shows us how a service orientation in one of his courses was introduced and practiced. Matthew Berndt describes how student affairs and academic affairs planned and implemented together a creative Career Development Program linked by a Service-Learning design. The last article in this section discusses the importance of deciding to evaluate what you set out to do. The editor, with Nancy Hemesath and Sister Grace Ann Witte, presents excerpts from an evaluation design created in a first-year Service-Learning program.

The final section pushes the edge for many of us, as the editors introduce us to some "next generation" possibilities. Are we willing to put more and more influence into the hands of developing imaginations in our communities, with students, and among our faculty as we link service and learning in our curriculum and programs? CIC is not suggesting by including this material that these are necessarily the prescribed next steps in the journey. As the *Journey To Service-Learning* continues, we see the next generation suggestions made here as possibilities for consideration, adaptation, or implementation. Indeed, there are many that will be or have already been acted upon.

There is in this book, and its rich collection of experiences, an overarching sense that Service-Learning *works*. Service-Learning *makes a difference*. It transforms and enriches student learning. It can have the same effect on faculty development. It can renew administrators' commitments to students, values, and the educational mission as a whole. And overall, Service-Learning can help institutions fulfill the explicit commitments of their missions to help their various communities—be they churches, neighbors, other colleges, the nation, or society as a whole—and to learn as institutions from that experience. Service-Learning is a powerful educational movement that speaks to the heart of the mission of most liberal arts colleges and universities today.

Also implicit throughout this book is the inherent value of *community*. Service-Learning is fundamentally about working with others for the betterment of all. That sentiment reflects a founding principle of the Council of Independent Colleges. It also guides and informs other current CIC programs—among them, efforts to help economically disadvantaged students succeed in college; drawing participants in college teacher education programs into collaborative work with local schools; and helping colleges in urban areas find effective ways to contribute to their communities. The CIC concept of community extends also to our long-term programs designed to link historically black private colleges with fellow private liberal arts institutions throughout CIC. Another set of CIC initiatives links CIC colleges via information technology in a virtual community. And of course the Council itself is a community, of colleges and their leaders, banded together for the common good.

It is my hope that, taken as a whole, the stories, lessons, and passions shared in this publication will stimulate conversations among administrators, faculty, students, community residents and community leaders as we all seek to find ways to link the dilemmas of our world order/disorder with creative learning approaches. CIC is committed to support the linking of service, which makes positive contributions to the life of communities, and learning, which inspires and prepares young people and those they work with to be able citizens and lifelong learners.

Allen P. Splete
President
Council of Independent Colleges
Washington, D.C.
September 1996

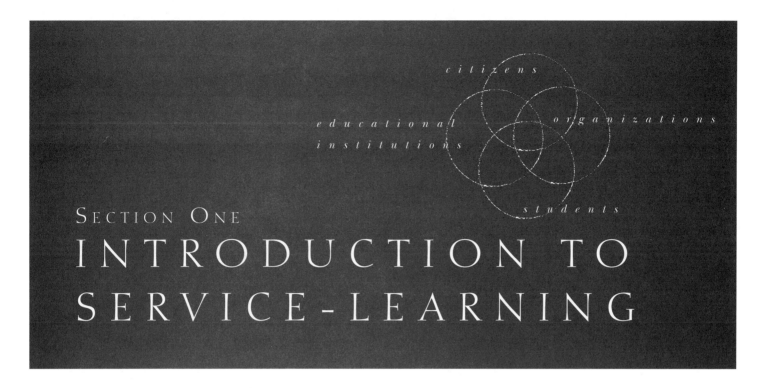

INTRODUCTION TO SERVICE-LEARNING

Service-Learning

... is the coming together of all four parties as teachers *and* learners, beneficiaries *and* contributors.

CITIZENS
as teachers/learners
contributors/beneficiaries,
includes:
    individuals
    families
    groups
    neighborhoods
    communities

EDUCATIONAL INSTITUTIONS
includes all types:
    trustees/board
    alumni
    administrators
    faculty
    student services
    other staff

ORGANIZATIONS
student mentor/supervisor as:
    direct provider of care
    technology support staff
    policymaker/top manager
        in
    private, public, nonprofit
    and community-based
    organizations

STUDENTS
including their:
    exposure experiences
    capacity-building opportunities
    practice and responsibility

CHAPTER 1

AN INTRODUCTION TO
SERVICE-LEARNING

Or, An Open Letter To College And University Leaders Committed To Creating Conditions For Students To Contribute And Learn

BY ROBERT L. SIGMON

Service-Learning is rooted in these fundamental intentions and actions:

1. The desire to and practice of contributing (serving, caring, loving, and being connected).

2. The desire to and practice of learning and growing.

Service-Learning is based on a premise that when these fundamental human desires are linked, each is enhanced and each enhances the other. The Wingspread document on "Principles of Good Practice for Combining Service and Learning" claims, "Service, combined with learning, adds value to each and transforms both."[1]

I believe that establishing conditions for students to engage with others in a shared search for doing what needs to be done (Service) and pursuing what needs to be learned (Learning) is important work for colleges and communities at the end of this century.

As you consider and/or develop policies and systems for creating conditions for students to continue their journey contributing and learning in settings away from campus, the following observations are outlined for your consideration.

Robert L. Sigmon is president of Learning Design Initiatives, Inc.

The Community and The College

The word "service" in Service-Learning comes first intentionally, for the tasks defined by a specific individual, group, or community situation set a primary context for a Service-Learning activity. If a group is unable to define a task, then the task is to decide, not to engage or to work with the group to define a concern that the student and faculty can jointly work on with the citizens.

In my experience, a major strategy for higher education faculty and staff is to locate passionate, committed and competent individuals in communities who care about well-being, opportunity, and fairness for their neighbors. Then, I would suggest, build relationships and listen for common ground for joint work and learning. As you listen to what is desired, also listen for ways the community can contribute to what is important for the students to know and be able to do when they are enrolled or graduated.

When the desires to contribute and to learn are practiced by a student—in an internship, a field study assignment, an action-research project, an independent study, a cooperative education venture, a summer job, an immersion experience, a tutoring or mentoring role, a voluntary action project, or a full-time job—the prospects for significant contribution and learning are high. In a recent study of private liberal arts colleges, faculty suggested that they have major hopes for more student self-direction in their learning. Service-Learning has enormous potential to assist students with their self-directed learning.[2] Prospects for contributing and learning are even higher when the persons with whom the student interacts in the process are also engaged in a contributing and learning stance (e.g., citizens with whom he or she engages, faculty members who assign some credit, agency representatives who offer some supervision).

For a faculty member and an institution of higher education, this suggests that a Service-Learning type of activity can be initiated from one of four levels:

1) the citizens in a community setting who have defined tasks and who invite the assistance of students and faculty;

2) students who define their own interests in contributing and learning in a beyond-the-classroom setting;

3) faculty who want to include a service activity in an existing or new course; or

4) linking all three levels in the design work.

The challenge for faculty is to develop relationships with communities—listening to their situations, engaging in conversations, and asking for assistance. In other words, what is it that folks in a community can contribute to the learning of students? What is it that students can contribute to the community? Once these interests are stated, then the faculty task is to figure out how the academic disciplines of choice can be called on to respond to the community situation, the student's own interests, and how the disciplines can be enhanced by engagement with the situation.

This suggests that an experiential learning pedagogy which is able to connect what is known in an academic discipline, what is required in a community, and a student's own personal interest, will often emerge as the teaching-learning style of choice. The direct experiences of the faculty, the student, the citizens, and the organizational contacts with a common task will define what is to be contributed and taught, what is to be gained and learned. Each party brings something to the dialogue that enhances each of the other parties' sense of contributing and teaching, being contributed to and learning.

Key Principles

When each of the parties views the other as contributor and beneficiary in a Service-Learning situation, a mutuality and reciprocity principle emerges as primary.

In a Service-Learning experience, each participant is server and served, care giver and care acquirer, contributor and contributed to. Learning and teaching in a Service-Learning arrangement is also a task for each of the partners in the relationship. Each person is presented with the option to clarify personal learning goals while at the same time respond as teacher to the learning goals of others as they mutually address a common situation.

Service-Learning has enormous potential to assist students with their self-directed learning.

Within a Service-Learning framework, the use of power and authority necessarily are different from most teacher-student and supervisor-worker relationships. Faculty and agency supervisors generally are in positions of power over students and citizens in communities. In a Service-Learning arrangement, the power is shared with the citizens in the community, who are definers of their situation, and with the students, who are partners in defining their learning agendas. Traditional authority roles of faculty and agency representatives are not discarded. However, in a Service-Learning arrangement the issue of who defines and assesses what is to be done and what is to be learned is shared by the citizens and students with the agency staff and faculty.

Experiential learning theories abound. In this century, William James, John Dewey, David Kolb, Paulo Freire, Jane Vella, Allan Tough, Donald Schon, James Coleman and others have spoken eloquently of learning that grows out of engagement with the realities of communities and work settings. Fundamental to most of them are the notions that learning is highly idiosyncratic for each learner, that each learner develops a major way of learning and many minor ways, that direct experience creates extraordinary opportunities for learning, that careful reflection on experience is essential, that mutuality/reciprocity in relationships is a key component for learning, that dialogue is essential for most learners, and that sequence has potential for enhanced contributing and learning.

Within a Service-Learning framework as a way of engaging citizens and students in contributing and learning, action and knowledge are connected and reinforce each other. A concern for "objective truth" as a norm in classroom pedagogy gives way in Service-Learning to exploration, reflection, and involvement in a recurring action/reflection pattern.

Most community situations call on multiple disciplines for assistance. For example, in a tutoring activity the disciplines of English, economics, social policy, public health, history, psychology, and mathematics are potential contributors to how well students and tutees understand the specifics of the tutoring task and the context in which the tutoring is taking place.

Processes and Systems

In Service-Learning experiences, as this chart suggests, three major forces come together:

One, the student is attempting to connect his or her self-directing desire to contribute and learn in some kind of voluntary or for-pay situation with citizens, often connected to some kind of organization or institution.

Two, the college or university is attempting to figure out the most appropriate way to teach and enhance learning. The limited amount of prior connection with communities and their interests has often resulted in a mistrust between higher education institutions and community. A possibility for overcoming this separation is rooted in seeing the relationship of knowledge to public action, exploring the new places outside the academy where knowledge is being generated, and gaining a fresh perspective on what constitutes excellence in teaching and learning.

Three, organizations in the private and public spheres are keenly challenged by the growing awareness of institutional violence toward workers and customers. The extremes of poverty and affluence; the awareness of increasing disparities among peoples; the destitution of millions of citizens; and the frantic, stressed nature of so much of the workplace environment for those with jobs are challenging the goods and services providers of this country into rethinking and redesigning workplaces and relationships with customers or clients. In the language of "customer service" and "learning organization," Service-Learning is on the agenda of employers.

Could it be the case now that higher education's relationship to the growth and learning of people and organizations in this country, particularly those in their own neighborhoods, is the primary challenge and opportunity for higher education and its neighbors today? Service-Learning is one approach for developing the groundwork and creating the conditions for both colleges and communities to be contributors and learners as we all strive to promote the common good.

When the fundamental desires to contribute and to learn are linked in a conceptual and programmatic design in which all parties to a work and learning task are viewed as contributors and beneficiaries, as teachers and learners, then these three cultural forces are joined at some point in the journey.

Service-Learning arrangements will inevitably challenge those involved to engage in the realities of each of these arenas. Service-Learning is not a panacea nor direct answer, but a way of engaging in the dialogue about what is worth doing and worth knowing now and for the future.

Possible Outcomes

The parties who choose to engage in Service-Learning relationships will be equipping themselves with approaches to problem stating, relationship building, listening, designing, reframing, learning, teaching, team building and struggle, visioning, task completion, new task development, leadership, community building, reflection, and inner spiritual development. These are all capacities that each of us can acquire as we collectively seek to create the conditions for more just relationships among us, more able self-directing learners, more capable builders of community, and more able citizens at all levels. (For a valuable list of student outcomes, see Richard Slimbach's chapter in this book, "Connecting Head, Heart, and Hands.")

With these capacities and attitudes evolving, the hope is that conditions will be established to transform many institutions so that we can enable those with whom we associate to make strong contributions and learn at the same time.

As these institutions become more humane and just, the hope is that a society of just relationships will emerge where each person has the opportunity to thrive to the best of his or her abilities.

A Framework for Higher Education

Within a traditional liberal arts academic framework of passing on accumulated knowledge via classes with teachers who primarily lecture and assign readings, to what degree and depth is service-based experiential learning, as defined above, appropriate? A several-step approach may help focus the question.

A first step can be to locate the primary focus for seeking to link service with learning in your community and college. There are several possibilities:

- *Only with the students.* If so, are we wanting to create self-directing learners? active and competent citizens committed to just relationships among all people? productive workers? critical thinkers? scholars?

- *Primarily with how faculty teach and arrange learning environments.* (e.g. On curriculum development, or on multi-discipline approaches.)

- *Assisting communities and institutions to deal with concerns on their terms* and inviting them to teach students.

- *Creating and supporting learning environments throughout society.*

- *Influencing public policy issues* affecting the well-being of the Earth and all citizens?

- *Encouraging higher education to be more proactive and engaged* with the communities and institutions of society.

These options are not meant to be exclusive. It is entirely possible to focus on two or more of these issues simultaneously.

A second step can be an extended conversation within the college and within the community about the nature of "service." What does it mean to care for the brother and sister in this decade and in the future? What are the patterns of "service" we have grown up with and practice? What is working well in these relationships? What is not working well? What do traditionally "serviced" people feel and think about the traditional "servers?" What happens when these two groups meet together to plan collaboratively for their mutual well-being?

A third step is to be aware of existing patterns of connections between the college and the wider community. Who is doing what? Seeking what? As defined by whom? Via what kinds of relationships? What are faculty doing? What are students doing? How does the community contribute to educational purposes and functions?

A fourth step is to connect these concerns of Service-Learning to ongoing dialogues in higher education about educational reform, about new ways to teach and learn, about governance, about the New American College, or any other important conversations alive in your situation.

A fifth step is to just do something—plan, implement and assess something that links the desire to contribute with the desire to learn among as many potential partners as possible. Reflect on what you intended and did, and the outcome. Then decide if you want to try something else, improve on what you have done, or forget it.

A sixth step would be to develop or activate your own institutional mission and policies, defining what you intend to do in linking this desire to contribute with the desire to learn in a context of the wider community.

A seventh step would be the evolving of your own unique, distinctive organizational framework for arranging for the college to be engaged with the community as partners in creating maximum conditions for all citizens to contribute and to learn. Each institution and community will find distinctive ways to work out this partnership. No one blueprint or definition can be or should be adopted. The journey is unique in each circumstance. You will find throughout these pages stories of how others have initiated, sustained, and evaluated their quests.

REFERENCES

1. Honnet, E. and S. Poulsin. Wingspread Special Report: "Principles of Good Practice for Combining Service and Learning." Racine, Wisconsin: The Johnson Foundation, 1989.

2. Serow, R. and R. L. Sigmon. "Survey Results: Service-Learning at Private Liberal Arts Institutions." *The CIC Independent,* October 1995: 11.

CHAPTER 2

THE PROBLEM OF DEFINITIONS IN SERVICE-LEARNING

Why No One Definition Works

BY ROBERT L. SIGMON

Among individuals who have become passionate promoters and evaluators of Service-Learning experiences over time, a common trait is that we have been dismayed by the inequities in much of society and are compelled to struggle to address the injustices and promote more just relationships. Likewise, we talk about having been "over schooled," told what to study, when to study it, and how well we have studied it by teachers and experts. We have sensed that we have a capacity for self-initiated experiential learning as well, and have sought ways to create options for this kind of learning in and out of the formal schooling framework.

As we have faced the public tasks and work we have chosen, and worked at creating experiential learning opportunities in a Service-Learning framework, we have increasingly come to believe that this framework has much to offer communities and their citizens, public and private organizations, and educational institutions and their constituents at all levels. The notion of Service-Learning is nothing new in human experience, it happens to be a label given to the coming together of these two notions: our innate desire to contribute and our desire to learn and grow as human beings.

A distinctive aspect of the evolving nature of the "movement" of Service-Learning is that no one definition will work for everyone. This suggests that we each, as individuals or groups, can have conversations across the boundaries of race, age, gender, institutional alignment, and economic well-being to uncover our own way of thinking about and defining Service-Learning. If the assumption holds for you and those you choose to work with that there is a human tendency to want to contribute and to want to learn and grow, then how do these two tendencies play out in some limited fashion in your situation? For me, Service-Learning or service-based-learning language captures the idea well. I hope no one definition or set of standards will become the "true test."

Since 1985, Service-Learning language has been used to describe quite different kinds of programs. *Community Service-Learning* has tended to focus on citizenship development for students, often with a limited focus on learning and outcomes for those with whom they are serving and learning citizenship from in the communities. *Academically-based community Service-Learning* focuses primarily on relating theory to practice, most often through the means of a professor adding a small service assignment to a course. Other variations have been noted such as *career-based Service-Learning* and *service-based leadership studies. Strategic academically-based community service* is a phrase used by some to align the community and the college in a social transformation stance.

In 1994, the Council of Independent Colleges published a short paper, "Linking Service With

Learning," which attempted a framing of four common emphases in the linking of service with learning in private liberal arts higher education:[1]

SERVICE - learning focuses on the service as primary and learning as secondary.

service - LEARNING focuses on learning goals, with service secondary.

service learning acknowledges that each is separate and important, but not linked.

SERVICE-LEARNING frames the reciprocity issue, that all the partners in the experience are servers and served and are teachers and learners. Service-Learning assumes that colleges are living parts of communities, that the location of learning and serving is often beyond the classroom, and that communities have much to teach students and faculty.

Rarely written about is the potential for Service-Learning in the for-pay work force, either public or private. Since many college students work for pay, the potential for creating Service-Learning opportunities within these settings is very high. In the workplace environment of this decade, customer "service" is a buzz word, as is "learning organization." The notion of this kind of "service" is rarely considered by many working with Service-Learning programs.

In my experience, the following story illustrates where many of us in higher education are with respect to our reasons for wanting to contribute and learn.

A practitioner in the Service-Learning field told me recently that in high school she had been involved in a number of school- and church-related service projects, mostly based on a "I am blessed and you are not so blessed, so I want to help you out" principle and a social peer group principle that "service" was the thing to do.

Somewhere in this process of trying to contribute, an idea was born and questions were raised about "why serve anyway?" What difference does it make if we do it or not? Who gets helped and who gets hurt in the process? And all of a sudden, a reflective moment occurs and in many cases some learning.

My friend went on to explain that when she was in college, a well intentioned group sought to tutor and help out in an area high school setting. The initiative came from college students, who planned what they wanted to do and went searching for a place to do it. A high school's administration said, "Sure, come on, we need x and y." Upon getting into the situation, the students realized that x and y were not what was wanted. And the school realized that these college students were more trouble than they were worth. Neither group knew how to connect with the other. The dilemma was organizational. My friend learned from this, noting that the college administrators and faculty were not involved in a potentially significant activity. The religious organization on campus had taken the lead and supported the effort. The public school leaders were not clear about how the college students could be involved in a mutually helpful way. She also learned that the college students were there to find a way to contribute. They were searching for ways to unleash a natural urge. My friend discovered that the learning potential in the college-school linkage was almost totally ignored by the teaching faculty at that time, 20 years ago.

In my own experience, the urge to contribute led me to the Punjab region of Pakistan for three years as a lay missionary with the Methodist Church. Living with wonderful people in a village in the Punjab who, by our Western standards, would be called very poor, I realized what my friend had realized. I was there for my own need to contribute and serve. The learning dimension emerged in powerful ways, but was recognized later.

Out of these moments when individuals and collections of individuals realize that something is worth doing in a time and place with other people and/or the natural environment, the possibility for Service-Learning is present. To contribute and serve well, we ask what it is that we need to know and be able to do in order to deal with the situation at hand. Once into the experience, we stop periodically and ask, What is going on here? We begin reflecting on our experience. As the work and relationships tend to ease up and reach some closure, we wonder about what the experience meant to us, to others, and to the general public good. When we venture into yet another framework with problems or work to be done, we draw on the experience of what we have done before, what we learned from it, and what we do and do not want to have to face again. This is another way of defining Service-Learning.

But, you may ask, *what is* service in Service-Learning? When asked how does one know one has served well, Robert Greenleaf responded, "Do those involved in the relationship become wiser, freer, healthier, more autonomous and more disposed to serve?"[2] Within this Greenleaf phrase is the notion of mutuality and reciprocity. Greenleaf used a motto over and over—"To serve and be served by your experiences in the world." So service is not one-way: "I do to you, I fix you, I help you." Service is two-way.

Reflecting over the past 30 years with students who have been "serving" others and learning through their experiences, the overwhelming response has been, "I was helped a lot more than I helped," and, "I learned a lot more than I taught."

This common theme is a link to asking a key question: "What about the learning part of Service-Learning?

Learning by doing as a notion has been around for a long time. John Dewey has influenced many Service-Learning practition-ers.[3] David Kolb has been an interpreter of this phenomenon with an experiential learning theory which speaks of four points on a circle of experiential learning.[4] First is the concrete experience or work that we do, then our observations and reflections on that experience, followed by making sense of it (abstract conceptualizations or generalizations) and, lastly, deciding to move into a new situation or a new approach to an old situation (active experimentation). Donald Schon's study of how professionals learn unveils an "Action-Reflection" process that informs much of the learning side of Service-Learning.[5] Paulo Freire's work on learning from the context in its wholeness has been a major contribution to many Service-Learning advocates.[6] The work of Robert Greenleaf, in his Servant Leadership writings, suggests that listening to others is a fine way to learn and to serve. The self-directed learning research of Allen Tough and his colleagues suggests that from early adulthood to old age, most of us are self-directing learners.[7]

As we each frame the questions—about which we are curious, for which we need to know some specific piece of information, around something that is just fun to explore, or in some cases on issues that are thrust upon us—we are masterful at drawing on our prior experience, experimenting with trial and error approaches, seeking out help from experts, courses, books, and friends, and finding among these methods ways of learning that we need to know in order to complete a task.

So, how do you want to link service and learning? Definitions are by necessity fluid and emerging, for the life of each of us is evolving and growing as are the lives of communities and organizations. The moral of this chapter is that you can look at the definitions in the literature and practice, but the creative expression that awaits you and those you care about is in the conversations about what it means in your situation(s) to link the desires to contribute and learn for all the parties involved in these service-based learning enterprises.

REFERENCES

1. Sigmon, Robert L. *Linking Service with Learning.* Washington, D.C.: Council of Independent Colleges, 1994.

2. Greenleaf, Robert. *Servant Leadership.* New Jersey: Paulist Press, 1977.

3. Dewey, John. *Democracy and Education.* New York: Macmillian, 1916.

4. Kolb, David. *Experiential Learning.* Englewood Cliffs, N.J.: Prentice-Hall, 1984.

5. Schon, Donald. *The Reflective Practitioner.* New York: Basic Books, 1983.

6. Freire, Paulo. *Pedagogy of the Oppressed.* England: Harmondsworth, 1972.

7. Tough, Allen. *The Adult's Learning Projects.* Toronto: Ontario Institute for Studies in Education, 1979.

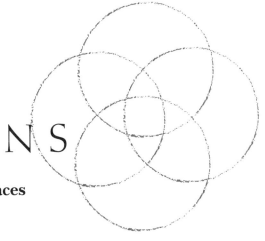

CHAPTER 3

DESIGN CONSIDERATIONS

Building Relationships Between The Academy And Workplaces In Service-Learning Programs

BY ROBERT L. SIGMON

Developing and sustaining partnerships between educational institutions and business, public agency, non-profit, and community-based organizations in order to produce serving to learn and learning to serve outcomes is a challenging, complex matter.

The anatomy of a Service-Learning partnership that includes educational groups and work/service settings is shown in Chart One. This anatomy includes two primary axes. The vertical axis is the personal linkage of citizens with students. The horizontal axis focuses on institutional connections between colleges and community- based organizations. The other arrows indicate four other major relationships in a Service-Learning anatomy.

Chart One

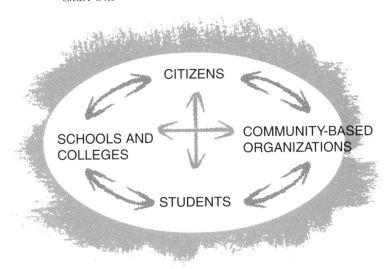

The aim of this chapter is to suggest a planning framework for including the perspectives of each of the parties in the Service-Learning anatomy, with the expectation that paying attention to the planning framework will enable all the participants to arrive at relationships and program designs that are congruent with what is important to do and learn about in each situation.

Six Starting Places for Service-Learning Design Work: A Student Perspective

Six major forms of linking service with learning are practiced on most campuses in varying degrees. Each form presents opportunities for student service and learning.

1. *Work-Based Learning.*

   Estimates suggest that over one-half of college students work for pay during their undergraduate years. Many workplaces speak of customer SERVICE and being a LEARNING organization. There is increased potential for linking service and learning when students work for pay. This is a vastly under-explored form of Service-Learning.

2. *Voluntary Action-Based Learning.*

   Students traditionally have been actively involved in short-term, charity-oriented voluntary action. Increasingly these programs are adding a more reflective component and seeking more mutuality in the relationships. These types of programs and activities are fertile ground for the journey to Service-Learning.

3. *Classroom-Based Learning.*

The dominant form of teaching and learning in undergraduate education is finding the inclusion of experience-based learning to be both a challenge and an opportunity. That is, how can prior experience, work experience, and volunteer experience already in place be seen as important contributors to classroom-based learning? And as more conscious planning for including service components in courses emerges as a fast growing enterprise, the Service-Learning approaches suggested in this book become strong allies for classroom-based learning.

4. *Service-Based Learning.*

When locally defined public tasks are seen as a unique way to promote learning as well as good service, then these mutual goals are energized. Beginning with social dilemmas and public issues as a learning strategy is a challenging opportunity for colleges, faculty, students, agency staff, and citizens.

5. *Self-Directed Learning.*

Most initiatives begin with a single person and most colleges yearn for ways that students can become more autonomous, self-directing lifelong learners. Given the Service-Learning anatomy partnership and its necessary relationships, an emphasis on program design for student-initiated service and learning has merit.

6. *Co-curricular-Based Learning.*

Leadership development, career exploration, and student affairs tasks of managing the living arrangements of student lives all present a forum for contributing and learning in the style of Service-Learning. The challenge is to explore these connections and create conditions for healthy service and learning to thrive in as a part of the co-curricular work of the campus.

Four Questions

As a general guide for relationship building and maintenance, program design, and program evaluation, four planning questions can be asked:

WHO?

SEEKS WHAT?

AS DEFINED BY WHOM?

VIA WHAT KIND OF RELATIONSHIPS?

First, a look at each of the primary entities in the anatomy. The responses outlined in the following four charts are examples of what might be included after the four planning questions. The blanks on the right-hand side of the page are for you to complete from the vantage point of your own position and perspective. In Chart Two, for example, alongside the "Who" column, write in the particular individuals or groups that students will be working with in the program or course. Then next to the "Seeks What?" column, show what those particular citizens are saying that they want or desire.

"As defined by whom?" may cause you to stumble somewhat, for we often find other agents expressing what it is that those to be served want or need. And finally, the fourth planning question focuses on the "relationship" patterns that already exist or that can be created as all the parties begin to work together.

As you use these worksheets on the next several pages, you should have a clearer picture of strengths in your relationship patterns and areas where some focused attention would further improve relationships.

Chart Two

CITIZENS

	EXAMPLES	IN YOUR SITUATION
WHO?	- Individuals - Workers - Families - Neighborhoods - Functional groups/communities	_____ _____ _____ _____ _____
SEEKS WHAT?	- Opportunity for work and leisure - Capacity building for self-sustaining social and economic life - Capacity building for being a part of active community life - Individualized goals/objectives (e.g., jobs, relationships, literacy, parenting skills)	_____ _____ _____ _____ _____ _____ _____
AS DEFINED BY WHOM?	- Families or groups of citizens organized for realizing own goals or purposes - Individuals	_____ _____ _____
VIA WHAT RELATIONSHIPS?	- Private business - Public agencies - Not-for-profits - Community-based organizations - Educational Institutions - Students	_____ _____ _____ _____ _____ _____

Chart Three

WORK PLACES
AND COMMUNITIES

	EXAMPLES	IN YOUR SITUATION
WHO?	- Businesses (large, medium and small)	_____
	- Public agencies, tax funded	_____
	- Not-for-profit service organizations	_____
	- Community-based organizations	_____
	- Small community groups	_____
SEEKS WHAT?	- Return on investment or profits	_____
	- Production of high-quality goods/services	_____
	- Productive, satisfied & growing employees	_____
	- Stable social and economic order	_____
	- Critical thinking and loyal employees	_____
	- Just relationships	_____
AS DEFINED BY WHOM?	- Boards of directors	_____
	- Top management	_____
	- Marketplace	_____
	- Voting public	_____
	- Membership of organizations	_____
VIA WHAT RELATIONSHIPS?	- Citizens: buy the goods and services and provide the labor	_____
	- Educational institutions:	_____
	- produce future employees	_____
	- provide basic and applied research	_____
	- Students: prospective employees link between new knowledge of academy and workplace	_____
	- Training opportunity to shape students	_____
	- Part-time production workers	_____

17

Chart Four

EDUCATIONAL INSTITUTIONS

	EXAMPLES	IN YOUR SITUATION
WHO?	- Kindergarten-fifth grade - Middle schools - Secondary schools - Community colleges - Undergraduate colleges - Graduate schools - Continuing education programs	_____ _____ _____ _____ _____ _____ _____
SEEKS WHAT?	- To produce citizens who think critically - To produce basic and applied research - To practice excellence in teaching - To survive, innovate in teaching and learning	_____ _____ _____ _____ _____
AS DEFINED BY WHOM?	- Boards of directors/boards of education - Administrators - Faculty - Alumni - Students - Parents of students - Funders-public and private	_____ _____ _____ _____ _____ _____ _____
VIA WHAT RELATIONSHIPS?	- Citizens-pay bills & send their children - Students-passive? active? - Workplaces-partnerships at some levels providers of funding	_____ _____ _____ _____

Chart Five
STUDENTS

	EXAMPLES	IN YOUR SITUATION
WHO?	- Kindergarten-fifth grade	_____
	- Middle	_____
	- Secondary	_____
	- Community college	_____
	- Undergraduate baccalaureate	_____
	- Graduate degree	_____
	- Lifelong learners	_____
SEEKS WHAT?	- Good grades and graduation to next level	_____
	- Learning how to learn	_____
	- Participation in public life	_____
	- Capacity and skill development	_____
	- Establishing friendships	_____
AS DEFINED BY WHOM?	- Curricula designed by faculty	_____
	- Situations in the world	_____
	- Students themselves	_____
	- Parents	_____
VIA WHAT RELATIONSHIPS?	- With parents	_____
	- Peers	_____
	- Workplace settings	_____
	- Teachers and schools	_____
	- Citizens/neighbors	_____

Chart Six

ANATOMY OF A UNIVERSITY-COMMUNITY SERVICE-LEARNING PARTNERSHIP

This chart, "An Anatomy of a University-Community Service-Learning Partnership," is designed to follow up the work you have done in sorting out who seeks what as defined by whom via what relationships on the previous charts. In this chart you can begin to see the relationships within a Service-Learning experience. Here you can see each of the dyads and the network as a whole. A major assumption emerges that each of the parties seeks to be a part of this serving and learning arrangement and is able to see the connections among the partners.

Partnerships are organic, complex, and interdependent systems. They share some of the characteristics and behaviors of natural ecosystems. They consist of both human and physical resources, are affected by limiting factors such as time, space, and money, and each group of individuals plays a vital and unique role in this community. As organic entities, partnerships are ever-changing—growing, developing, reallocating, or deteriorating, thus needing constant care and attention. A small change in only one part of the system can mildly or profoundly affect another, or even impact the whole. This analogy provides a framework on which to reflect, evaluate, and improve our school and community partnerships. For this exercise, look at a partnership as a biologist looks at an ecosystem, by examining the pairs of interactions that take place to better understand the dynamics of the whole. The model below is greatly simplified compared to the partnerships with which you work. The vertical axis shows students and citizens. The horizontal axis shows the sponsoring organizations. Look at the assumptions, perceived limits, and possible opportunities in the six pairs of relationships which are contained in a typical school and community partnership. For your situation, fill in the blanks for the four sectors on the facing page and complete the exercise as outlined.

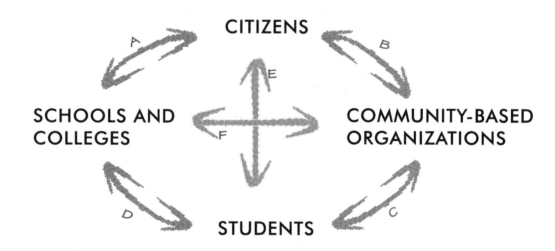

Chart Six, continued

I. Please fill in specific names for your situation, e.g., students, agencies, citizens, and academic units/faculty.

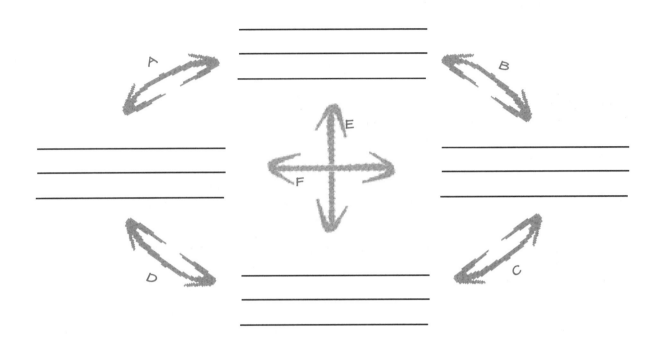

II. After completing the exercise in Part I, above, describe and comment on the six operating relationships among the four parties in the Service-Learning anatomy in your situation.

A _____

B _____

C _____

D _____

E _____

F _____

(This worksheet is a modified version of an original design by Jennie Niles and Robert Sigmon first used at a National Society for Experiential Education workshop on Partnerships, November 1995.)

Conclusion/Discussion

These Service-Learning design tools suggest a framework for considering the unique contributions each sector makes to a partnership in connecting contributions with learning. When each of the sectors is given full consideration for what it seeks out of the relationship, who is defining the terms of the relationship, and via what patterns of communication across the personal and institutional boundaries, then a Service-Learning partnership can be experienced for the benefit of all participants.

The desire for fairness and being at home in the universe wherever we live offers educators and workplace managers opportunities for creating partnerships so that we can learn to serve and serve to learn throughout our lifetimes. In the hands of developing imaginations of workplace and education leaders working within creative partnerships, signs of hope for a sustainable future will be clearly visible.

As some high school teachers told me recently, we must realize that learning is a 24-hours-a-day, seven-days-a-week enterprise, and that people caring for each other is likewise a full-time enterprise. The desire to contribute and to learn is constant in most of us. We are connected. Each tiny impulse from every one of us has the potential to control or transform individuals, relationships with another person, group norms, and the entire human community. If the conditions are arranged to minimize control and domination and build up the opportunities to contribute and learn, then the good society that Robert Greenleaf spoke of may have an opportunity to flourish.[1] A paraphrase of his vision is:

> *If a good society is to be built, one that is more just and more caring, and where the less able and more able serve one another with unlimited accountability; then the best way is to raise the performance of institutions as servants, and sanction natural servants to serve and lead.*

Creating partnerships which promote service-based experiential learning opportunities within businesses, public agencies, nonprofit and community-based organizations is a challenge for employers and educators at all levels. Use, adapt, or ignore these tools as you wind your own path along a road to link service with learning as an institution, in academic courses and within the lives of individual students and citizens.

Once you have followed through on exploring **who** is seeking **what,** as defined by **whom,** via what kinds of **relationships** in a Service-Learning venture, issues emerge for how to structure the supportive and sustaining framework for programs.

Listening to and observing some of the distinctive practices and emerging intentions of the 30 colleges in the CIC *Serving to Learn, Learning to Serve* program, a framework for creating a leadership structure emerged (see Chart Seven).

At one level is what Robert Greenleaf calls "conceptual leadership." Generally, this would include the college trustees and top administrators who make determinations about the degree and depth of Service-Learning activity that fits within the overall mission of the institution. Faculty also have a key role in helping to determine this direction.

The other level is what Greenleaf calls "operational leadership." Within a Service-Learning program, this can consist of those who make it work, who do the tasks of organizing, sustaining and reviewing the programs. Again, there is a critical role for the faculty and their influence in linking service with the curriculum.

To build partnerships with the community, a partnership council will bring to the table all the voices that need to be present when programs are being planned, implemented, and evaluated.

A critical dimension of many programs has been the creation of a Service-Learning office and the employment of a seasoned practitioner with experience in both community and academic matters.

On many campuses, students are strong players in the operational side of leadership

REFERENCES

1. Greenleaf, Robert; *Servant Leadership.* New York: Paulist Press, 1977.

Chart 7

LEADERSHIP STRUCTURE POSSIBILITIES

CONCEPTUAL LEADERSHIP

BOARD OF TRUSTEES

Establish vision and mission for distinctive service and learning opportunities for campus. Create conditions for programs to flourish.

OPERATIONAL LEADERSHIP

PARTNERSHIP COUNCIL

Bring together citizens, community-based organizations, non-profits, public entities, private business, faculty, and students to build relationships, explore mutual interests and capacities, establish guidelines, plan support, and assess processes and outcomes.

FACULTY

(have both a conceptual and operational role)
Create curriculum which includes linking service
    options with learning
Develop contacts with community
Develop reflection tools
Co-design courses with other faculty
See self as learner and contributor
Conduct research and publish on topic of service-
    based learning

CENTER FOR SERVICE-LEARNING

Staffed by seasoned agent with community and academic experience, assisted by upper level students. Tasks for Center:
1. information center
2. technical/logistics resource
3. relationship building among all parties
4. agreement negotiations with off-campus groups
5. recruitment/publicity
6. training and assessment
7. special projects coordination
8. problem solving
9. grant writing/fund raising
10. recognitions/awards
11. create library on Service-Learning
12. encourage writing and publications
13. communicate
14. inventories of activities and records
15. nurture all campus staff as service-learners

CAMPUS ADMINISTRATORS

Design overall structure for Partnership Council and Center for Service-Learning, arrange for resources, provide oversight, and offer encouragement.

Editor's Note—Scattered throughout the book are edited versions of journal notes from Robert Sigmon, including letters and reports of conversations he has had with other Service-Learning practitioners and some of his own reflections. The first three appear at this point to illustrate Service-Learning practice via concrete stories.

Journal Entry 1

Exposure, Capacity Building, and Responsibility
Three Distinctive Frameworks Of Service-Learning Programming For Students

I am often challenged by conversations with Service-Learning practitioners. For example, today a friend called and her main line of agitation went something like this: "A dilemma keeps bothering me in this linking of service with learning. The approach assumes a level of maturation beyond the experience of many college students. A service concept of caring for others through their self-defined requests for assistance and an expectation that the student be "served" by those they are serving is a framework many students have not experienced before. Likewise, expecting students to be self-initiating learners and to rely on discovery learning places them in another situation for which they have little experience. Given these two observations, are we not doing students a great disservice in promoting service-based learning before they have enough exposure and capacity to handle tough situations and self-directed learning? And are we not inflicting unprepared, inexperienced young people on others who have enough troubles to deal with anyway?"

To clarify my own thoughts, I tried in my journal to respond as if I were writing my friend a letter.

Dear Anne:

You have nailed a major concern. My response is to focus Service-Learning strategies on the bosses, mentors, preceptors, and community organizers—the primary actors in business, public service, human service, and community-based organizations. These are the persons with influence and power, who can shape a student's experience.

These are the persons who can establish the conditions for students to glimpse how to serve and learn in the midst of the human condition.

Journal Entry 1

In working with organizational leaders and staff, educational institutions can clarify with "out-there educators" the level of student being encouraged to work and learn alongside these preceptors. Three levels of students are most often encouraged to undertake Service-Learning experiences:

a) Students who are limited in their awareness of the realities beyond their own community, and who need EXPOSURE experiences. Exposures to the realities of people different from them; to organizational frameworks for dealing with those realities; to raising questions about their own values, stereotypes and customs; and appreciation for diversity and the possibilities for understanding the connected nature of life.

b) Students with some exposures, but with limited capacity to contribute much. In these circumstances, CAPACITY BUILDING is the primary aim. Students are presented with opportunities to develop capacities to contribute and develop competencies as they serve within situations of misfortune or injustice.

c) Given that students have been exposed and have honed their capacities, they then are prepared for intensive RESPONSIBILITIES, still under supervision of citizens they are serving or of organizational preceptors, which test their understandings and capacities to contribute and be contributed to, to teach and learn.

Each of these levels requires a different kind of preparation, support during the experience and assessment of the outcomes.

When Service-Learning programs focus on clarifying the framework for the students being encouraged to engage in service-based learning activities, then the successful preceptors are better able to match the experiences available with the level of student readiness. So, preparing the preceptors for their roles as Exposure arrangers, Capacity builders and overseers of Responsible student agents is a critical factor in overcoming the dangers of sending students into situations for which they are not prepared or capable of handling. The challenge is for the "preceptors" and the on-campus Service-Learning organizers to develop and carry out specific "training" programs for preceptors. In some areas, these preceptors are granted adjunct faculty status for their teaching role with students.

Some programs can be designed to include all three levels in one summer or semester. For example, a tutoring program can begin with some exposure visits and conversations and readings. A training period to learn tutoring skills and techniques for relating to others can follow. And then a responsibility with one or more students can be arranged.

For a four-year liberal arts college committed to engaging students with service ventures beyond the campus, sequencing experiences is a process worth thinking about as you plan. And paying attention to the

Journal Entry 1

increased high school focus on Service-Learning resulting in students with exposure and capacities is warranted too.

Arranging for exposures to public, private, and community settings in which people in communities are invited to "teach" students about their realities is one way to organize the Exposure part. Freshman orientation, Break Aways (short forays from academic courses) and self-initiated exposures are some of the ways these Exposures can be arranged. Time for individual and group reflection is essential following these experiences. By placing ourselves in a position of being served, we serve. Pointing this out in service-based learning is a critical pathway along the journey to Service-Learning.

Requirements for establishing capacity-building experiences range from concrete skill development to sophisticated analysis of public issues to capacities of self-understanding and cultural awareness.

Responsibilities and practice opportunities, the third level, are determined by a match between what a community or individuals indicate they desire and the capacities of a student service-learner. Negotiating what each desires and can offer is the key factor in these kinds of service-based learning arrangements.

As I thought about my colleague's quandary and my notes to myself to clarify a response, two recent debriefing interviews with students came to mind and I looked back in my journal notes for those reflections, noted in the next two journal entries.

Journal Entry 2

Contributing and Growing in a Course
A Student Perspective

I had a chance to ask two students about their experiences doing Service-Learning in a course. Sue responded to my question about how they got started.

Dr. L in a Religion and Public Education course assigned Rob and me to work as a team to get involved in some public education issue that would result in something useful being contributed to the community, be the subject for a class presentation at the end of the semester, and help us learn from people in the community.

Rob chimed in:

With direction from Dr. L and a school board member, we decided to learn all we could about the issues, people, institutions, and organizations involved in a school board decision to build a new public school in a city park next to our college. The city park separated the college from an African-American community. The issue was controversial and had been debated for 20 months when we entered the story.

We were surprised that as we got into the project, our relative inexperience and being strangers became an asset. We sought out the initial contacts by stating that our aim was to learn as much as possible about the wide web of organizations and people involved in the decision to build a school in a city park. This openness and framing of the issue, the way we did it, invited those we were talking with to open up and share a lot of information and feelings with us.

I asked Rob and Sue about what skills and capacities they developed over the semester.

Well, as we moved about we got more and more confident to ask questions, follow up leads, feel comfortable talking with all shapes and conditions of people, find data, sift through data for its reliability, and begin to see patterns and themes in the findings. As we obtained more and more information and began to see some patterns, we realized that we were devoting a lot of attention to thinking about systems. We started going to the library to find out about complexity like this. We were surprised at how our capacities to be data gatherers and confident interpreters evolved steadily throughout the semester.

Journal Entry 2

At this point the conversation shifted to an earlier statement they made about doing something, or contributing something useful to the community.

This is the place where we really struggled. We talked with over 60 people from 45 organizations involved in the decision. Along the way we had to combine our intuitive and logical processes in producing a paper and chart outlining the complex set of relationships of all the parties involved. We identified key issues, named the major conflicts, and made our own assessment of strategies for proceeding. Our most prized product was an innovative mapping of the relationships of all the parties. This chart became a major element in the next stages of the dialogue in the community. Here is where the struggle came in. We felt a deep responsibility to the school board member who gave us our initial charge and who was available from time to time to listen to us. But we also felt compelled to share the information with the wider community, for two major institutions were responding in heavy-handed and unfair ways to block the process of planning for the school as well as intending to stop the process and the project. Our own college was an obstructionist group, using influence and raw power, even threats, to subvert what had begun as an open, community-wide dialogue. We found ourselves caught in a bind. Do we share our findings fully? Do we let the cat out of the bag that our own college has not been very honorable in this process? These obstructionist tactics were unknown to many in the local community and the teachers and parents of the 85-year-old school. We looked for help from some of the religious groups involved in the debate. These church leaders ducked for cover. The school board member was delighted to have the information, and suggested that sharing the full paper widely would be unwise. But he recommended that we share the innovative chart showing the complex web of relationships involved in this public issue. We were really surprised that in our class discussion of our project, the class was split about the ethical, political and practical consequences of withholding some data and sharing other data.

We did not share all the information, but we did share the chart which became a useful tool for some of the parties who were involved in the debate. We both were really sad about our own institution's role and attitude.

Rob continued:

And our own lack of courage to speak out hurt me, but we sensed that the local public and private groups involved had to work out the issue ultimately, and it was not our role at that time and place to cause ripples and name names." Sue perked up, *"You can bet that when I move into a new community from now on, I will have tools for listening to the community and learning from them about what matters to them.*

As they talked, I kept asking myself, "Did they provide a service? Did they learn? Did the linking of this service project in the context of a religion and education course add to the service and to the learning?" The school board member and many of the parties involved said they appre-

Journal Entry 2

ciated the analysis shown in the chart. The professor is using their work and process as a case study in his classes. Rob and Sue wanted to keep talking about what they had learned, particularly about the richness of working as a team. Rob volunteered that:

This was the first time in my schooling career that I have had a chance to work with someone else on a learning project. We really complemented one another and I know we accomplished more and learned more than if we had done it alone.

Sue interjected:

I learned more in that one semester than from any other one semester course I've had at the college. And one other comment. I was hurt by and fascinated by the very limited awareness and involvement of the religious communities in the processes of public education decision making.

Rob responded:

I learned that we were good data gatherers, good listeners, good integrators of diverse material. But in spite of that, I am really alerted now to my own fragility and helplessness at times in the light of powerful forces operating in a community.

At this point, I had to move on to another appointment, thrilled with the learning that had occurred and expectant of a challenging future for these two students. Again, the pattern of moving from exposures to capacity development to a sense of responsibility seemed to hold true as I reflected on what I had heard from them.

Journal Entry 3

A Student Reflects on a Year-Long "Stop Out" Service-Learning Experience

Ruth decided to take a "stop out" year her junior year in college. She had tutored her first year in a public school kindergarten and then in her sophomore year had worked as a volunteer with a grassroots community organizer in a small town near the college. She told me:

For a whole lot of reasons I needed to be away from school, have something practical to do. I was really lucky when my friends in the community where I volunteered ask me to come and help them start their own co-op child care center for pre-kindergarten children and an after-school program.

Ruth negotiated with her parents and her college advisor and the decision to "stop out" was carefully planned. A professor of sociology offered to make an independent study option available to Ruth for the year. She declined. Ruth, white and 20 years old at the time, told me what she did next:

I was able to rent a third floor walk-up room in the home of a saintly matron in the town, whose large home was on the boundary of the African-American working class neighborhood of the friends who had asked me to come work with them. I was raised in an upper middle class family with almost no contact with mill workers, day laborers, maids, or underemployed or unemployed men. The harshness of the reality of single mothers who wanted to work, but could not afford child care or did not trust the day care available, or did not have a mother or aunt or neighbor who could care for children during the day, disturbed me a lot. I became aware of the barriers people faced every day in making ends meet and raising their children.

I had some rude awakenings as some white citizens in the town spread rumors about me and tried to block the development of the child care center, citing codes and rules. My own protected early life was exposed for its isolation and prejudice. You know, I didn't even know anything much about group work, child care issues, or the cultural nuances of the community in which I was working.

Exposures to the current realities and the dreams of the community residents highlighted her early talking. Ruth then began to talk about what she had actually learned to do during the year.

Journal Entry 3

As we took leave of one another that afternoon, she told me, "I think all students should have a year to do something like this as a required part of a liberal arts education."

Ruth continued:

I decided not to take an independent study, but did on several occasions consult with some professors about issues I needed help with. You know what really pleased me most in that whole year? The trust relationship with some of the mothers and with several of the women in the white community. What really turned me on was the realization that the women I was working with were all learning and growing just like I was. As that little tiny building that became the center for child care work emerged as a habitable space, I also learned a lot about contracting, building codes, structural issues in buildings, and tenacity.

Having a chance to work on an "invitational" basis with women and children in the neighborhood, Ruth felt an immense sense of *responsibility*.

When the building was ready, I was asked to be the first director until someone in the community could get free from their present job and prepared to do the child care job.

See what I mean by the trust factor? By the time I went back to school after spending almost a year in the community, the mothers had organized themselves, had secured a full-time teacher, and had withstood the threats to close the center for not meeting all the standards set by some state agency. Relationships were developed with DSS and the Health Department. The community college is now offering a child care continuing education class to 10 mothers twice a week.

Ruth was a tired, but confident, and clearly self-directing young woman at age 21 when I talked with her about her experience. Gaining exposures to her own cultural heritage and another group's cultural heritage, developing capacities at multiple levels, and having responsibility within a context of support and struggle were powerful service and learning experiences for Ruth.

As we took leave of one another that afternoon, she told me:

I think all students should have a year to do something like this as a required part of a liberal arts education.

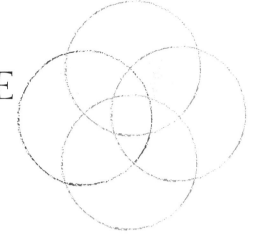

CHAPTER 4
THE REFLECTIVE ARTS

BY ROBERT L. SIGMON

The art of reflection is a vitally important exercise that assists students to derive meaning from their service experiences. This essay suggests three ways to approach reflection in which all parties involved benefit from their Service-Learning experiences.

Reflection in Service-Learning has something to do with the ways we each are able to state and think about what matters most to us. Once we are able to state what matters, we often want to share it with others. As we engage in working and reflecting together, we want to talk about how the work is being done and how we are feeling about it. We often find that others may not be in a listening mood at that moment, or that they listen in such a way that challenges us to rethink what really matters to us.

Reflection can be a private thing—for example, writing in a journal or just describing an experience. Reflection is often done in small groups talking about what each has done or not done in particular circumstances. Or reflection can be mulling over something for a long time, with spaces between the mullings. An experience in a Service-Learning activity may just sit there in its raw form, unreflected upon for weeks, months, years —and presto, all of a sudden you find yourself behaving in a new way, responding to something in a way that you never have before, and you ask, where did that come from? In asking, you discover that a long-ago or recent experience sat unnoticed for a time but had informed you to the degree that when confronted with a situation, you behaved in a new way. Moshe Feldenkraise says that most truly important things are learned this way.[1] There was no script, no curriculum, no teaching, just the experience and time.

Recently I have been introduced by my son-in-law, Paul Castelloe, to three forms of how people talk with one another about experience or what matters to them.[2] These underlying themes in the journey to Service-Learning involve not only the students, but each of the other parties outlined in the chapter "Design Considerations." Each of the three forms is introduced here in oversimplified terms with an attempt to relate the form to reflective practice within Service-Learning experiences.

I. **Open conversations** have at their core a concern with interpretation, openness, and a willingness to examine one's own interpretation of an experience or a series of events for their accuracy and fairness. Interpretation is stressed over objective truth in what some call a hermeneutic approach. Here we just put it out there, our ideas, our beliefs, our interpretations of what we have experienced and thought about rather than believing that we are stating some fundamental objective truth(s).

In reflection as interpretation rather than expressing objective truth, we most likely are able to remain open to other interpretations. We may not change our way of looking at a situation, but we can at least hear, respect and recognize interpretations of others. We can then respect others in a form of mutual trust that they will similarly hear us but not necessarily change their interpretations. In open conversation reflection on Service-Learning experience, the possibility exists for being open to

37

multiple interpretations and enlarging our own interpretations. This is not argumentative, combative, do-it-my-way conversation. It is simply sitting, sharing, listening, and seeing what happens.

For students in Service-Learning experiences that are new and challenging, such as the exposure type (see Journal Entry 1 in this book), this form of reflection has merit. Consider the potential value to a student, faculty member, citizen in a community, and an organizational representative if they would take the time to sit together periodically in a Service-Learning activity and simply share their interpretations of what mattered to them in the situation in which they were all involved. The potential for enriching, challenging conversation among these parties is unlimited.

If you are a citizen in a community or a representative of a public or non-profit organization involved with a student, or a student or faculty confronted by a difficult circumstance, ethical dilemmas can arise that require more than just sharing interpretation and listening to others. For example, I once was involved with an environment health studies student who embarked on a study of prior warnings of OSHA inspections in textile mills. A lone middle level OSHA staff member was a key advisor and sanctioner of the study as well. When the data were being collected with the assistance of workers in the mills, political pressures and threats were mounted against the school, the dean, and me, the Service-Learning coordinator. Just providing our interpretations of the experience was not enough. The unevenness of the power relationships that emerged was stifling to communication. We backed down and were shut off from completing the project as initially planned.

II. **Undistorted communication** as discussed by Jürgen Habermas in his writings about discourse ethics is concerned with the ways that relations of power and domination determine what participants in conversations can and cannot say.[3] My own interpretation is that most conversations in a Service-Learning reflection with faculty and/or agency contacts would result in distorted communication. The professor has power over a student which can distort the way the student speaks or does not

speak about certain things. A community agency representative, in speaking about those being served by the organization, has a power relationship over both a community resident and a student —in that the services can be cut off or a student's internship or research or service task can be terminated. A student's credentials or economic status may overwhelm those with whom the student is

---

Is the "common sense" cultural meaning of teaching shifting from "I control what you will learn" to "Let's engage together in a quest connected to linking knowledge and action in the world toward the end that just relationships are sustained"?

---

working. And in some instances, community organization leaders can intimidate faculty, students, and agency representatives. In the case of the environmental studies student, the political leadership of the state and the university leadership clamped down in strong terms and interrupted a process of contributing and learning at one level. The workers decided not to take any action to change the situation. The faculty were quiet. I was disturbed, but worked to understand and communicate with all the parties what I thought the options were in the situation.

So, Service-Learning situations deal with unequal relationships. The challenge for all the parties in a Service-Learning reflection practice is to be aware of these power relationships and openly state them, explore their distorting properties, and search for ways to overcome any perceived inequalities.

An ideal option to overcoming the distorted communication pattern is suggested by Habermas in what he calls an "ideal speech situation." Three rules or principles of a "ideal speech situation" can be paraphrased as follows:

1) anyone is allowed to participate in the conversation;

2) participants are allowed to question any assertion; introduce any assertion; express their attitudes, desires, and needs; and

3) participants are not prevented from questioning, introducing, or expressing themselves by any covert or overt coercion.

This "ideal speech situation" envisions an interaction process without open domination, self-interested or strategic behavior, or the more subtle barriers to communication that result from self-deception. Was the environmental studies case story a likely place for this kind of communication? My interpretation was and is, no.

Given the chance at hindsight, what could we have done in the environmental studies case as those with power were in no way willing to practice undistorted communication? Do we simply go passive and say "why should they, when the process seems to work well from their perspective?"[4]

III. **Contesting Common Sense Cultural Meanings,** referred to by Laclau and Mouffe as hegemonic articulation, is a complex idea and a third way to think about reflection with Service-Learning experiences.[5] As examples, consider these two contested common sense cultural meanings that are alive in the American experience today.

a) Is husbands' violence towards wives defined as "wife battering" or "the reality of boys will be boys?"

b) Is the equation of motherhood (but not fatherhood) with nurturance and home life defined as "the core of women's oppression" or "the core of family values?"

In the first example, feminist efforts have reframed the issue which has resulted in a shift in cultural meaning. Where American society once used the latter "common sense" definitions (marital violence as "boys will be boys"), we now usually use the former, "wife battering."

In the second example, the struggle over common sense cultural meaning is as yet undecided, a struggle that feminists may be losing.

Contesting points of view struggle over cultural or societal meanings in many different areas—not only in male-female relations, but in relations between black and white, poor and rich, gay and straight, young and old, credentialed and non-credentialed, teachers and learners, served and servers. These struggles over "common sense" definitions can force the attention of groups with a lot of power who otherwise tend to refuse to attend to the claims and needs of groups with little power. In Service-Learning situations, reframing contested common sense issues is suggested as useful when attempts at open conversation or overcoming distorted communication have failed.

Faculty, when credit and graduation are at stake, hold enormous power over students. Yet many faculty say they want students to be more autonomous and more self-directing.

When students seek to contribute and learn in a community context, they usually are discovering information, sensing issues and struggles, being confronted with their own biases and prejudices, humbled, affirmed in what they do know and care about, and become more whole persons and learners in the process. Much of what is being experienced by students is not in the experience of the faculty member. The student's perspective is not often fully considered in its totality because the professor does not know how to engage it. The teacher is focused by tradition on the content of a course within an academic discipline. The fullness of the student's Service-Learning experience is often not fully appreciated when the arrangement is controlled by the faculty and the quest for learning the discipline's content is primary. If we want students to be more autonomous and self-directing in their learning, and the traditional teaching approach is domineering and controlling, then how do we frame the issue in terms of a cultural struggle and/or institutionalized power?

Is the "common sense" cultural meaning of teaching shifting from "I control what you will learn" to "Let's engage together in a quest connected to linking knowledge and action in the world toward the end that just relationships are sustained"?

In the context of reform in higher education, the contested ground is the meaning of teaching. Is teaching a passing on the accumulated wisdom of the past via lectures, reading assignments, papers, and exams? Or does it also include creating environments in which action and knowledge are linked in the course of student self-discovery with assistance from experienced "teacher facilitators" and "experienced practitioners?" Service-Learning experiences provide one avenue for colleges to better understand an experiential learning role and style of teaching in private liberal arts education.

Agencies and businesses hold enormous power and influence over those they serve, their own employees, and students when students are invited in to serve and learn with them. Do we create "service systems" in order to maintain dependent people in a lesser posture? Or do we as a culture want to promote capacity building and self-reliance and community for all? Who is prepared to raise this concern in the context of local controversial issues and then also create the conditions for each party to reflect about the nature of their relationships in the ensuing communications? Students are often caught in a double bind when they see passive acquiescence and are puzzled by the heavy-handedness of the alignment of power and systemic practice of keeping people down. On the one hand, if a student raises too many questions, the agency representatives become uncomfortable and can close out the student from involvement. On the other hand, if a student tries to speak on behalf of the citizens, she or he becomes suspect of a kind of advocacy that keeps dependency intact and fails to see the task as supporting the development of skills and capacity for the citizens themselves to speak their truth in their own voice in their own time.

In the context of reform concerns within social policy related to dependency and entitlements, will the common sense meaning become "capacity building" policy for all citizens or continue to be rooted in "service delivery?" Service-Learning experiences with solid reflective practices involved have potential to help frame this common sense issue and contribute to its meaningful dialogue.

In this analysis, searching for new common-sense meanings or definitions is an interpretive struggle in the larger context of public policy and day to day practice in higher education and community work. If the dominant groups in the Service-Learning framework, primarily the faculty and the agency contacts, are willing to truly open themselves to the views of students and citizens, then open conversations and "ideal speech situations" are preferable. But if the dominant groups refuse to be open, then the struggle over social and cultural meanings seems a useful way of working with and against domination. By focusing on policy-oriented cultural common-sense definitions rather than role or personal/physical struggle, all the parties have an opportunity to ensure that we retain a sense of our shared humanity even as we struggle against each other, and that our struggles against each other do not deteriorate into hatred, physical violence, or total alienation.

As a faculty colleague recently commented to me, "We intend that students recognize complexity so that they are not satisfied with serving in the soup kitchen. We want them to ask the tough questions about social policies, cultural attitudes, personal histories, and economics that create the climate for making it necessary to have soup kitchens...." Will the common sense meaning in linking service and learning shift from dominance of faculty and agency staff to "shared partnership with students and citizens?"

In Service-Learning activities, reflective practices are crucial for all parties to understand more fully the consequences of their positions and behaviors, and their impact on communication about what matters. As students, faculty, citizens with whom students interact, and organizational representatives engage jointly in Service-Learning activities, the reflective practices employed may well be informed by the three modes of communication and reflection proposed in this essay.

What can be envisioned through the utilization of open communication, "ideal speech situations," and contesting common sense cultural meanings is a team in which each is contributor and contributed to, teacher and learner, and where there is no distorted communication, all are free to listen, share, interject, and express the best that they know and feel at the time.

REFERENCES

1. Feldenkraise, Moshe. *The Case of Nora*. Toronto, Canada: Fitzhenrg and Whitehead Limited, 1977.

2. Castelloe, Paul E. Jr. *A New Way of Traveling: Changing the Practice and Culture of International Tourism.* 1996. Manuscript submitted for publication.

3. Jürgen Habermas has written about discourse ethics, also called communicative ethics (Habermas, 1971;1984;1987; *Knowledge and Human Interests.* Boston: Beacon Press, 1971; *Theory of Communicative Action, Vol. 1: Reason and the Rationalization of Society.* Boston. Beacon Press. 1984; *Theory of Communicative Action, Vol. 2: Lifeworld and System: A Critique of Functionalist Reason.* Boston: Beacon Press, 1987).

4. Rehg, William. *Insight and Solidarity: A Study in the Discourse Ethics of Jurgen Habermas.* Berkeley: University of California Press, 1994.

5. Laclau, Ernesto and Chantal Mouffe. *Hegemony and Socialist Strategy: Towards a Radical Democratic Politics.* London and New York: Verso, 1985.

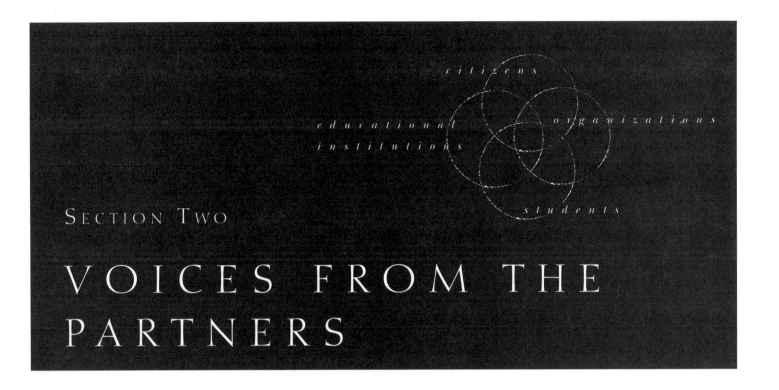

SECTION TWO

VOICES FROM THE PARTNERS

INTRODUCTION

citizen:
Why don't these groups ever ask us what we want or need? I don't have time to be taking care of volunteers.

professor:
Our course goal states: To give students the opportunity to see the face of homelessness firsthand through community placements. ...We did not ask the homeless people themselves if they were willing to educate us.

agency rep.:
I am aware of the mothers' resistance to students. But I need community support and donors, and that comes from the personal experiences. The waiting list is long all the time.

student:
What do they think of us? Why do they think we come? Do they wish we'd leave them alone?

Voices of citizens, community contacts, students, and faculty members are highlighted in this section. The material here follows from the supposition (outlined in the previous section in the chapter "Design Consideration") that *relationships* are vitally important if a Service-Learning experience is going to result in all parties being learners and teachers, contributing and contributed to. This section shows relationships coming together, with groups collaborating to create conditions where each is learning and teaching, serving and being served.

The two concluding journal reports in this section, reflecting conversations with two faculty members, raise salient questions and offer sound advice for those beginning a Service-Learning journey and also for those who have been on the trip a while.

CHAPTER 5
AMONG TRUE PARTNERS

BY JUDY HARVEY

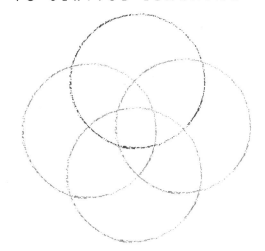

As a Service-Learning enthusiast, I spend much of my time encouraging faculty to add a service component to existing classes, developing issues-oriented Service-Learning courses, and supporting students in their first service experiences.

My enthusiasm is two-fold. As an educator, I'm interested in profound learning—learning experiences that take a student to the edge of what they comfortably know. Exciting things can happen when students are asked to interpret experience in the context of academic-based learning. A strong Service-Learning placement can facilitate that intense learning as well as motivate students in new ways.

I'm concerned by the ever-increasing gap between the people who have access to goods and resources and those who do not. I'm dissatisfied with the inequities of our society. As a concerned citizen, I'm interested in justice. Middle class people can easily live their lives without having significant, personal contact with people from a lower socio-economic group. It is essential for us to understand the complicated elements that contribute to the disparities in our society. What will motivate us to find ways to narrow that gap if we have insulated ourselves from its existence?

A New Course

As I write this, a new course linking service and learning entitled "Homelessness" is being offered for the first time this semester at my institution. As coordinator of the class, I schedule faculty from five disciplines to teach different components of the course, lead discussions on the reading, and supervise the required 54 hours of field work in programs serving homeless people. Students are asking the questions I had hoped they would ask. They're uncomfortable with the lack of options and services. They're concerned about the health and safety of the homeless people they're getting to know. They're angry about the magnitude of the problem and they're confused about where the solutions might lie. They realize this is not one problem neatly packaged as "homelessness." They see the poverty which clearly links all homeless people. As second semester seniors, they wonder what their chances are in this economy as we witness the societal upheaval that comes with the change from an industrial society to a service economy.

This course is a successful venture. Developed in response to student interest and initiative, 15 students and seven faculty members have worked together at various points over the past two years to develop this course. The course was full after the

Judy Harvey is Director of Internships and Service Learning at Guilford College in Greensboro, North Carolina. Guilford's work in the area of homelessness is partially funded by a grant from Learn and Serve America: Higher Education, a program of the National Corporation for Service. Thanks to Carol Clark and Katrina Knight who shared thoughts and advice, and students Heather Adams, Thea Anderson, and Carolyn Howes who conducted interviews.

first morning of pre-registration and had a waiting list of 14 students.

Still, I am left with a nagging discomfort. One of our course goals states: "To give students the opportunity to see the face of homelessness firsthand through community placements." We negotiated partnerships with community agencies serving homeless people. We even started our own tutoring program for children which we run four nights a week at the family shelter. However, we did not ask the homeless people themselves if they were willing to help educate us. The "face of homelessness" mentioned in one of our goals is comprised of real live people who never once have been asked if they are willing to let us see their faces, to hear their stories, to learn from their experiences. We did not ask, "Are you willing to be our teachers?"

We bring with us our imperfections and our individual limitations when we come "to serve." We measure the homeless against our stereotypes, we challenge our prejudices, we re-think our assumptions. This work of refining and reshaping ourselves is important work for us to do and we are often not at our best while doing it. Rethinking our world views and facing other people's pain can make us grumpy and defensive. It is not easy for our students to tread at the edge of unfamiliar territory. Some students hold on to negative assumptions about poor people who are facing homelessness. "Haven't they ever heard of birth control?" challenged one student during a class discussion as we talked about our work at the family shelter. How does it feel to be a single homeless mother and to be "served" by a middle class college student who is silently judging your life?

The moms are tired and stressed. Each day brings another set of obstacles and there is no reason to expect that tomorrow will be any easier. They often yell at their children and all too rarely give the children the quiet, positive attention the young ones crave. It isn't that they don't care about their children. They care fiercely. But this group of single, homeless moms faces more difficulties than anyone should have to face in one lifetime. Low-paying jobs, if they have a job at all. Raising the kids alone. Continued poverty. A racist society. Some are fleeing violent relationships. Others face substance abuse and addiction issues. No family to

serve as a safety net of protection to face all of these problems. No real hope that it will ever be any different. Surviving is what they think about. Possibly the last thing they want are "do-gooders" underfoot. They have had their fill of well-meaning intervention by professionals.

Midway through the semester, some students begin to ask: "What do they think of us? Why do they think we come? Do they wish we'd leave them alone?" One student reports her embarrassment when a mom asked her why she came to tutor at the family shelter: "I was embarrassed to tell her the truth. I told her I came for a class, but I didn't want her to know it was a class on homelessness. I told her I came for a psychology class. I didn't want

It is not easy for our students to tread at the edge of unfamiliar territory.

to embarrass her or make her feel bad about my reasons for coming." Another student reported that a man at the night shelter for single adults had been reprimanded by a staff member in front of the student volunteer. "The staff member told him I was here to help him out of the goodness of my heart. Here he was, a grown man being reprimanded like a child. I felt ashamed to have my work thrown in his face."

We decided to informally ask a few homeless and formerly homeless people how they felt about the volunteers who worked in the programs through which they are served. We talked to moms who lived in the family shelter last year and who now reside in subsidized housing. We talked to moms currently living with their children in the family shelter. We spoke with homeless and formerly homeless single adults who used the shelter system as well as a range of other services available to homeless people.

Lowest on the mothers' list of desirable help were one-shot special events planned by well meaning volunteers. School groups, Sunday school classes, sororities, and youth groups. "Why don't these groups ever ask us what *we* want or need?" complained one past resident of the family shelter. "They act so uncomfortable and it's like they want us to be friendly so it'll be easier for them. I don't have time to be takin' care of no volunteers." This mother reported that some parents refused to come out of their rooms while volunteers were in the shelter. Others, she said, participated reluctantly at the encouragement of the shelter staff.

Conversations with the director indicated that he was aware of the mothers' resistance to these activities, but he feels obligated to say yes to the community groups who want to plan special events for the families. He needs donors and community support and he knows that a personal experience with a homeless family is one of the best ways to get continued support for this desperately needed program. The 15 available rooms are always full with a long waiting list of families needing shelter.

Another negative aspect of the presence of volunteers are people's feelings of being on exhibit. "Sometimes I feel like I'm in the zoo," complained one mother of four. "I reckon the volunteers just want to get a good look at some homeless people." Another formerly homeless woman added, "Even though you don't see a notebook, you know those students are taking notes. It makes me feel kind of strange to think I might end up in somebody's psychology paper." "I don't want to be somebody's class project," said a young single woman in a tired voice.

In spite of the pitfalls involved in trying to serve well, important connections are often made. What then, in the eyes of those being served, allows a connection to form? Commitment, sincere caring and concern, and response to self-identified needs are recurring themes. "I was kind of standoffish at first. But those students came to tutor our children several nights every week for the whole eight months I was living in the shelter. That was some help I needed. I was so tired at the end of the day and I don't always feel sure I know about the kids' homework," remarked a 36-year-old mother of two. "It took a while," added a mother of three school-age children. "But we talked to each other about different things...besides kids...so I learned a little

about the students in a personal manner. They just kept coming back."

A single man who has been homeless for four years explained, "It's extremely demeaning to be homeless. Have you noticed how the sparkle in the eyes of many in the shelter is gone? The light just goes out after so much discouragement. What we really need is love and acceptance so we'll feel valued. It's hard to value ourselves when we feel so low."

Although the people we serve teach us well, many are not aware of their important role. "I wasn't aware that I had anything to give," remembered one formerly homeless woman. This thought was echoed by others.

Three of the people we talked with were aware of their importance. Two former residents of the family shelter had asked tutors to continue working with their children after they moved to their own apartments. A year-long working relationship—initiated by mothers—has mutual benefits for mothers, children, and tutors. The question, "What do the college students learn from you?" at first brought a surprised look to one mom's face but with only a pause of a few seconds she said, "What did the college students learn from me? Well...basically how one can have something in life and go to not having anything...that one day you may have a home and the next day you may not...and I feel like by you all coming into our homes even after the shelter, this gives you another insight of how we are doing, how we are progressing." The second mom reported, "Students learn from us more insight about homelessness from our situations. You students get a variety of views on how poverty might be or how something like this might happen to someone. We help you understand the world."

One homeless man, a dedicated advocate and organizer, was clear about his role with the students. He came to campus to speak to classes and to share a meal with students. He proded and nudged our assumptions about what homeless people need. He enticed us to join him in his work. He had a long list of possible projects ready for students in the course on homelessness. He invited us to host a meeting of the state-wide self-help network for homeless people. He drew us in and we became friends. "I guess I'm just a born teacher," he commented happily after one successful session with students. With great sadness we watched him walk away with all his earthly possessions on his back to find the piece of pavement that was to serve as his bed that night.

We are learning lessons which can be applied to our work here from our experience with poor communities in a semester-abroad program in Mexico. Our institution's relationship with Intercolonias, an organization of poor communities near Guadalajara, Mexico, has taught us a great deal about this issue of reciprocity. They demonstrate a model for negotiating mutual interests and jointly planning for the learning and the doing which has important implications for our work at home.

Each fall we send a group of students to Guadalajara for the semester. Students in a community development course are required to work in one or more of the Intercolonias communities. This relationship was forged very carefully by a faculty member with a great deal of Latin American experience. She knew that a charity model would be of no interest to the people living in these communities. Extensive ground work and many conversations led to a three-hour meeting in which she was questioned about our motives, our college curriculum, and the history of our institution. We were deemed "allies" and the relationship began. The faculty member who negotiated the relationship said, "For the first several years we were always 'on trial.' We needed to please them, prove that we were who we said we were, and to build trust."

The organization of Intercolonias is based on a model of popular education in which members of these communities are educating themselves and others for social change. Their short-term goals are to obtain city services such as garbage pick-up, schools, and paved roads. By working together to achieve their immediate goals they learn about structure, process, and prepare themselves for the long-term goal which is to create a democratic and just society. Their methodology includes four steps: to see, to analyze, to act, and to celebrate. Evaluation is an important part of each step for it is here where much of the learning occurs. Even the celebrations are evaluated!

Everyone involved is clear that the students are not there to teach, but to learn. The residents of the communities decide what the students will do. Each semester the partnership is evaluated. The communities are free to decide to terminate our relationship, but for now we even have a place on the organizational chart.

Two concepts are helpful in understanding how this reciprocity occurs. "Convivencia" means "to live with or get together in order to get to know." These communities recognize that in order to collaborate and to work together there must be informal times to build community and to strengthen communication. Convivencias and fiestas are essential to the communities' ability to work for change. Relationships are strengthened. Spirits are rejuvenated. The work continues and improves because people grow in their ability to work together. Our students are included exuberantly in these wonderful occasions. A one-way relationship of serving is not in the realm of possibilities here.

The second instructive concept is that of solidarity. The faculty member in charge shared this example. "We were leaving Guadalajara for the semester and the students had some clothes they didn't need. We wanted to share the clothes, but we didn't want it to be charity. So I asked the leader of Intercolonias if we could share the clothes, that it would be a shame to throw them away. He agreed that we could give the clothes in solidarity." To be in solidarity means a recognition of the giving as support of shared goals, not as an act of charity. We are in this together. Today I am fortunate to have something which is needed, but tomorrow I may not be so fortunate. Small gifts of self from people who have little become more important than large gifts from people with material abundance.

The example of the Intercolonias communities and the homeless and formerly homeless people who answered my students' questions remind me of the limitations of charity and the narrowness of a paternalistic service model. Perhaps our first step towards improvement can be to recognize the rich possibilities available to us if we expand our notions of what is feasible when people truly collaborate and work together as equal partners.

What a tremendous responsibility it is to send our students into the community! I will continue to work to reduce that small, nagging discomfort that even successful Service-Learning ventures bring to me. My resolutions are firm. I will do my best to send my students into the community with careful awareness. I will prepare them to do no harm and to support them in their sadness when they realize the obstacles faced by their new acquaintances. I will listen and respond to what we are told by the recipients of our service.

My hopes are many.... May we respond to the potential for good present in each human being. May we approach each person, no matter their current situation, with the respect he or she deserves. May we do a better job of communicating the important role individuals play in our lives. May we be grateful for the connections when they are made and open to the possibilities for collaboration among true partners.

The Community Impact of Service-Learning: A Conversation with Lynn Rupp

Recently several West Virginia Wesleyan College education students were involved in a tutoring class of learning disabled middle school students. The college students tutored, maintained contact with the students, and encouraged them with notes and special treats. It was easy for the college instructors to see the results in the students. They were practicing what they were learning in the classroom and gaining a wide range of experience in dealing with at-risk youth. Some of the college students even caught the spirit and spent many more hours than required or continued the experience even after the class ended.

The middle school teacher shared her observations with Lynn:

"We had anticipated that the middle school youths would certainly benefit academically from the additional tutoring. What we had not anticipated were some of the hidden attitudinal changes. Students who had never expressed any interest in education began to ask how one gets into college. Others had perceived college was too expensive. Yet the college students, often from the same background as those who they tutored, talked openly about how they financed their education. They talked about places they lived, places they traveled. Most importantly they talked about the choices they were making in their own lives. For the first time some of the LD students began to practice on their own some of the study strategies taught by the college students. I believe that more has been accomplished with these six students in one semester by these college students than in two years of having me for a teacher."

One reason why these college students were so successful with this group is because they too are learning disabled. They understood these middle school students much better than most teachers. They knew the

Lynn Rupp works with students who serve and learn in the schools near West Virginia Wesleyan College, where she is Assistant Professor of Education. This account is taken from a conversation with Lynn.

avoidance techniques, they understood the frustration, and yet they modeled possibilities for these students.

It is far too early to say that these middle school youths have had their lives changed, but what is possible to say is that these college students were able to offer the care, patience and support the overextended teacher wanted to give but did not have time to give. Perhaps the missing component which the service-learning college students offer to the community is that often-missing combination of time and compassion.

CHAPTER 6

VOICES FROM THE CITIZENS IN THE COMMUNITY

BY DAMITA J. DANDRIDGE AND BARBARA S. FRANKLE

LeMoyne-Owen College, a historically African-American college in Memphis, Tennessee, is, like so many urban institutions today, embedded in a neighborhood fraught with challenges. The peacefulness of the Georgian-columned campus faces an area of poverty, dislocation, violence, and low academic aspiration among the residents. Across the street is a public housing development optimistically named for the college when it was constructed half a century ago. LeMoyne Gardens now houses 2,401 people, two-thirds of the population of a census tract representing a median family income of just $5,142. Only 45% of the population over 25 have completed high school. Among the children, more than three-quarters of the first graders in the district fail to achieve even partial mastery in reading comprehension, as measured by the Tennessee Comprehensive Assessment Program. After having faced a stressful day at school with the odds of achievement and success heavily against them, these children return home to an area so threatened with violence that the police target the district with special nightly randomized sweeps.

Urban institutions can respond to changing neighborhoods by building either fences or bridges. LeMoyne-Owen College has chosen, after some years of insulation, to become a true neigh-

bor. In the words of NBC's Bryant Gumbel, who presented the Institution's Community Outreach Program to young males on the "Today" show, LeMoyne-Owen College is "an oasis of learning in an otherwise barren landscape." Over the past several years, the college has combined several efforts in an extensive, coordinated program. The Social Weavers Service Learning Project is integrally tied to the wider community incentive, with the greatest thrust in the Family Life Center, which houses the holistic Family Life and Revised Real Men Experience Project (FLARRE). Focusing on youth, FLARRE offers mentoring, social, and cultural educational activities for adolescents in the neighborhood. FLARRE draws more Service-Learning students than any other program as it combines a chance to better the neighborhood, and to work with children. After receiving significant training in violence prevention, conflict resolution, mentoring strategies, and problems of substance abuse, the college students work directly with the neighborhood youngsters and their families.

The goal of FLARRE is to prevent violence in the community. The kinds of violence potentially faced daily in the community affect both the physical and spiritual life of a neighborhood confronted with apparent hopelessness and stunted dreams. The mentors want to bring hope and purpose to youngsters more often faced with apathy or despair. Bearing witness to the ways this program can affect the life of the neighborhood are the voices of the residents. Grateful parents testify to the new

---

Damita J. Dandridge, Esq., is Service-Learning Coordinator and Barbara S. Frankle is Associate Dean for Academic Affairs at LeMoyne-Owen College in Memphis, Tennessee.

visions and prospects for growth which the mentors bring.

Mrs. Olan Anderson, a mother of a FLARRE child, recognizes the challenges her youngster must face, and the assistance the project offers:

This program to me has meant that our children are being enlightened on various alternatives that can make a difference in their lives if they are focused on a particular goal. Life is more than a struggle with crime, drugs, and alcohol that we find so prevalent in our community. As a citizen/parent of this community, we are in great need of the type of experiences that FLARRE has committed to bringing to us on a weekly basis as a reminder that there are more appropriate channels of conquering the many obstacles that face us in our everyday lives. I will continue to serve this program in all respects of helping my children as well as others get the message out that our children are somebody. In my weekly observance of attending seminars and orientation of parents, this program has made every effort to bring in individuals from all walks of life to give encouragement and to build the self-esteem of our children through various activities to help their development.

Sandra Mitchell, mother and Gardens resident, sees FLARRE as concretely benefiting her whole family, providing them all with new skills and hopes:

I think FLARRE is a good program. It helps my children to be good citizens in the community. It teaches them to respect others that are older than them. It also teaches them to learn how to communicate with others, to speak out, because Derrick and Broadie are very shy kids. Derrick has learned to speak out a little more and try to participate a little more: but, I enjoy FLARRE myself; it helps me to be a better person and a better mother for my children. The mentors are good teachers for the children of FLARRE. They teach them about drugs, sex, and violence. They also teach them to do the right things in life. But we need more parents to come out and participate in FLARRE.

Not only the parents are aware of the hope FLARRE offers. The children are the focus of the whole village which is LeMoyne Gardens, and their

growth inspires the entire community. Rose Woolfork, president of the LeMoyne Gardens Resident's Association, reflects upon the importance of FLARRE for all the neighbors when she says, "The residents in the housing development are eager to learn, serve and give to the community, the mentees at the college are hope for the young kids. I feel that the mentees have taught the mentors that they (mentors) are the light that shines before them."

The neighborhood school which serves LeMoyne Gardens also welcomes the reinforcement FLARRE offers its students. In acknowledging the gains of one child, Cummings Elementary School Principal Robert Terrell recognizes the benefits to all the youngsters in his care:

The college mentors and mentees from Cummings Elementary School are developing new understanding about serving and learning. At Cummings Elementary School, we see the difference in our students. One student has stated that his grades improved thanks to the love and kindness of his mentor. The youngster told the mentor that his act of caring made a significant difference in his life. Just because the mentor asked why this young man wasn't making good grades, the child pulled them up. This was a revelation to the college mentor that serving in the most seemingly small way may be the prevalent factor in a young person's life.

The mothers applaud the help the mentors give their children. In their words resonate the hope, the love, and the faith that the college students give when they touch the lives of their community:

My son is currently involved in the Family Life and Revised Real Men Experience Project. This is a program I am very pleased with. I feel that the mentors and the college teachers have done an outstanding job in contributing their time to the little children who are in need of guidance.

Jackie Boone

The Family Life and Revised Real Men Experience has made a difference in the lives of many young boys and girls in our community. I am appreciative and thankful that the staff and mentors for this program have made a sacrifice in giving up their time, talents, and abilities interacting with our children...I applaud LeMoyne-Owen College, Dr. Bailey, mentors, and staff for their unselfish love, time, and patience in making a difference in the lives of so many boys and girls in our community.

Olan Anderson

Our students learn the rewards of giving. As Maurice J. Jones poignantly reveals:

I have felt so needed and loved in this program.

Statistical assessment and sophisticated evaluations may tell us that Service-Learning achieves academic goals, but words like these far more tellingly help us know we are indeed laying the groundwork for better futures for our young people.

CHAPTER 7
THE COMMUNITY AND SERVICE-LEARNING

Reflections From Coalition-Building In Western North Carolina

BY THOMAS PLAUT, SUZANNE LANDIS AND JUNE TREVOR

Those of us who believe Service-Learning is an important pedagogy also believe that the university cannot be an ivory tower set apart from the world around it. The university, in our view, is an integral player in the life of a local community, an agency among sister agencies.

Planning for Service-Learning begins with the question: "Who defines the realities and relationships in which we seek to have students learn and grow?" In reality, this question should be "who comprises the community?" Who are the people whose daily work and lives will intersect with (and possibly be enhanced or hurt by) students involved in Service-Learning?

Once we know who "the community" is, and how its members experience and define their world, then we can begin to develop working definitions of our common strengths and needs. Once community and agency people understand that college faculty really listen and that our agenda is to truly hear their agenda, then we can begin to dialogue about a common, collaborative future. We can begin to talk about goals and formulate collective action to reach those goals. Collective action comes after a detailed process of inquiry, reflection, and building personal relationships and trust. A meta-

morphosis is required—from community residents' view of us as faculty at "the college" to neighbor. (One of the nicest compliments one of the authors received came from a rural farm woman whose husband was dying of cancer. After talking for several hours about our hospice program, she confided "when the medical center told us you taught at the college, I figured you didn't know nothing, but they said 'Tom's just country folks like us,' and you are.")

When we move from visioning and planning into action, roles and relationships must be clear and explicit. This is especially important for students in Service-Learning situations. When a student at Mars Hill finally begins a Service-Learning project, she or he has a contract which spells out specific activities and learning objectives, how their work will be evaluated and who will do the evaluating. The contract is signed by the student, a faculty advisor and community/agency member. These parties meet periodically to evaluate how each of them is conforming to the agreement.

Mars Hill College's three decades of experience with service and learning suggests the need for and the reality of interdependence in campus-community relations. As individual students work with public and private agencies, so must college faculty and staff. The institution must join with community organizations in the collaborative creation of a vision for the community, together with the goals, objectives, and ultimately the action that transforms them into reality.

Thomas Plaut, Ph.D., is a Professor of Sociology at Mars Hill College. Suzanne Landis, MD, MPH, is the Director of the Family Practice Center in Asheville, N.C. June Trevor, MSW, works with the Western North Carolina Community Health Research Services.

Much of the Mars Hill College faculty involvement in the Madison Community Health Project was possible only because of the W. K. Kellogg Foundation funding of the community-based initiative described in this article. The foundation provided critical support between 1989 and 1993. Long before that, however, college faculty had

People understand their own health needs and that they need to have a voice in identifying those needs and in identifying the services that address those needs. So, at bottom, it's the community that drives the consortium.

-Madison Community Health Program project director.

worked in the development of a primary care medical service (Hot Springs Health Program), the Rape Crisis Center, Hospice, Habitat for Humanity and Community Development Clubs in Madison County. Faculty had served on community and agency boards of directors, been elected to local public office, and involved students with residents in conducting community-based research. In the 1970s, the college operated "Community Development Institute" under the direction of its Academic Dean, Richard Hoffman. The institute enabled students and faculty to work hand in hand with local agencies engaged in the War on Poverty. The college's "Appalachian Scholars" built mountain trails, camp sites, and trout streams with the U.S. Forest Service; rehabilitated houses; tutored children; and cut, split, and carried fire wood off the college farm to people in need. There is a longstanding Mars Hill tradition of both faculty and student community service. When the Kellogg

Foundation evaluated Madison County as a possible grant recipient in the winter of 1989, they found a tradition of community service, collaboration, and networking already in place.

What we discuss as a case study here is a process of faculty-community collaboration in a Community Oriented Primary Care or "COPC" project in Madison County, North Carolina, that began with the W.K. Kellogg Foundation funding in July 1989. After a brief overview of the project and its outcomes, we list our sense of the requirements for campus-community networking and coalition-building, which can also facilitate student Service-Learning.

Community Oriented Primary Care

The "Community Oriented Primary Care (COPC)" model was developed by Sidney and Emily Kark in South Africa in the 1940s. Community Oriented Primary Care begins with an assessment of the health needs of the population of a defined geographic area and then involves both professional and community members in designing, implementing, and monitoring interventions designed to meet identified needs. The community is at the core of COPC theory and practice. Community members define strengths and needs. In dialogue with medical and human services professionals, they determine health-related interventions. (Kark 1981; Nutting 1990; Overall 1989; Shaler, 1993; Trostle 1986).

Applying the COPC Concept to Madison County

I. The Idea of Community. Since COPC begins with a community assessment, our first task was to determine what people in Madison County, a rural Appalachian county of some 17,000 people in western North Carolina, meant by the word "community." The county's three postmasters were asked to map resident-defined communities within their zip code areas. Their maps were validated and refined by local informants. Communities turned out to be defined as small mountain neighborhoods, based on traditional kinship ties and land holdings. A total of 72 units were identified, along with 350 "community helpers" (defined as people whom residents of a specific community would call if they needed advice or assistance). For many residents, the county is not as much their community as is the traditional, kinship-based mountain "cove." This presented a problem for the COPC process: Which community is "the community?" For the purposes of the project, Madison County became a "community of communities." We decided to talk to as many communities and groups as possible, and invite all interested parties to join the project's "Community Advisory Board, " the group that would decide how the Kellogg monies should be spent.

II. Assessing Community Strengths and Needs. How could information be obtained from residents? "These people have been surveyed to death," one local resident said. "They're tired of being asked if they're poor." This aversion to surveys was widespread. Community-based small group interviews were chosen as a non-threatening and effective means of obtaining community perceptions of health, health-related behaviors, and services delivery. The fragmentation of the county by its mountainous geography, its 72 subjectively-defined communities, its various agencies, and schools and the project goal of community-based change required that as many groups as possible be included in the research process. Consequently, 40 focus groups were conducted: seven with teachers; eight with social services, mental health and community support personnel (the sheriff's office, Extension Service, day care and congregate meal site staff); 11 with medical providers and 14 with community groups. The group interviews were conducted between August and December 1989, involving 416 county residents. The setting for each group was its own turf, be it a school, a fire department garage, a church, or an office.

In addition to focus group results, aggregate data was gathered from federal and state health and human resource agencies and from county agencies such as the Department of Social Services, the Health Department, schools, and the Hot Springs Health Program. Assessment results were given to the Madison Community Health Project Community Advisory Board, or "The CAB."

Interventions

In the winter of 1990, the CAB began a series of grassroots interventions:

- Support for parents of newborn children in a pilot school district by specially trained lay volunteer women recruited by the PTA. (The CAB chose the district because of its active PTA organization)

- Flu and pneumonia vaccinations for people over 65

- Annual health fairs for seniors reaching over 500 people each year

- Forums for high school seniors on AIDS, stress, and stress management

- A newspaper column on health issues, written on a rotating basis by CAB members

- Publication of two resources guides, one for parents and a second for the elderly

- Co-sponsorship of a series of forums on national health care and insurance reform

- An oral health/dental sealant program for school children

The CAB scored a major success in September 1992, when it received a $220,000 grant from the U.S. Department of Health and Human Services to finance a 911 emergency telephone system (to replace a maze of 13 different emergency numbers) and emergency and injury prevention training for county residents. The grant not only provided important and needed services, but made a clear statement to the people whose anger and frustration was manifested in the group interviews at the start of the project in 1989. It provided evidence that their concerns had been heard and had sufficient impact to win a competitive national grant (there were 260 applications for 27 awards). A year later the CAB won an additional $270,000 to further develop the emergency system (Plaut, et al., 1993). The combined efforts of the county health department director, college faculty, and a private medical program director led to a $175,000 grant being obtained in the summer of 1995 for a two-year Diabetes and Nutritional Counseling Education Program.

The trust between agencies and flexibility in work patterns was demonstrated when the grant writing team was able to change the designated recipient of the funding from the health department to the private medical program without creating any arguments or concerns about "turf." The point was to benefit the county at large and not an individual agency.

By the time Kellogg Foundation funding ended in the summer of 1993, the CAB had reconstituted itself as The Madison Community Health Consortium. By December 1994, its membership had grown to 60 and its energy was sufficient to command the presence of the chair of the county commission and school board members. Its membership included virtually all health and human service agencies, private medical practices, a number of Mars Hill College faculty and staff and community groups. It networked these agencies and groups and created trust and personal relations based on a shared history of collective decision making and action. It provided an opportunity for Mars Hill College to become a trusted peer among local agencies and groups, breaking down some of the fear and distance that so often separates colleges from the communities that surround them. When a film crew interviewed the health department director about the impact of the consortium, she replied:

It's probably the best thing that ever happened to Madison County—the best thing that's ever happened to the health of the people of Madison County. We have had an impact on just about every segment of the population. We have taken on projects that impacted health needs that were identified by the community. That's where it starts and that's the only way you're going to make a difference.

COPC and Service-Learning

Students have been involved in many activities of the Madison Community Health Project and Consortium:

- acting as recorders in COPC group interviews

- entering evaluation data into computerized statistical packages

- developing bibliographies on community organizing and coalition-building

- helping set up and run the senior health fairs

- attending and observing CAB/Consortium meetings

- designing, conducting, and writing up the results of evaluation surveys (a process which ended in a dissertation for a MPH student)

- helping in a "Festival of Trees" fund raising weekend for the local hospice

- interviewing senior citizens about perceived barriers to health care

- helping design and build walking/exercise trails

- being asked to conduct CPR classes as part of the 911/rural health education project

- assisting community volunteers to readdress every home and business in the county for the "Enhanced 911," computerized response emergency system

- designing and conducting recreation activities for senior citizens

- interviewing women about barriers to mammograms

- students from medical schools accompanying local providers on their rounds (due to the coordinating efforts of the Mountain Area Health Education Center, which served as a lead partner in the COPC project)

- medical students researching resident breast-feeding practices, adolescent drinking and driving, child abuse, tobacco use among children, resistance to mammograms, depression in the elderly, and the use of automobile seatbelt child restraints.

Students have been networked through the consortium into other agencies, such as the Hot Springs Health Program and Madison County Hospice. One student conducted interviews and developed a slide show explaining the hospice program. Others have been trained and certified for hospice volunteer work. Students remember these experiences as the most vibrant and memorable in their undergraduate education:

I really didn't know what I wanted to do with my life before my internship with the Hospice (arranged through Consortium networking). Now I know I want to be in health administration and my internship was a big plus in getting into graduate school.

Faculty and staff at Mars Hill College developed these Service-Learning options through various actions:

- helping write the original COPC grant (and a number of other grant proposals—some funded (911, Diabetes/Nutrition), some not)

- playing a central role in conducting the original COPC assessment, including gathering aggregate data, conducting focus groups, and mapping the community in terms of resident definitions of "home" communities

- conducting basic data entry and analysis for agency research projects

- serving on the project Community Advisory Board and facilitating decision making at CAB meetings

- working in CAB-directed interventions

- emphasizing the availability of college resources (library, computers, Internet access, research design and data entry, recreational facilities) to local residents, groups and agencies

- serving on agency and community boards

- working with agency/community persons and students to create Service-Learning contracts.

Beyond the COPC project, faculty service on agency boards and networking has enabled student Service-Learning in a variety of roles:

- tutors for school children

- data gatherers and analyzers for the Madison County Health Department, Buncombe County Probation and Parole, Pre-Trial Release Services, and other programs

- investigators and case summary writers for both district attorneys and public defenders, as well as for pretrial release programs

- fund raisers and builders for Habitat for Humanity

- organizers of a "teen court" experiment for juvenile offenders

- assistant probation officers (with their own case load, thereby not only serving and learning, but providing relief to a badly overloaded system)

- counselors in a training school for juveniles

- counselors for a Rape Crisis Center (students developed fund raising activities that have provided the agency with some $5,000 additional annual income)

- members of the Boards of Directors for Madison Habitat for Humanity and the Rape Crisis Centers of Buncombe and Madison counties.

Students have been motivated for work in these efforts in several ways. While a few volunteer simply in the spirit of volunteerism, the majority must complete a specified amount of community service to meet scholarship requirements. Classes take on collective projects. A class in Appalachian studies, for example, helped a community historian gather data by conducting interviews. These kinds of efforts pose problems in terms of transportation, scheduling, and differing levels of study skill and motivation. Some of the more sophisticated work involving data gathering and analysis have been built into senior seminar projects. For example, a senior sociology student recently conducted the required data analysis and surveys for the Madison County Health Department as part of a biannual community diagnosis required by the state of North Carolina.

The college has a special program for community service, funded by the Bonner Foundation of Princeton, N.J., in which 80 students are enrolled and required to complete 10 hours of community service each week and 240 hours in the summer, for which they receive a $3,700 stipend. As freshmen and sophomores, students tutor at-risk youths in local schools. During their junior and senior years they perform services in major cities, the National Parks Service, the National Forest Service, and third world countries during summer and Christmas holiday breaks. Mars Hill Bonner Scholars are now networked with Bonner Scholars at 20 other colleges and are taking leadership roles in the ongoing evaluation and development of the Bonner Service-Learning program. Mars Hill hosted the first meeting of the National Bonner Student Coalition in January 1995.

Several other tuition scholarships are combined to form a group of 75 "Mars Hill Scholars," who must complete 280 hours of community service before graduation. These students begin their college careers with a retreat in which they spend three days working with the National Forest Service, building mountain trails and campsites. Their service projects then vary according to individual interests, ranging from tutoring and/or being a Big Brother/Big Sister to teaching literacy to adults, building and rehabilitating housing, conducting recreation programs for senior citizens, and organizing multi-campus fund raising and other services for agencies such as the "Helpmate" program for victims of family violence, or the Rape Crisis Center. Upperclass scholars have moved into positions of leadership and planning as voting members of agencies' boards of directors.

Suggestions for Reflection

At the outset of the development of a college or university's Service-Learning initiative, faculty and administration would do well to make use of the COPC process described above and join with community organizations and agencies in an ongoing assessment of community strengths, needs, and networks, and the creation of a common vision for the future, together with some proposals on how to achieve it. The assessment can become a blueprint for where and how students can best join in the organic process of unfolding community life and can minimize the confusion and damage caused by "parachuting" students into other people's social worlds and agendas.

Service-Learning offers great opportunities for both students and the community, but it requires continuing institutional investment and commitment, predicated in the knowledge that much of a college's vibrancy for teaching and learning is dependent upon its engagement of the world outside the campus. Working in collaboration with community groups and agencies, perhaps in the context of a community coalition, can maximize the potential for Service-Learning projects.

REFERENCES

Kark, Sidney. *Community-Oriented Primary Health Care.* New York: Appleton-Century-Crofts, 1981.

Nutting, Paul. *Community-Oriented Primary Care: From Principle to Practice.* Albuquerque: University of New Mexico Press, 1990.

Plaut, Thomas, Suzanne Landis and June Trevor. "Focus Groups and Community Mobilization: A Case Study From Rural North Carolina." *Successful Focus Groups: Advancing the State of the Art,* edited by David L. Morgan. Newbury Park, CA.: Sage, 1993.

Plaut, Thomas, Suzanne Landis and June Trevor. *"Enhancing Participatory Research with the Community Oriented Primary Care Model."* The American Sociologist, 23, 4. 1992.

Shaler, George. An Assessment of the Madison County Community Oriented Primary Care Project's Community Advisory Board. Chapel Hill: Health Behavior & Health Education Department of the University of North Carolina, 1991.

Shaler, George. "Putting the Community Back in COPC—The Madison Community Health Project." A Master's Paper in the Department of Health Behavior and Health Education, The University of North Carolina at Chapel Hill, 1992.

Trostle, James. "Anthropology and Epidemiology in the Twentieth Century: A Selective History of the Collaborative Projects and Theoretical Affinities." *Anthropology and Epidemiology,* edited by Craig R. Janes, et al. Boston: D. Reidel, 1986.

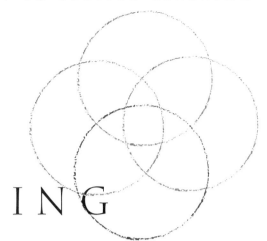

CHAPTER 8

THE VOICE OF STUDENTS IN SERVICE-LEARNING

BY RALPH CORRIGAN

*I*n response to a perceived institutional need at Sacred Heart University to introduce Service-Learning
to fellow faculty members, Professor Corrigan was
asked to present a brief talk about what he had encountered in the writing class of freshmen who had been involved in a Service-Learning experience. Each week
during the semester, students went once a week to a site,
either an urban school, a soup kitchen, a shelter, or a community center in Bridgeport. He says, "by presenting a
chronological overview of the students' experiences and research in their own voices, I hoped to demonstrate to my
colleagues that Service-Learning engaged students in ways
that were not possible in a traditional classroom setting,
and that it was a substantive academic experience worthy
of their investigation. This chapter is a reworking of that
talk."

The voice of authenticity is often missing in student writing. Invariably, students parrot back information gleaned from secondary sources, and as a
result their writing lacks the immediacy that comes
from first-hand experiences. But Service-Learning
changes this dynamic. Instead of rehashing what
they have learned from books and articles, students
become engaged and often moved by the people
they encounter on site, which translates into a different writing "voice"—the voice of authority.

Parker J. Palmer, in his article "Is Service-Learning for Everyone?" alludes to this when he com-
pares the popular image of the "apathetic" college

*Ralph Corrigan is Professor of English at Sacred Heart Uni-
versity in Connecticut.*

student with what occurs when those same students
are involved with Service-Learning:

> *The dominant image of students in too much faculty
> discourse is that they are withdrawn, apathetic,
> almost "brain-dead" when it comes to learning—and
> the blame for their condition is placed on poor public
> schooling, television, and the breakdown of high
> culture. But an alternative diagnosis of their
> condition suggests that student "apathy" is a
> function of their marginality: because society has
> pushed the young to the sidelines and has given them
> little sense of purpose and worth, students believe
> they have few resources to bring to the educational
> process. For faculty who reject student-bashing,
> Service-Learning is an empowering tool that can
> help bring young people from the margins into the
> center, giving students both a social purpose and a
> sense of personal worth in the process of learning
> itself.*

(in *Rethinking Tradition,*
edited by Tamar Y. Kupiec)

Palmer is right on target. Service-Learning
causes a shift in the content and even the style of
the writing as students become immersed in the
day-to-day, on-site activities. What follows are a
semester's worth of chronologically arranged excerpts from the journals and papers of a freshman
English class.

On one level the selections show what happened
to the sensibilities of the students as the semester
progressed; on another level, my hope is that the

passages give evidence of an emerging authenticity in the writing voices of the students.

First and foremost, Service-Learning activities take students and faculty out of the protective environment of a university setting and place them in what for many is unfamiliar territory. Even after—or perhaps because of—a classroom lecture on personal safety, students are apprehensive about entering inner-city schools and community agencies. One student wrote:

I got my first taste of the real world three weeks ago on my first community service assignment to the Hall Neighborhood House in Bridgeport to help in the fight against adult illiteracy. There I was, an 18-year-old college student from a small town in Maine, traveling to an inner city where poverty and crime are seen every day on the streets to help adults with their reading, writing and math skills.... I was about to leave my peaceful life and head into a world totally unknown and contrasting from my own. It would certainly be an unforgettable experience. As we drove out of the Sacred Heart parking lot and down Park Avenue, the thoughts raced through my head. Where was this place? Am I going to get shot? What about the people I'm going to help? Are they going to look down on me for who I am? Total chaos raced through my head for our 15-minute ride. I saw run-down houses, boarded-up shops, garbage lining the streets, graffiti everywhere, and people pushing carts.

Jill Beaudoin

Another student put it this way:

While conversing on a street corner in Bridgeport, a van with about 10 young men pulled up ready to volunteer with Habitat. Then a few more cars packed with volunteers pulled up beside us. The majority of these volunteers were disturbed youths who really had tough times in their lives. Some were heavily involved with drugs, crime, violence, and several of them did not even attend school. I kept thinking to myself, here I am standing on a street corner in the middle of Bridgeport. What did I get myself into?

Michael Dobosz

But once the initial shock of witnessing poverty for the first time wears off, students are genuinely moved by what they see. One student wrote in her journal:

I now knew how Dorothy in "The Wizard of Oz" must have felt when she landed in Munchkin Land. When the car entered Bridgeport I knew that I wasn't at home in Keene, New Hampshire, or at Sacred Heart University for that matter. There were run-down buildings on either side of the street.... But what really got to me was that to some people this was a standard of living. It was life. Buildings that looked as though they were fit to be condemned had people calling them home.

Service-Learning is all about "taking a plunge"—about making a commitment, then moving our students to a different place. It affords students the opportunity to rethink issues, to grow and mature, to be of service to others, to develop a sense of their self-worth, and to take pride in their efforts. It is education at its best.

As the students start to hear the voices of people in the community, they begin to question what they are seeing and their own responses. The same student who wrote the journal piece above, continues:

It is no longer unusual for me to see people clutching at plastic shopping bags full of bottles as if they were their last worldly possessions. I don't find it strange when a man comes up to me asking for bread or a tea bag or sugar and smells of alcohol or urine. And I don't stare at the women or children who are wearing clothing that is too small for their scrawny arms and legs.... I'd like to think that I've opened my mind and my heart, and tried to put myself in their shoes. But it was very difficult—possibly because I'm so sensitive—because more than ever I realized that the people that I once looked at with disgust and fear...they are human. It really hit me when one lady started to play the piano...it was incredible. The kind of playing that takes years to develop. Somewhere, someplace, these people have relatives...have family...have a past.

Joy Graves

Along with the realization that real lives are behind the statistics reported in the newspaper articles, the next stage inevitably follows. The students come to know the people they work with on a one-to-one basis and find that emotional ties begin to develop. One football player writes:

As each session passes, I grow closer and closer to the students. For me, personally, this has grown to be more than just a college English class. This is now more personal. I want to help these children succeed in life. I want to make a difference in their lives. I believe that I have made a difference with a little girl named Nija. Just this week she told me how she wanted me to be her adopted father.

Jason Dion

But identifying with the poor and the disadvantaged carries a price for college students, as is apparent in the following excerpt:

Today our eighth grade class was about to have a Valentine's Day party. The night before, I had stayed up preparing cards for all my students. As I walked through the classroom door I was overwhelmed with all the boys and girls exchanging their cards with each other and also with me. I wasn't about to let them down. I began passing my cards out to all the enthusiastic children when I suddenly realized that one of my favorite students was absent on that much awaited day. I asked a boy, "Where is Pedro today?" He whispered in my ear, "Le tiraron un tiro enfrente de su casa." This means that they shot him in front of his house. Chills traveled throughout my body. I wondered if he was alive. I could have lost my composure right there, but I couldn't ruin their party. That experience was a bitter taste of reality for me.

Tim Aucoin

Such experiences stun the Service-Learning students. Then, after they process what has happened

in discussion groups and in their journals, the students often are moved to action.

In a Monday class, I read parts of articles from the New York Times about proposed federal spending cuts to educational programs. The next day, my students arrived at the elementary school where they worked in an after-school program, and discovered that the program was cut back because of a lack of funding. That same day, a student delegation called me on the phone, demanding to see me at nine o'clock that evening in my office to talk about what they could do about the situation. Here's how one student processed the incident:

The Bridgeport school district has signed the death warrant for our future. They have canceled an after-school program due to some financial difficulties. This program was very important to all those involved with it, from the staff, to the volunteers, to the families, and most of all to the children it served. Many of the children involved have nowhere else to go after school because their parents work. These are young, impressionable, and relatively naive minds. To leave them unsupervised is to leave them as prey to the evil the world around them holds. When I first heard about this, I was sickened, horrified, shocked, outraged, and terrified beyond what I thought was imaginable....

We, the country as a whole, have been part of a mass genocide much larger than that of the Holocaust. It is a suicide of our own future, the exact ramifications of which will not be known for many years. What makes this situation more devastating is that we are not even fully aware that we are committing such a heinous crime. This offense has reached national proportions due to the careless actions of our national, state, and local leaders. But the blame should not rest solely on the heads of our officials. It rests in our hands as well. After all, it is our responsibility to insure that the needs of the country are being addressed properly by those in charge. We should be electing people who will look out for the best interests of the country and not their own interests.

Sande Baer

Soon students are reflecting on and wrestling with national issues, not because they haven't thought about these issues before, but because their experiences are causing them to think about these issues in new ways. On-site commitments force them to rethink old positions or, even more to the point, the positions of their parents that they've automatically assumed as their own.

Here is one student working her way through this new awareness:

I used to think that the majority of people dealing with poverty had brought it on themselves. I figured they all did drugs or dropped out of school because they didn't like it. I thought if they just tried harder and got a job—any job—that they could stop sitting at home collecting welfare checks.

I certainly realize now that these ideas are way off. What about the children who are born into poverty? Did they bring this upon themselves? Many of these children born into poverty will end up living in poverty all their lives. They'll go to public schools where few of them will be lucky enough to have teachers (even one) like Mazie Muniz who actually cares for her students. They'll just go through the motions of getting a minimum education. Since nothing better is expected of them, they'll drop out of school or get pregnant at 15. Others will try to make something of themselves by selling drugs to get rich. There is so much room for these kids to end up going in the wrong direction. I do believe that it is up to the individual to decide what kind of life to lead, but then that idea has been put into my head by very caring adults. What if no one ever believed in me, or said they were proud of me? Would I still feel the same way?

Hope Morrison

There is an "engaged" tone to the above passage because the student, frustrated with our flawed system, is asking questions about issues that now matter to her. Another student writes:

It seems as though the Republican "Contract with America" and welfare cuts are inevitable. As much as I wish I could make it mandatory for all those proposing the cuts to work in a soup kitchen, I know that this is not possible and can only hope that some might see that they are not reforming welfare but rather they are wiping out hope for many.

As a college freshman I don't know much in comparison to what I will know when I graduate with the Class of 1998. But I do know that the government that I believed was established to help and better the people of the United States is now letting down and overlooking a population of people who I have worked with extensively over the past semester and have come to care a great deal about. This semester started out just like the last one, and I was taking just another English class. But all that has changed. Through talking to Mike Jones, hearing about baby Emily's HIV test, and researching welfare it has become a lesson in life.

If there is one thing that I have learned this year and will take with me as I move on it is that one person can make a difference. No matter how small the deed…one person will make a difference. So…I look back on the lessons I have learned, the people I have met, and the feelings that I have felt, and realize that I have become a bit more empathetic and much more human.

Joy Graves

When it begins to dawn on the students that their presence makes a difference, that people actually count on them to be there and are appreciative of their efforts, they are amazed. Many register difficulty grasping the impact they have had on people:

As I walked into that final day at the Winthrop School, I had no idea what to expect. I thought the children were not even aware that it was our last day, but I was strongly misguided. When we walked by the doors of the library we noticed that they were hiding. We opened the doors, and the children were hiding behind the front desk. All of a sudden, they all jumped out, a few with roses in their hands, and screamed "surprise!" I could not believe my eyes. Were these children actually going to miss us? Did we really have that much of an impact on their lives? I felt a tear come to my eyes, and was very moved by it all.

I then sat down at my regular table, and one of my girls, Lorissa, handed me a rose, while the others smiled, waiting for me to open the card that was attached. As I opened it, I still could not believe that they went through all this trouble for me. The card read that they just wanted to say that they loved me and thanks. I couldn't believe it.

Jillana Grundy

Another student writes:

Many do not realize the rewards and benefits of seeing people so grateful for helping them understand something as simple as the multiplication table. We do not realize how much we take for granted until we experience it first-hand. We can listen to the stories that community service volunteers tell, but the feelings do not really hit home unless we get the chance to experience it ourselves. It is amazing how much of a difference one person can make in another's life.

I look back now at my experience at Hall Neighborhood. I wonder, what if I never had signed up for this class? All the people and experiences would have been gone forever. I treasure those moments now. The odd thing is that these people don't even think or realize that they have touched my life. I find myself daily thinking about the people I have met there. I wonder where they go after they leave Hall Neighborhood, or if they are still healthy and alive from all the crime that is such a familiar sight to them. I look back and I am thankful for everything I have gained.

Deirdre Hynes

One student talks about changing her major because of her Service-Learning experiences:

I loved working with the children. I loved it so much, that I am considering changing my major from Sports Medicine to Elementary Education. Children today have an extremely hard time trying to have a safe and "normal" childhood. It seems as if all children have to grow up at least 10 years faster because of all the drugs, poverty, violence and even death. I feel that if I were to become a teacher, I would want to teach in an inner-city community, because that is where the demand is for people who really care. By teaching, I feel that if I could make a difference in just one child's life, then my job has been fulfilled.

Karen Hennig

And then there are the emotions felt when leaving the work site for the last time:

Service-Learning student Kim Sousa, who works with the children at Merton House, agrees: "During the time you spend with the kids, you aren't aware how close they have become or how they have touched your life. You only begin to realize and understand it after you can't be with them anymore." Those who

think that the children's faces will be easily forgotten should look in the desk drawers and on the walls of the Service-Learning students. What they will see is a semester's collection of drawings and crafts made by the children. These objects are being kept as living memories of the children they have become attached to.

Kendra Laptik

Another student presents a letter to his cooperating teacher on the last day of his Service-Learning experience:

Toward the last few minutes of the day, I presented my letter to Mazie. She broke down in tears in front of me. We hugged each other. She thanked me continuously for all my help.

Finally, as we got ready to leave Winthrop, I looked down the hallway for the last time, walked past the steps with the kids running by. The school would always be here and so would the spirit of these children.

It all came down to hugging a little girl on the front steps of the school. It was my last gift from the kids.

Jim Pane

Still another student writes about how his learning experiences over the semester changed him:

I feel as though the lessons that I have learned through my Service-Learning class have been priceless. I never imagined that I would be walking away from a college English course that has changed me in so many ways. Not only did I learn the correct way to cite a quote, but I also discovered that I love to work with children. And I also found a caring side to my heart that has never emerged before this class.

Jason Dion

These students are not apathetic and not "brain-dead." They are real people, discovering their own voices while engaged in an educational process that empowers and transforms them.

Service-Learning is all about "taking a plunge" —about making a commitment, then moving our students to a different place. It affords students the opportunity to rethink issues, to grow and mature, to be of service to others, to develop a sense of their self-worth, and to take pride in their efforts. It is education at its best.

CHAPTER 9

FACULTY ON
SERVICE-LEARNING

Why do liberal arts college faculty chose to spend time and effort on promoting and implement
ing Service-Learning within their own courses, departments, colleges, and communities?
The Council of Independent Colleges' innovative Serving to Learn, Learning to Serve
project brought together many of these faculty in 1994-95. Some of them chose on their own to develop statements about why they do Service-Learning. These statements are printed here in their original or edited versions with each author's permission.

Sources And Watershed Events:
Why Do I Do Service-Learning?

BY JOHN REIFF

When I was a sophomore in college, my philosophy professor, John Silber, assigned the class a field
research project. Alongside reading Plato,
Descartes, and Kant, we were expected during our
Thanksgiving and Christmas breaks to go back to
our home towns and learn about low-income housing. We were to interview people who lived in a
poor neighborhood, then try to talk to their land-
lords and to city officials responsible for enforce-
ment of housing codes. As a child of privilege, I
found myself drawn into a world I had driven by
but never seen.

One bitterly cold West Texas afternoon, the tem-
perature about 12 degrees and the wind blowing
hard, I found myself inside a one-room house.
Roaches thronged upon the walls and floor and on
the chair I had been invited to sit on. The only
heat came from a gas space heater with a pot of
food cooking on top of it. My host showed me a
picture of her husband, recently killed in Vietnam.
She told me how, after cleaning people's houses all
day, she came home and helped her children with

*John Reiff is Associate Professor of American Cultures at
Tusculum College in Greenville, Tennessee.*

their homework, so they could succeed in school.
She worried that they didn't understand what you
need to know about life: "What do you do when
you reach the end of your rope? You tie a knot and
you hang on." After she got them all through high
school, she planned to go to school herself—to
learn to be a nurse, so she could return home to
the Navajo reservation and give health care to her
people, whom she described as in great need. As
the interview was ending, she remembered the
food cooking on the space heater and ran to pull it
off; it was burning. I apologized for distracting her
from her cooking, and she tried to make me feel
better: "It's all right. At least this way, we got to
keep the heater on a little longer," and she turned
off the heater.

This was not a typical "Service-Learning" experience, but it was a kind of Service-Learning. It was I
that was served, and I had the opportunity to learn.
This woman not only helped me with my school assignment; she taught me to see—to see in those
wretched conditions her courageous and compassionate spirit.

Two years later, I set up an independent study
with an artist, Don Weismann. I wanted to learn
about making art, and I didn't want to compete
with students in regular studio art courses, I bar-
gained with him to get his help and advice if I kept
a journal recording my efforts at creativity. The
first piece I made during the week I was deciding
to file as a conscientious objector; it was in clay—a
cannon supported by a wheel on one side and on
the other side a boot, stomping a prone figure into

the ground. In making it, I needed something to dig out and smooth the clay between the cannon and the boot; I searched through the house, and finally found a spoon whose handle did the job. When I presented the piece and the journal to Don, he smiled and said, "You have discovered the need for tools. I thought about telling you about the kinds of scrapers and shapers that people who sculpt clay use, but I figured that if you were attentive to the work, it would define for you the tools that were needed." At that point I gained an insight into the creative dialectic between worker and task that went far beyond my piece of clay; I also, for the first time, encountered the teaching power of dialogic reflection on experience.

A year later, I had the good fortune to be asked by my draft board to tell them why they should designate me as a conscientious objector. Gripping my notes like a shield, I told them that my upbringing in the Southern Baptist church had taught me that all human beings had infinite value, and that I was called to affirm life, to use my life to create, not to destroy. This was a watershed moment for me, defining both the importance and the meaning of service in my life.

Two streams have come together in my life—one focusing on service, the other on learning through experience. Service affirms life, building connections among people that can help sustain them. Experience connects the learner to the complex realities of the social world. In both of these streams, the most important elements have been the people and situations I have encountered directly. The stories above are only some of the most important influences; others would include my parents, my students, my supervisors at the youth and family counseling center where I worked for a year, and Molly Rush, grandmotherly smasher of nuclear nose cones.

Various writers have also helped guide me toward Service-Learning. Central among them were John Dewey, whose *Education and Experience*, read when I was in college, helped me articulate a rationale for the experiential education I had come to believe was so important; James Agee, Studs Terkel, and Robert Coles, whose attempts to render with clarity and compassion the lives of people quite different from them helped me focus on the importance of experience that bridges gaps between

people; and Fran Peavey, whose *Heart Politics* shows how a life can move through different chapters searching with others for a shared good, and how reflection on that action can lead to insight.

The Value & Rationale For Combining Service And Learning: Personal Reflections

BY FREDRIC A. WALDSTEIN

During the past several years I have been trying to recreate some of the excitement about learning (and teaching) that I have experienced over the years as an active participant in various community settings. "Learning by doing" combined with an element of service has rekindled that excitement in me. I spend much time thinking about why this is the case. What is it about this pedagogy that makes it more stimulating than the traditional classroom dynamic? Several themes seem important in creating that excitement. I would like to identify some of these and attempt to explain their significance to me at this point in the evolution of my career.

Professional satisfaction demands that the teaching/learning experience be meaningful and enjoyable for me personally. To be successful, the

Fredric A. Waldstein holds the Irving R. Burling Chair in Leadership and is Professor of Political Science at Wartburg College in Iowa.

experience must be something to which I am personally committed. Perhaps that to which I am most committed is teaching our students the value of taking responsibility for their communities and making them better through public action. In fact, that is the definition of leadership that Wartburg College has adopted. This theme permeates all courses I teach. At the risk of sounding apocalyptic, I believe the survival of our democratic system is dependent upon our ability to encourage our students to value democratic engagement in the public sphere. We are, among other things, educating students to lead lives as productive citizens. I pursue this daunting challenge using certain pedagogical "tools" that are symbiotic with the concept of Service-Learning, broadly defined. I will focus on some of these.

A strong sense of civic responsibility depends on something Daniel Yankelovich identifies as "public judgement," a concept to which he devotes an entire book.[1] Public judgement refers, at least in part, to the capacity of citizens to employ skills of critical inquiry to make informed decisions about that which is in the best long-term interests of the polity at large. This is a normative value judgement. It is one I accept as reasonable.

Yankelovich refers to the work of the German sociologist, Jürgen Habermas, to develop the belief that education is critical to attain the capacity for public judgement.[2] Learning as a process has an emancipatory effect. It encourages one to participate productively in the marketplace of ideas. This, in turn, encourages active participation in the public sphere and can lead to what Carole Pateman defines as participatory democracy, a form of democracy that can transcend politics and permeate all aspects of society.[3]

Crucial to the evolution toward participatory democracy is the encouragement of certain ground rules which facilitate its development. The dialectical theory of reasoning is compatible with emancipatory learning because it accepts as fundamental to the growth of knowledge the exchange of competing ideas and information as necessary to reach a higher order of knowledge.

Critical to the quality of dialectical reasoning is the civility of the discourse practiced in the dialogue. The free exchange of competing ideas can be chilled quickly if individuals are fearful that their expressions may cause them to be ostracized or otherwise discriminated against. This, consequently, is a handicap to attaining public judgement.

The traditional academic model whereby the expert teacher instructs the ignorant student to become educated like him/herself is largely counterintuitive to emancipatory learning. A more democratic, collaborative approach of shared inquiry, as articulated by Paolo Freire, is the concept of dialogical education.[4] The student and teacher are co-inquirers, each bringing different background characteristics that will make the inquiry richer than if only one individual is perceived to be the source of knowledge and wisdom.

Combining service and learning is compatible with my teaching objectives, as are the means identified as important in achieving them, both in traditional academic and nonacademic venues. Francis Moore Lappé and Paul Martin DuBois have synthesized much of this thinking into a "workbook for doing democracy" that is highly accessible to a broad audience.[5] Of particular value is their insistence that democracy is a process, not an outcome. Similarly, education, especially emancipatory education, is a dynamic process. The goal of the educator in this context is to create opportunities for the student to engage in reflective self-discovery that encourages her/him to remain engaged in the learning process beyond the formal academic experience.

A combination of community service with a reflective, analytical component is one means of promoting emancipatory learning by employing dialogical education, the dialectic, and civil discourse. This can occur if students are given the opportunity to identify and encounter actual challenges faced by a community, develop a plan of action to address them that includes collaboration with members of the community, undertake the plan of action, and reflect upon the outcome and the implications of the outcome. In this model the broader community becomes the classroom and the teacher. The instructor becomes a co-inquirer who brings his/her experience to the project, but initiative remains with the students.

There are certain disadvantages associated with combining service and learning. It is more complex logistically to execute than the traditional pedagogy. Also, many faculty members are not comfortable with evaluating student performance. It is not a model of learning to which most academics have had significant exposure. But the literature in this area is growing and the more one employs this pedagogy the more likely one is to find tools for evaluation with which one feels comfortable.

The advantage of this model is that it has the potential to expose students to the worldwide communities into which they will graduate in a context that encourages successful interaction within their respective communities. This, in turn, may encourage students to become actively engaged in their communities as a means for personal education and self-fulfillment that is consistent with the underlying values of a democratic society. The result can be mutually rewarding and satisfying to teacher, student, and the community at large.

NOTES:

1. Yankelovich, Daniel. *Coming to Public Judgement*. Syracuse, N.Y.: Syracuse University Press, 1991.

2. See, for example: Jürgen Habermas. *Knowledge and Human Interests*, translated by Jeremy J. Shapiro, pp.301-317. Boston: Beacon Press. 1971.

3. Pateman, Carole. *Participation and Democratic Theory*. New York: Cambridge University Press, 1970.

4. Freire, Paulo. *Pedagogy of the Oppressed*. New York: Continuum Publishing Co., 1970.

5. Lappé, Francis Moore and Paul Martin DuBois. *The Quickening of America*. San Francisco: Jossey-Bass, 1994.

The Source Of Service: An Autobiographical Bibliographical Exploration

BY WILLIAM R. REYER

The deepest element of God's command to protect human life is the requirement to show reverence and love for every person and the life of every person.

—John Paul II, ***Evangelium Vitae***, 72

The essential focus of Service-Learning is theological in my view, rather than civic or cognitive-developmental. While many view the Service-Learning movement as a means for creating good citizens or aiding students in their journey from dualism to committed relativism, for me the relationship of self to service is, fundamentally, an expression of the triangular relationship between oneself, one's neighbor, and one's image of the divine. By preparing for service and doing service and reflecting on service we become more adept at "show[ing] reverence and love for every person," which—despite what one may think of his gender and population politics—John Paul II rightly sees as "the deepest element of God's command to protect human life."

Before I turn to those texts which have been instructive to me regarding the nature of service—drawing from them themes related to the Service-Learning movement—I wish to pause a moment to consider what your needs may be in reading such a self-indulgent document as this. What practical information, in addition to inspiration and provocation, may be of use to you? Valuable Service-Learning, besides incorporating the three-step process of preparation, action, and reflection, functions, it seems to me, at three levels: the practical, the social, and the spiritual.

William R. Reyer is Professor of English and Director of the Honors Program at Heidelberg College in Ohio.

Anyone wishing practical advice for the creation of Service-Learning programs at the collegiate level will want to turn to two sources for direction: the institutional mission statement of one's own college and to the three volumes of *Combining Service and Learning: A Resource Book for Community and Public Service* (Kendall and Associates) published by the National Society for Experiential Education. The mission statement will serve as the well-spring for any rationale statements or program mission statements that may be required. The *Resource Book* will provide models, theoretical discussions, and more. For example, Heidelberg has received permission to include the 10 "Principles of Good Practice in Combining Service and Learning" in our Honors Program Handbook. A recent evaluation consultant noted in her comments that these 10 principles will provide the basis for an assessment device which we will construct to measure the success of our students' Service-Learning experience.

Since I am by training a student of literature and not of sociology or political theory, my reflections on the manner in which service functions at the social level have a literary cast. This is not at all unfortunate, however, since the two works which have enriched my understanding of service as a social phenomenon also introduce two of the important themes in the dialog developing around Service-Learning: civil disobedience and healing. Henry David Thoreau's classic "On the Duty of Civil Disobedience" reminds us—and our students, should we use his essay as one of the preparatory texts for service—of the importance of individual influence. Thoreau's essay also introduces a question which requires courageous dialog in any school which institutes a Service-Learning program: what is the relation between political advocacy—protest—and service? John Paul II's statements on abortion, euthanasia, and the death penalty in *Evangelium Vitae* reflect the importance of this question as well.

The focal purpose of the Service-Learning movement is not political action, however, but individual acts of healing. In *Beloved*, her novel which explores the ambiguity of acts of moral decision, Toni Morrison creates a character who embodies service to the community, Baby Suggs. Morrison renders a scene of combined grief, reconciliation, and self-reclamation which serves as an inspiration for anyone who would enter into service to others. To the community of escaped slaves and their families which she serves, Baby Suggs offers her heart and a sense of reality:

> *Baby Suggs, holy, offered up to them her great big heart. She did not tell them to clean up their lives or to go and sin no more. She did not tell them they were the blessed of the earth, its inheriting meek or its glorybound pure. She told them that the only grace they could have was the grace they could imagine. That if they could not see it, they would not have it (88).*

Service concerns itself with individual and social healing. Through the character of Baby Suggs, Morrison reveals that the one who would serve must have a keen sense of reality as well as a big heart. It is this combination of attributes that responsible Service-Learning programs require.

One cannot separate the practical and social concerns from the spiritual perspectives which under-gird them, of course. One cannot hear the passion and power of the Black Gospel recordings of Marion Williams like *Surely God is Able* (Spirit Feel - 1011) without hearing the passion and power of her faith. Her work in Philadelphia introduces two additional themes into the Service-Learning dialog: What is the relationship between service and faith-witnessing; and what is the relationship between service and artistic performance? The first of these questions must be considered in the light of an institution's and an individual's faith tradition; the second must be considered to permit uniquely gifted individuals to express their gifts through meaningful service.

Service stems from need, of course, and need—regrettably—finds its root in suffering—both human and environmental; and who cannot doubt that suffering, along with being itself, remains the great mystery? The Poet of Job unfolds for us the need to admit the mystery of suffering so that we may have courage to serve in its midst. Job himself, like Thoreau, reminds us that individual integrity is a precious possession, the successful guardianship of which makes us fit for service to others—as Job served his friends at the poem's close. Finally, the Voice from the Whirlwind in the majestic Hymn to Creation (chapters 38 - 41) reminds us that the Earth is not ours—its exquisite fabric comes from a source other than our hands. The themes of the mystery of suffering and the human being's co-creaturehood with the rest of the natural world are themes that anyone who would devote herself or himself to service should encounter in this great poem.

I offer these themes and comments on enriching texts, realizing that they arise from dialog with fine minds and compassionate hearts: colleagues from my home institution and the CIC Service-Learning Alliance. I offer them for any support they may lend to beginning Service-Learning programs which may strengthen the developing moral sense of our students: "…it is always from this intimate sanctuary of the conscience that a new journey of love, openness, and service to human life can begin" (John Paul II, 43).

Philosophical Foundations/ Perspectives For Experiential Education

BY GARRY HESSER

As a product of Boy Scouts, 4-H, church youth groups, Y-Teens and parents who valued and exemplified community service, I suppose you could say that I was born into "Service-Learning." But my first self-conscious involvement came at Phillips University in 1960, when an OT professor challenged a group of us to form a "First Mile" club to serve the elderly in the county home and nursing

Garry Hesser is Professor of Sociology and Urban Studies and Director of Experiential Education at Augsburg College in Minneapolis.

homes, attending to basic needs like shaving the men, talking, and doing things that the staff did not have time for. We met every Thursday morning at 7:00, to discuss and reflect on those experiences. Then, there was the field work I did in a public housing apartment in New York City and the OEO program working with Native Americans as a sociology graduate student, all of which enabled me to learn the value of combining learning and service. As a teacher, my initial experiences derived from encountering the transformed students who returned from Philadelphia, Detroit, Portland, San Diego, some of whom talked me and my family into living with them in a community service house at the College of Wooster, where each student initiated and assisted in a community service endeavor and we all designed a course on "Community" ['72].

This led me into Rosabeth Moss Kanter's book on *Community and Commitment* and the works of Roland Warren on community and community organizing, thus helping me to integrate my own background in the sociology of community and the meaning-making journey which all of us took as co-learners. Simultaneously, I was re-engaging in the efforts of the Ecumenical Institute in Chicago, finding their effort to synthesis "all that was known" about communities, faith, and global realities both stimulating and overwhelming. The Institute's "5th City" enterprise in Chicago's West Side and around the world and their pushing the edges of envelope of theory and practice intensified my own valuing and learning from a "praxis" form of education.

Then, a book and a community of experiential educators literally focused and fundamentally altered my life. Nadinne Cruz loaned me a copy of David Kolb's *Experiential Learning* (1984) when I became the President of the Higher Education Consortium for Urban Affairs (HECUA). Kolb's synthesis of Dewey, Piaget, Lewin, Freire, et al., coupled with my re-introduction to the National Society for Experiential Education (NSEE) seemed to turn on "all" the light bulbs. NSEE's *Strengthening Experiential Education in Your Institution*, coupled with the mentoring of Sharon Rubin, Jane Kendall, John Duley, Robert Sigmon, Jane Permaul, and the Cornell Field Studies staff in the NSEE consultant training process refocused my professional life on the role of experience as a catalyst in effective teaching and learning. The years of serving on the NSEE Board (two as its President), during the time that the Wingspread Principles and the two-volume *Combining Service and Learning* were written, brought me into continual dialogue and collaboration with those who were instrumental in the re-emergence of Service-Learning as an educational enterprise and movement. Freire's *Pedagogy of the Oppressed* and the *Politics of Education* came alive when I had the opportunity of a lifetime to spend three days with him and William Foote Whyte (*Street Corner Society* and *Participatory Research*) in an American Sociological Association teaching workshop.

The opportunity to begin attending AAHE annual conferences in conjunction with meetings of the NSEE Executive Committee put frosting on the cake by introducing me to the words and writings of Donald Schon, *The Reflective Practitioner*, and a former seminary classmate, Parker Palmer, *To Know As We Are Known*, and the research and writing of Pat Cross, *The New Students*, Derek Bok's *Higher Learning*, and Ernest Boyer's *Scholarship Reconsidered*, where the focus was upon how students learn as well as on what they should learn. As I conducted faculty workshops as an NSEE and Campus Compact consultant and continued to teach Service-Learning classes and coordinate the Internship, Service-Learning and Cooperative Education staff and faculty, my own learning curve stayed on high. Thanks to Jane Kendall's pulling together the voluminous articles on *Combining Service and Learning*, published by NSEE, we have access to a never-ending gold-mine of resources, complemented by the Praxis series by Jeff Howard, et al., out of the University of Michigan. Sharing my syllabi with colleagues in workshops, reading the journals of my interns and introductory sociology students engaged in combining service and learning, and working in my city neighborhood and visiting the seniors in the nursing home whose board I chair, all continue to transform my own teaching and learning with life as the "textbook" and the challenge and delight of always being and living in an experiential learning cycle and process.

Grassroots Biblio-Biography To Service-Learning/ Community-Building

BY A. KAY CLIFTON

I was introduced to widening circles of reciprocal giving by my parents' modeling and invitation. Mom led the way to gardening and neighborly exchanges. Dad led the way, usually with other friends of the family, to woods, fields, and streams for hunting, fishing, and gathering (some animals, but mostly fruits, nuts, and decorations). Mom showed us that much preparation must be done for youth groups, such as Scouts, to facilitate personal growth and interpersonal/group understanding. I recognize a deep internalization of an abiding Scout motto: "Leave places better than how we find them." Dad introduced me to his version of civic service when he took me on his wartime, neighborhood air raid rounds. We not only checked on "lights out" but we also stopped in to visit those who lived by themselves. Our family grocery store was both a business and a service—people bought groceries, of course, but also traded jokes, political and sports opinions, and family problem-solving. Our family of six was parented by both Mom and Dad, and since we were all introvertish, conversations were probings and reflections. All this occurred within Methodism (work is a calling to improve the world) and an MYF with fun, community service, and wise, caring adults for reflection. Most of my readings have developed appreciation for these roots and sought examples for rebuilding our world communities.

My parents sent me to Iowa Wesleyan College, presumably to curb some restless and rebellious spirits they had spotted. I did not reject my roots, but instead began to ask why others had not been as privileged as I was with regard to quality of life

A. Kay Clifton is Professor of Sociology and Social Work at the College of Mount St. Joseph in Cincinnati, Ohio

and why this same quality of life was disappearing for all of us.

My philosophy professor was the first one to let me know how privileged and protected I was. I met him crossing campus one fall day and he said, apparently knowing I was considering pledging, "Sororities discriminate, you know!" I retorted naively but proudly, "Oh, I don't think we (I had made a tentative choice) would." "It's in their national charters," the professor said, "find out about it. Think about it."

That was 1956 and I have been finding out and thinking about it for almost 40 years. My mind was beginning to be opened to social, cultural, ethnic, and gender diversity by the earlier works of two women anthropologists: Ruth Benedict, *Patterns of Culture*, and Margaret Mead, *Coming of Age in Somoa* and *Sex and Temperament in Three Primitive Societies*. These books also linked biology, personality, social structure, and cultural patterns in my mind as interdependent explanations of human, and even other animal, behavior. I wandered around among these majors until a text, *Social Psychology* by Lindesmith and Strauss, wove them all together with social linguistics. My philosophy of life, learning, and service is woven with interdisciplinary pursuits.

I was eager for the 1960's books on social justice: Harrington's *The Other America*, King's *Why We Can't Wait*, Carmichael and Hamilton's *Black Power*. The latter led most social scientists away from the post-WWII authoritarian personality explanation of prejudice and discrimination to one that focused instead on social structure and cultural patterns, with the introduction of the concept of institutional racism. It was, however, *The Autobiography of Malcolm X* that so vividly explored the effects of these social forces upon the lives, families, and communities of oppressed peoples. To these books were added several general critiques of industrialization/modernization: Paul and Percival Goodman, *Communitas*; Jacque Ellul, *The Technological Society* (I recommend his *Technological Bluff* to students today). I was not finding alternatives in books, but instead in the interactions and pamphlets of social movements: free speech, civil rights to black power, anti-war, and by the late 1960s feminism and then ecology with the first Earth Day in

1970. Ecology, social justice, and feminism have increasingly joined paths in the pursuit of personal, family, and community revitalization. My ecology knowledge began with learning to identify, and for this Golden (for beginnings) and Peterson Guides to trees, wildflowers, insects, mammals, etc. are indispensable. When you can name them they are no longer just weeds or bothersome and you can begin to note their connections to one another and to us. Country living added more gardening experience and books: Rodale's *Organic Gardening Encyclopedia* and Ruth Stout's *No Work Garden Book* offered alternatives to the growing chemical approach. Louise Riotta's *Companion Planting* relayed folk knowledge about plant and insect connections that are useful for gardeners. And recently, Gary Nabhan's *Enduring Seeds* affirmed that natives had been developing applied natural science about plant and animal connections for thousands of years. Before that, Bateson's *Steps to an Ecology of Mind* was the first academic book to legitimize my sense of the intricate connections between humans and the rest of nature. His later *Mind and Nature* continues the story. For me, then, Service-Learning should not only work for social justice, but also help build a sense of place with its accompanying knowledge and responsibility.

Feminism started with Betty Friedan's *The Feminine Mystique* and continued with books, speakers, and consciousness-raising groups. These helped make sense of three, then four, and now five and a half decades of experience. One example in the late 1960s, relevant to a philosophical stance, will illustrate my point. Many people were looking for alternatives and a speaker at the university was explaining what we might learn from Eastern religions and philosophies that were not so egocentric. I was very interested, and still am; however, I suggested during the Q and A that many of these value-orientations existed among women and why not look for home-grown expertise. He of course, as men were inclined to do then, paternally suggested that my idea was "nice" but not well-researched. I cited the work of Florence Kluckohn on variations of value orientations and the work of Dorothy Lee that indicated that others beside women had self-concepts that connected with nature and human others. He said he had never heard of them, which, of course, dismissed both them and me. It would not take long before academic feminists would begin providing more well-known research that has certainly convinced me that many Western women, while living for centuries within patriarchies and growing materialism, have retained significant threads of a non-Eurocentric world view. A landmark book is Carol Gilligan's *In A Different Voice*. With this affirmed, women began recognizing their links with nature, with one another internationally, and began critiquing modernity. Griffin's *Women and Nature* began the re-examination and Merchant's *The Death of Nature* examined how the development of the current mode of science left behind the cooperation between humans and nature. A major international voice is Vandana Shiva, whose books describe and explain the failure of much third world development: *Staying Alive: Women Ecology and Development, The Violence of the Green Revolution,* and my favorite, *Monoculture of the Mind*. International ecofeminism is an important ingredient for community-building.

A final set of readings comes from social change anthropologists and sociologists. Some documented the negative effects of modernization on indigenous peoples: Turnbull's *The Mountain People*, Farley Mowat's *The Desperate People*, Kottak's *Assault on Paradise*, and Chagnon's *Yanomamo: The Last Days of Eden*. And sociologists began to suggest that the vulnerabilities of American society could be the result of what most thought was its genius—industrialization and modernization: Bellah and friends' *Habits of the Heart*, Stivers' *The Culture of Cynicism*. And even more important, some of these social scientists and many other activists have begun organizations to rebuild both indigenous and modern communities. Helena Norgerg-Hodge's *Ancient Futures* tells the demise and rebuilding story well for overseas. And Broad and Cavanagh's *Plundering Paradise* details the importance of the struggle for the environment to the survival of many of the people of the Philippines. In the United States, sociologist Etzioni's *The Spirit of Community: Rights, Responsibilities and the Agenda*, and his journal, *Responsive Community*, explore the emerging ideas necessary for transformation. And many ecological and social justice activists, here and abroad, work with these ideas to improve their neighborhoods and communities. Those who have received the Right Livelihood Award—the alternative Nobel Prize—are described in Seabrook's *Pioneers of Change: Experiments in Creating A Humane Society*. For continuing working models I have found two journals useful: *In Context* and *The Neighborhood Works*. Transformative Service-Learning needs to introduce students to these ideas and actions.

Journal Entry 4

Faculty Observations
Linking Students with Learning and Service in Asia

I was intrigued by some notes that arrived from a professor who regularly takes liberal arts students to India and Sri Lanka. Having also lived and worked in the Asian subcontinent, I was reminded of my experiences and their impact on my subsequent years of living and working. He wrote:

I take students to South Asia not to learn about South Asia within the abstract patterns of academic disciplines such as sociology or history or economics or political science. We go there to have experiences which will dislocate the values and patterns students have developed either consciously or unconsciously up to this point in their lives. One of these kinds of experiences can be loosely defined as service. Most of the Service-Learning which fits the standard conventions of service as outlined by the service program takes place in Sri Lanka with the Sarvodaya movement, an indigenous, Buddhist, Gandhian village development movement which believes people should be supported in helping themselves and should not have others do their work for them. Here, the students are not encouraged to do long-term construction projects.

But the students do join in a weekend-long shramadana, or village work project, such as building a school or clearing roadsides or cleaning weeds out of an irrigation pond. But even as they do this they realize that the labor is not of great significance. What is important is the American student's presence. The tensions between rich and poor in the village break down when foreign guests join in a project.

My friend was clear that it would be very hard to justify the students paying $2,500 to fly over and provide $50 worth of labor over a six-week period. A better option would be to send the $2,500 for materials for schools and latrines which they could build themselves.

The service which can be justified is our presence. At the heart of service is not the work done, it is the empathy that students feel for someone, which in turn makes the students want to care for them and help them, which leads to work with them. Both in the shramadanas and the home stays of about five days, students spend night and day talking with people, playing games, sharing perspectives, working with people and finally caring for the people they stay with and missing them very much when they leave. This intensity goes both ways. In most cases it stays with the students for life and it stays with the families they visit for life. In a world which is divided in a north and south way between the rich and the poor, a week-long stay in a village leads to empathy and caring on both sides which will last a lifetime and perhaps lead

Journal Entry 4

people on both sides to put their money or their vote or their labor to the service of healing the gap between countries caught in poverty and countries caught in affluence.

These are two examples of the kind of service he feels is appropriate on these trips to Asia, examples which can be measured in hours. Throughout the visits to Sri Lanka in village after village the students talk and play and answer the same questions over and over again. The professor has coined a name for this—intermittent service. Students seem to do it with a good heart and patience over and over again.

This is a kind of service that cannot be done through the mail. You have to be there to do it. In this situation, the students do raise money before the trip and each student contributes several hundred dollars as part of the cost of the trip for projects which the service organizations use for good purposes. So buildings get built and village outreach projects get funded as a result of the student visits.

He has an unusual twist on the academic credit part of the experience.

It is hard to separate learning through the experience of service from learning through the experience of everyday life. The center of service is developing empathy and caring.

Students develop empathy and caring when they listen to each other's stories in class. Likewise, students develop empathy and caring when they open up to Sri Lanka and India and try to put themselves in the shoes of the people they are visiting. The traditional service work that students do in their home country is really an excuse to get close to someone and to listen to them and to respond to them while working with them. Figuring out a way to grant credit in the traditional sense of grading papers and tests is not possible. What I look for is this essential empathy and caring dimension, particularly how each student relates to his/her fellow students and to those with whom they are visiting.

In further talking with my friend, it turns out that he has changed his entire way of teaching when back on campus.

Last summer I participated in a CIC-funded faculty workshop on the pedagogy of experiential learning. It had a great impact on me. But a large part of the impact was listening to my fellow teachers and becoming aware of their presence and motivation, to learn what motivated them as teachers. It is their presence I carried with me and still do. I think it was the best teacher training workshop that I have attended on or off campus during my 30 years of teaching. It helped me stop pretending that I was doing academic learning on these trips to India. I have written a completely different syllabus and am open about what I think is really happening to students on these trips rather than what an academic council thinks should be happening. The sharing within the Service-Learning Workshop has led me to conduct all of my classes in an experiential way.

Journal Entry 5

Teaching and Service-Learning

While reading a CIC project report, I picked up the phone to explore some points of view of a faculty member who had prepared the report.

My faculty friend reported that over the past year of exploring the issues and concepts of Service-Learning, that the more basic issue, and the one that "catches" teachers, is that of what makes for good teaching and good learning. The discussion that has been taking place on her campus, especially this past year with the help of the CIC grant, has developed into a broader discussion about teaching and learning. She was surprised that when teachers discover that Service-Learning improves the quality of the teaching and learning in their courses, they become willing to extend the extra effort necessary to implement Service-Learning and become more satisfied with the work they are doing as teachers.

She was really clear that Service-Learning is not a methodology for everybody, yet was equally clear that the conversation benefits all faculty members. One of the current goals at the college is to draw more faculty members into this discussion.

I was not surprised by her commenting on a major obstacle in the delicacy of the "town-gown" relationship there. The suspicion of "outsiders" is strong and, in many cases, well-founded. Having once worked in that area of the state, I know that that community, like many others in that part of the world, has been exploited and "burned" by many well-meaning outsiders. A trusting relationship between the college and the local community is important to nurture and difficult to develop given this legacy.

Another theme in our conversation did surprise me some, for most faculty are not willing to talk about it openly. She noted that the religious background of many of the students makes them predisposed and even experienced in "service" but not necessarily in "Service-Learning." She lamented how difficult it is for many students, even after a lot of reflection, to move from an orientation of "service to the less fortunate" to one of "Service-Learning" in which there is more mutuality. Without hesitation she was clear that encouraging that transformation is difficult, but it is perhaps uniquely a function that her college can provide.

Journal Entry 5

These two issues, the "town-gown" legacy and religious background of students, bring additional issues to the good teaching question, in her opinion. And at weekly cafeteria chat times, she reported, some of the faculty are spending time figuring out how the Service-Learning approaches they are trying and hearing about in other places can contribute to a more appropriate set of arrangements for the communities, the faculty and the students.

Here is another example of open conversations leading to expressing keen insights when faculty engage one another in reflecting on their own Service-Learning experiences.

citizens

educational
institutions

organizations

students

LINKING SERVICE
AND SCHOLARSHIP

INTRODUCTION:

In this section, faculty members share some creative and imaginative thinking about rationales and practices for linking service and learning within our network of colleges. John Eby makes a passionate plea for linking service with scholarship. Richard Slimbach outlines a detailed and elegant design for a departmental focus on outcomes for Service-Learning students. Yoram Lubling describes how a college set in motion a new course for pedagogy and how the department of philosophy took hold of it, and in detail shows us how a service orientation in one of his courses was introduced and practiced. Matthew Berndt describes how student affairs and academic affairs planned and implemented together a creative Career Development Program linked by a Service-Learning design. The last article in this section discusses the importance of deciding to evaluate what you set out to do. The editor, with Nancy Hemesath and Sister Grace Ann Witte, presents excerpts from an evaluation design created in a first-year Service-Learning program.

Journal Entry 6

Conversation With A Dean

The interests and missions of private liberal arts colleges and universities are well-served by Service-Learning principles and practices. I recently talked with a Dean of Academic Affairs about this and he clipped off four themes that suggest a systemic impact Service-Learning is having on his campus.

He prefaced his comments by suggesting that many independent liberal arts colleges have a message about service in their mission and some ties to a sponsoring religious community. These relationships are rich with potential for a revitalized undergraduate liberal arts education. He believes that Service-Learning, especially if it is integrated in the curriculum and into extracurricular affairs, brings the college and its sponsoring organization closer together and allows for the fulfillment of the mission of each.

He mentioned four barriers that he felt were being broken down at his institution as a direct result of intensified Service-Learning activity:

Boundaries between divisions. The Service-Learning Committee at his college is now a new standing committee, composed of faculty from a variety of departments, student affairs staff, and students. Every time this committee meets to discuss its collective purpose, divisional boundaries are crossed.

Boundaries between academic departments. Enriching contacts are being made across departments in the cause of Service-Learning, such as the collaboration of a feminist sociologist and a nursing faculty member on a course related to women's health.

Boundaries between the community and the college. The college has identified a few community agencies with which it has established ties and wants to maintain an enduring commitment. This is in contrast to the "clearinghouse" approach. They want the people in the community to know that their objective is that students and faculty have more than a "snapshot" experience. This helps teach about systemic social change as well as how agencies operate. The agencies involved also appreciate the

Journal Entry 6

college for its ongoing commitment to them, and the college is viewed as an enduring friend and supporter of certain community agencies.

Boundaries between students and faculty/staff. When students work shoulder to shoulder with faculty and staff, they come to know these college employees as real people and friends as well as mentors.

The dean reported that in the past year he had noticed that faculty in Service-Learning arrangements were being more innovative than their non-involved faculty colleagues. Faculty who incorporate Service-Learning into their courses were reporting increased motivation, more enriched writing, and better application of their course content to real issues. What faculty learn is that it is okay to move toward some alternative ways of teaching. The sparkle in my friend's eyes was hard to miss.

He went on to say that Service-Learning provides an opportunity for faculty to forge a synthesis of the three-legged chair of faculty activity: teaching, research, and service. Within the faculty and administration a growing consensus is being realized that leads to a consideration of the role of service to students in the promotion/tenure process.

He then spoke at some length about Service-Learning helping prepare students for the world of work where most problems are now dealt with by teams. Most student work in college is carried out and judged through individual activity. His business education faculty now understand the need to prepare students for team-based problem solving and are developing teaching tasks which require students to work on cases or real business problems by working in teams. As a result, much of their Service-Learning activity is done in teams of students, both in the experiential component in the community and in the reflection work done on campus.

The college has identified a few community agencies with which it has established ties and wants to maintain an enduring commitment. This is in contrast to the "clearinghouse" approach.

CHAPTER 10
LINKING SERVICE AND SCHOLARSHIP

BY JOHN W. EBY

Introduction

Higher education in America has recently come under some stinging criticism. Some critics perceive a decline in the quality of teaching and suggest that teaching and learning are not given adequate status and priority. Others criticize higher education for an ivory tower irrelevance which fails to address the needs of society. And others suggest that higher education is not adequately instilling values of community responsibility and service in students.

At its best, Service-Learning has potential to answer these criticisms. It contributes to the transformation of teaching and learning by developing a new pedagogy of engaged scholarship and bringing into the educational process the knowledge and experiences of community leaders. It makes available to communities the analytic, research, and knowledge resources of the college to address consequential community problems and provides creative and innovative student power to community agencies. It helps stimulate, shape, and form an ethic of service among students and faculty.

John W. Eby is Director of Service-Learning and Professor of Sociology at Messiah College, Grantham, Pennsylvania, since the fall of 1994. Preparation of this paper was supported by a grant from Messiah College. Substantial parts of the paper were presented as a Messiah College Faculty Lecture on April 11, 1995. Dr. Eby retains the copyright for this essay.

In many ways linking learning and community service builds on the particular strengths of small independent liberal arts colleges. Most include service as part of their mission. For many church related and Christian colleges, developing a service lifestyle is one of their core values. Many students have developed strong service motivation in their churches and communities prior to entering college. Scholarship at small colleges is already defined broadly and includes interdisciplinary approaches to issues. Teaching and student learning are central.

Educational leaders who are concerned about the mission and directions of colleges will be interested in Service-Learning because of the potential it has to revitalize teaching and learning and because of the potential it has to serve community needs. Community leaders will be interested because of the potential for Service-Learning to provide additional resources for working at community issues.

The Scholarship of Service

In response to a growing concern about education in America, the Carnegie Foundation for the Advancement of Teaching launched a study of what they sensed was a foundational issue, the meaning of scholarship. In 1990, Dr. Ernest Boyer, president of the foundation, wrote a highly acclaimed report, *Scholarship Reconsidered* (Boyer, 1990). He observed, "...in just a few decades, priorities in American Higher Education were significantly realigned...at many of our nation's four-year institutions, the focus had moved from the student to the professoriate, from general to specialized education and from loyalty to the campus to loyalty to the profession. We conclude that for America's colleges and universities to remain vital a new definition of scholarship is required" (Boyer, 1990, p. 13).

Boyer reclaimed as common ground the scholarship that underlies what has too frequently been a divisive polarity in the academy, the interaction between teaching, research, and community service.

He identified four kinds of scholarship: the scholarship of discovery, the scholarship of integration, the scholarship of application, and the scholarship of teaching. This report generated lively discussion at national meetings and on college and university campuses, fueling a movement to reform the academy. It had a major impact on refocusing attention on teaching and learning in an environment in which the quality of teaching at major research universities was a low priority. It emphasized the connections between the disciplines and between the disciplines and general education. It revealed what historically had been a central concern of the academy but had been neglected in recent years—the application of knowledge in responsible ways to consequential societal problems through service. "Service is routinely praised," he says, "but accorded little attention—even in programs where it is most appropriate" (Boyer, 1990).

Boyer observes that less than a century ago the words reality, practicality and service were used by the nation's most distinguished academic leaders to describe higher education's mission. He has articulated a vision for a New American College that "celebrates teaching and selectively supports research, while also taking special pride in its capacity to connect thought to action, theory to practice." He quotes Woodrow Wilson who, several years prior to his becoming president of Princeton University, said, "It is not learning but the spirit of service that will give a college a place in the annals of the nation" (Boyer, 1994).

This reconceptualization of scholarship in the academy is refreshing good news for private liberal arts colleges. They cannot and should not try to compete with major research universities in basic research. They can excel within this broadened definition of scholarship in the areas of integration, application, and teaching.

A Growing Movement

There is a growing movement to reflect this broadened conception of scholarship and to increase the relationships between colleges and their surrounding communities. While in the past many Service-Learning activities operated on the margins, many now are being fully incorporated into college programs and are integrated into the curriculum.

University of Maryland Baltimore, through the Shriver Center, has developed a multifaceted program as a prototype of the vision for a New American College articulated by Dr. Boyer. In addition to engaging students in community service work and Service-Learning, it delivers direct services to troubled youth through a professional staff and leads a consortium of public and private colleges and universities in Baltimore in an effort to develop capacity and infrastructure to support academic community service.

The University of Pennsylvania partners with West Philadelphia to create comprehensive university-assisted community schools that are educational, social and service delivery hubs. The Stanford University Public Service Center promotes student volunteerism and assists faculty in integrating service in courses. The Center for Public Service at IUPUI (Indiana University-Purdue University Indianapolis) supports academic units in maintaining quality collaborative partnerships with each other and their community. Gettysburg College, Cornell University, Bentley College, Calvin College, and many other colleges and universities have expanded their community service centers. Swarthmore hired a former organizer from the National Farm Workers Union to fill a professorship related to social action and community service. An increasing number of colleges are including a service requirement for graduation.

Organizations supporting community service are expanding. More than 500 colleges are members of Campus Compact. More than 650 are members of the student-oriented Campus Opportunity Outreach League. Ninety-three scholarly, professional, and service organizations joined forces to publish two volumes on "Combining Service and Learning" (Kendall, 1990). More than 1,900 faculty and administrators attended the 1995 Spring American Association of Higher Education meeting on the theme of the engaged campus. Representatives from more than 170 small independent colleges gathered in June 1995 at the Arthur Andersen Center to discuss implementation of Service-Learning under the sponsorship of the Council of Independent Colleges.

In many ways linking learning and community service builds on the particular strengths of small independent liberal arts colleges.

Scholarship on Service-Learning is increasing. With little effort hundreds of articles were located for this paper. The second issue of the Michigan Journal of Service-Learning was published in January of 1996. There are creative discussions of Service-Learning in disciplinary journals and professional meetings.

Because many Service-Learning programs are still done on marginal time and with resources scrounged from flexible budgets, there is a particular challenge for leaders of the college program to institutionalize Service-Learning. Service-Learning should become an integral part of colleges. Priority needs to be given to providing adequate staff and budget resources. Support structures such as transportation pools and facilitating infrastructure are important.

Perhaps the greatest challenge is to recognize the scholarship of Service-Learning, the scholarship of integration, application and teaching, on par with the scholarship of research in load allocations, tenure decisions and faculty reward structures.

Toward An Ethic of Service

Much of the interest in community service on college campuses is a response to a growing individualism and self-focus in American society shown in studies such as those by Bellah and Lasch which show growing individualism and self-centeredness in American society (Bellah, Madsen, Sullivan, Swindler, & Tipton, 1991) (Bellah, Madsen, Sullivan, Swindler, & Tipton, 1985) (Lasch, 1978). During the 1980s, Astin's study of the life goals of freshmen entering college showed a steady decline in support for values having to do with social awareness and altruism. Over the past 25 years the percent of students indicating that "being very well off financially" was very important or an essential life goal increased while the percent indicating that "developing a meaningful philosophy of life" declined (Astin, Green, Korn, 1987).

The most recent study shows that only 32 percent of incoming freshmen think it is important to keep up with political affairs and only 16 percent discuss politics frequently (Astin, et al., 1994). While previous generations of students battled "anger and frustration, the current generation battles feelings of "pessimism and alienation" when they think of politics and civic life as irrelevant to their lives (Creighton, 1993).

One of the goals of service on college campuses is to encourage altruistic values and civic service and to foster an "ethic of service" (Morton, 1993). These goals take on special meaning for Christian liberal arts colleges when they are related to goals of preparing students to enter the world as Christian servants.

Another reason that service programs have been expanded on college campuses is the revived interest of students in community service. More than 67 percent of students entering college as freshmen arrive having had some organized service activity as part of their high school experience. Several states mandate a service component as part of the K-12 curriculum. John Gardner, leader in the widely acclaimed freshman year experience, observed that students who have been involved in community service in high school face disillusionment when they encounter college campuses which may not support service activities (Gardner, 1995). Across the country, when a Service-Learning component is offered as part of courses and when necessary logistical support is provided, students eagerly volunteer.

There is a great deal of both empirical and anecdotal evidence that involvement in Service-Learning has major life-changing impact on students. Barbara Jacoby quotes students from the University of Maryland after participating in Service-Learning. "It gave my life purpose." "It benefitted me more than any classroom experience." "I don't take life for granted anymore" (Jacoby, 1994). A Messiah College graduate commented when visiting campus six months after graduation that, "Service-Learning was the most transforming experience of my college years."

Empirical studies show that participation in community service leads to personal, moral and civic development. One controlled experiment showed that students who participated in Service-Learning showed increases in a sense of civic responsibility, increase in international understanding, and decrease in racial prejudice (Myers-Lipton, 1994). Undergraduate ethics students who engaged in community service work as part of a course requirement scored higher on a test of moral reasoning than students who did not. By the end of the class 51 percent of the experimental group used principled moral reasoning while only 13 percent of the control group did. The Service-Learning students participated more in class discussions, showed increased sensitivity to social issues and increased understanding of persons different from themselves (Boss, 1994).

Other studies show that participation in Service-Learning increases student self-confidence, self-reliance, sense of self-worth, tolerance and leadership skills. Participation in community service contributes to self-empowerment, and to students becoming responsible citizens and developing career competencies (Cohen & Sovet, 1989) (Conrad & Hedin, 1991) (Hedin & Conrad, 1990) (Conrad & Hedin, 1990) (Cohen & Kinsey, 1994) (Coles, 1993) (Bransford, Goldman, & Vye, 1992) (Eyler, 1993) (Weaver, Kauffman, & Martin, 1989).

Students in service settings report that they learn discussion techniques, human relations skills, planning techniques, leadership skills, goal setting, and conflict resolution (Lackey, 1992). The recent study by the Harvard School of Public Health shows that the one variable which correlates least with binge drinking is participation in community service at least one hour per week (Gardner, 1995).

Because of the contribution service-minded students make to a college campus, some colleges make special efforts to recruit students with service motivation by offering service scholarships. Bentley College uses these scholarship students to provide logistical help for faculty to integrate service into classes. Gettysburg College has a group of trained student leaders supported by service work-study funds to work with faculty and local agencies.

There is a dramatic increase in the support provided for community service in colleges and universities. This responds to student interest, community need, and the recognition that involvement in service contributes to valued student outcomes.

The Learning Part of Service-Learning

In thinking about service in the academy, it is important to remind ourselves that colleges are learning communities, not service agencies. The primary justification for academically based service has to be pedagogical (Barber & Battistoni, 1993). Such scholarly service is serious, demanding work and requires the rigor and the accountability traditionally associated with research and teaching activities (Boyer, 1990, p. 22).

The central focus of the academy and the "bread and butter" of private liberal arts colleges are teaching and learning. The integration of service into the teaching/learning equation has great potential for renewing the educational process.

The term Service-Learning was coined by a Southern Regional Education Board program in 1967. The use of a hyphen reflects the anticipation that service and learning goals, while not of equal time, are of equal weight in the learning process. Each activity enhances the other for all participants (Sigmon, 1994).

"Service-Learning is a method and philosophy of experiential learning through which participants in community service meet community needs while developing their abilities for critical thinking and group problem-solving, their commitment and

Personal Thoughts About Service

In late March of 1995 in the elegant delegate dining room of the United Nations overlooking the East River as the sun set, Chinua Achebe reflected on international education and service in the keynote address at the annual meeting of The Partnership for Service-Learning. Achebe is the author of the novel *Things Fall Apart*, a moving story of the impact of missionaries on a traditional Ibo village in Nigeria (Achebe, 1993 (first published in 1959)). He commented on how harmful it is for villagers to be called upon to provide hospitality for "salvation dispensers" who work in ways that put people in the situation of "receiving without having the opportunity to give." A person coming to another group must come "not to convert nor to conquer but to build relationships. Go out to meet people not to save them" (Achebe, 1995).

Service has become such an ubiquitous term that it has almost lost its meaning. Almost any worthy activity can be called service. Part of the challenge of Service-Learning is to develop new understandings of service which build on the strengths of individuals and communities and which empower them rather than create dependencies.

The first act of service is listening. Service-Learning encourages a kind of service which learns and listens before it acts and which acts in ways that enable and empower rather than dominate and control. Such a service style respects the power and interests of the people with whom it works and becomes a partner with them to release the skills and resources and knowledge already present in the community.

Unfortunately there are service programs which reflect the triumphalism and ethnocentrism of Western culture and capitalism or the impositional stance of fundamentalist religion. The kind of community agency or program in which Service-Learning happens is of critical importance, particularly the structure of its relationships to its host community. The best kind of Service-Learning assignments are related to agencies or programs which have authentic roots in the community. It is best if the agency has a long-term presence in the community and if the activities in which the students participate are part of and contribute to long-term programs. Community people should have major influence on agency policy and practice. Work should emphasize interaction with community members. The experience should be long enough to allow building relationships and understanding cultural differences. Students

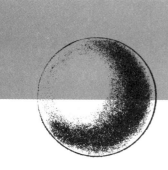

Part of the challenge of Service-Learning is to develop new understandings of service.

should use appropriate technology, resources, and principles of practice, and be in a relationship of accountability.

Service-Learning activities are particularly enriched when they are part of a broader ministry of a community agency or church that has authentic roots and a long-term presence in the community.

Service-Learning should give students tools to evaluate the service activity itself. Melanie Zuercher wrote the following analysis in her journal while on a Service-Learning project in Haiti.

Haiti has been called the dumping ground for North American relief. For all the tremendous amounts of money and relief materials sent to Haiti annually, the quality of life of the Haitian people has improved very little. Some is due to human error. Some is due to "mischanneling."...But most is due to what some groups term inappropriate relief: relief material distributed as handouts in non-emergency situations.

That type of relief given by missionaries has created a "beggar mentality" in places like Grande Riviere....

Far more serious is the fact that inappropriate relief diminishes the recipient's motivations to do for himself. When people are given what they need, very often their lives do improve as long as the source is available and active. But when the source dries up, they are as badly off as they were before...(Hess, 1994, p. 176).

Laura Noyes, a student at Messiah College, worked in a tutoring program in Harrisburg, PA. She wrote:

Contemporary educational research has clearly demonstrated the inefficacy of the factory model in which learning is based on time and not knowledge and instruction is based on guidelines and not individual needs.... Unfortunately [the program's] schedule continues the factory model concept after the formal school day ends. The children leave a long day at the factory-like school and begin another schedule" (Noyes, 1994).

Her insight and understanding is informed by classroom theory and enriched by her tutoring experience.

J.W.E.

values and the skills needed for effective citizenship. The core elements of Service-Learning are (1) service activities that help meet community needs that the community finds important and (2) structured educational components that challenge participants to think critically about and learn from their experiences" (Mintz & Liu, 1994).

Service-Learning is related to many things private liberal arts colleges have done for a long time. It is a type of experiential learning closely related to academically based field placements such as those in education and social work and to clinical experiences such as those in nursing. Many programs also make available practicum experiences.

It is the quality and intentionality of the reflective component which distinguishes Service-Learning from community volunteer service. This is particularly evident when Service-Learning is an integral component of academic courses. The Service-Learning experience gives existential meaning to course material. Course material provides a broader context for understanding the issues encountered in the service activity. The course provides theoretical perspectives, additional facts and links to other relevant material.

Service-Learning differs from internships in that internships are often oriented toward career issues rather than social service. Goals for internships include career exploration, professional development, self-assessment, and developing a philosophy of work. Internships include structured reflection.

The learning component in Service-Learning should be evaluated with the same rigor and standards used for other academic work. It is not only legitimate but important that students be awarded academic credit for Service-Learning. Credit guarantees academic integrity and accountability and allows for serious academic demands. Credit is not a reward for service but a reflection of learning (Barber & Battistoni, 1993). The awarding of academic credit symbolizes that Service-Learning is a valued and integral part of the educational program.

There are particular reasons for students to be required to cross social, economic, and cultural boundaries in Service-Learning. Working in situations significantly different from their own will give students the opportunity to develop skills of cross-cultural relationships and to reflect on their own experience and culture from the vantage point of another.

The service assignment in Service-Learning is a form of participant observation. All of the skills for participant observation are necessary to make it successful. The experience provides data for analysis. The service role gives entree to an agency and a community and is a legitimate reason for the student to be in the community. At best the student's service will benefit the agency and community and the agency and community will contribute to the learning of the student. For both partners there will be authentic opportunity to give and to receive.

Service-Learning supports a particular kind of learning. J. Lawrence Burkholder, president of Goshen College when the Study Service Trimester program (an acclaimed international education program that incorporates Service-Learning) was begun, makes the point that the difference between classroom learning and learning in cross-cultural settings is not one of substance but one of kind. What is learned on location in a traditional village of Nicaragua is essentially the same as what is learned in the ivory tower. The difference has to do with the form through which the liberal arts are presented—not a matter of content, but of form. In cross-cultural situations, humane studies are presented in the rough—in an unpackaged, unsystemized manner of a cultural labyrinth of sociology, art, music, religion and history—but not in the prepackaged forms of textbooks and science manuals. Cross-cultural education at its best is general education communicated in a general sort of way (Burkholder, 1989).

There is a dialectic of action and reflection in Service-Learning. This is similar to the learning most of us do throughout our lives. The service experience is an endless series of questions, puzzling and insistent. It is a curriculum formed and shaped by the issues that confront the student in the interplay of social forces and interpersonal dynamics. The student is not a passive observer but a participant in the action. So part of the curriculum evolves within the student as he or she observes, interprets and decides what to do. Part of the curriculum is the interplay of local and global forces and the conflicts of values. It includes the interactions between individuals and institutions, and institutions with each other. The whole mix of social dynamics and human choices is a rich social and ethical laboratory.

Scientists have long known that it is not adequate to simply teach students the results of science. They must provide settings where students can learn the process and joy of discovery by doing science. The service experience combined with reflection provides opportunity for students to cultivate their capacities for interpretation, discovery, and creation and to nurture critical and analytic thinking as they recognize competing theories and models (Weaver, 1990).

The service experience sets the agenda and provides the data for structured reflection. The student is driven to theory to find the patterns in the experience and the explanations that give form and shape to the chaos. Since most students begin at the individual level of analysis, reflection should take them to a systemic understanding. It will stimulate conversation and critical discourse around an investigation of social institutions, power relationships and value commitments. The knowledge gained will be contextual as well as general. A feedback loop will be created that will inform the conduct of service and frame significant questions.

This action-reflection dialectic requires a rather different kind of teaching than usually occurs in the traditional classroom where knowledge transfer is the prevailing model. In Service-Learning the teacher becomes a tour guide and mentor, a facilitator, consultant, and resource person. The agenda is dictated by the student and the situation. The method is collaborative, interactive, and dialogical. At its best, it empowers the student for self-learning.

Robert Coles recounts his experiences with a group of students working in an inner city summer tutoring project. He observed that students in service needed a wider perspective than the local situation could provide. He introduced them to great literature which prompted them to move from the particulars of the often exhausting, frustrating daily experience to a broader context and perspective which can easily be overlooked at the end of a day or at the end of a summer's work (Coles, 1994).

Parker Palmer observes that Service-Learning requires the interplay of intimate involvement and distanced reflection. It is a "dance between the objective and the subjective" (Palmer, 1993).

Service-Learning is particularly helpful to students as they develop higher levels of learning. The student's role shifts from a dependent passive one to one of greater independence and activeness. Students are encouraged to develop and use skills

It is the quality and intentionality of the reflective component which distinguishes Service-Learning from community volunteer service.

of analysis, application, synthesis, and evaluation (Duley, 1990). They are also encouraged to develop what King and Kitchener call reflective judgement. Reflective judgement is decision making and judgement done in situations of uncertainty. This requires the participant to bring together diverse values and data and make a judgement (King & Kitchener, 1994).

The effect of Service-Learning on students is significant. Implications for faculty are equally important. A survey of 250 faculty who use Service-Learning in 23 institutions in the state of Michigan revealed high levels of satisfaction (Hammond, 1994). They identified the following factors which motivated them to use Service-Learning. Service-Learning brings greater relevance to course material, encourages self-directed learning, and improves student satisfaction. Service-Learning is an effective way to present disciplinary content material and is an effective form of experiential education. These findings must be taken in perspective. Teachers who chose not to use Service-Learning, or who had used it and discontinued use, would not have been included in the study.

Though the faculty expressed high satisfaction and commitment to Service-Learning, they did mention several drawbacks. Nearly all of them said Service-Learning takes more time. A number of them mentioned difficulties coordinating many different tasks and many different people.

The impact of Service-Learning on cognitive learning has not been studied as extensively as the impact on values and personal and moral growth.

One study of students before and after participation in a Goshen College Study Service Term showed increased appreciation for reflective thought as measured by the Omnibus Personality Inventory. The data indicated that not only did the students retain their interest in reflective thought but they continued to climb compared to other students (Weaver, Kauffman, & Martin, 1989).

Markus and others did one of the few controlled studies on the question of academic learning at the University of Michigan in a lecture/discussion class in "Contemporary Political Issues." Two sections did 20 hours of community service while the others wrote a paper which required 20 hours of work. The "service" sections scored significantly higher on the course evaluation on the following items: learning to apply principles to new situations, developing a set of overall values in the academic field, developing a greater sense of societal problems, reconsidering many former attitudes, developing a greater sense of personal responsibility, and feeling that they performed up to their potential in the course. Class attendance of the service students was better. All students took the same midterm and final examinations and the examinations were graded according to a common set of standards. Students in the "service" sections scored 16 percent higher than the others (Markus, 1993).

Summary

Service-Learning does provide answers to some of the legitimate criticisms leveled at Higher Education. It incorporates the rich experiential knowledge of community persons and agencies into the curriculum. It involves students in relating to persons in need and in working toward solutions for consequential community problems. And it inspires students to develop an ethic of service and a set of values that extend beyond their own interests to the interests of others.

An often-quoted proverb, selections from two student journals, a quotation from Ernest Boyer, and a quotation from Bruce Herzberg capture the life and spirit of Service-Learning.

The proverb succinctly states a pedagogy of learning: *I hear and I forget, I see and I remember, I do and I understand.*

For Lenae Nofziger, the structure, culture, and spirituality of an Ebrie village in Coite d' Ivoire came to life in her experience living and serving in the village. Her observations were informed and directed by a formal lecture by an expert. She was able to see how religious beliefs and cultural patterns were reflected in the way the village was laid out. Her journal entry follows:

This morning James Kraybill, who's worked in West Africa for 15 years with the Mennonite Board of Missions, lectured about Ebrie villages, so I was excited to see if Petit Cocody, my Ebrie neighborhood, fit his model. I'd never noticed any organizing principles here before, but now I see that there were some (Nofziger, 1994).

Chris Sauder worked with the Perez Zelebon Ministry of Health Mobile Unit # 1 in Haiti as his Service-Learning assignment in a Goshen College Study Service Trimester. On this particular day they drove 1.5 hours off the main road deep into the mountains of rural Haiti. He wrote in his journal:

... A youth about my age offers to take me to the generator that supplies electricity for his house. Walking down the road, dusty now in the heat of the day, he suddenly asks, "Did you see the MTV music awards last night?"

"No," I stammered in disbelief. He did!

I recall one of the then seemingly pointless abstractions from Communications Theories class— Marshall McLuhan's notion that communication technologies are shrinking the world into a common culture in a global village.

The people here welcome us and our penicillin and condoms and nutrition charts. They bear no resentment toward our altering their way of life. They dream of Sears, Hitachi and True Value. They chase after the images of Hollywood and dream of Disneyland (Hess 1994, p. 178).

Bruce Herzberg, a professor of English at Bentley College, known for its strong business programs and for infusing its whole curriculum with Service-Learning, writes about the impact of Service-Learning on his students in a writing course:

What the students' final papers show, then, is a sense of life as a communal project, an understanding of the way that social institutions affect our lives and a sense that our responsibility for social justice includes but also carries beyond personal acts of charity. This is an understanding that has been very rare among Bentley students. Immersed in a culture of individualism, convinced of their merit in a meritocracy, students like those at Bentley need to see that there is a social basis for most conditions that they take to be matters of individual choice or individual ability.... Developing a social imagination makes it possible not only to question and analyze the world, but to imagine transforming it (Herzberg, 1994).

In a "Point of View" article in the Chronicle of Higher Education, Ernest Boyer shared a dream of how excellence in American higher education might be achieved if the academy took seriously his call for a new conception of scholarship and a new responsibility for social relevance:

What I am describing might be called the "New American College," an institution that celebrates teaching and selectively supports research, while also taking special pride in its capacity to connect thought to action, theory to practice. This New American College would organize cross-disciplinary institutes around pressing social issues. Undergraduates at the college would participate in field projects, relating ideas to real life. Classrooms and laboratories would be extended to include health clinics, youth centers, schools and government offices. Faculty members would build partnerships with practitioners who would in turn come to campus as lecturers and student advisors.

The New American College as a connected institution would be committed to improving in a very intentional way the human condition. As clusters of such colleges formed, a new model of excellence in higher education would emerge, one that would enrich the campus, renew communities and give new dignity and status to the scholarship of service. More than a century ago, the historian Handlin put it this way: "Our troubled planet can

no longer afford the luxury of pursuits confined to the ivory tower. Scholarship has to prove its worth, not on its own terms, but by service to the nation and the world." Responding to this challenge is what the New American College is about (Boyer, 1994).

REFERENCES

Achebe, C. *Things Fall Apart.* New York: Fawcett Crest, 1993 (first published in 1959).

Achebe, C. Keynote address at annual meeting of The Partnership for Service Learning at United Nations, New York: March 24, 1995.

Astin, A. W., K. Green, and W. Korn. *The American Freshman: Twenty Year Trends.* Los Angeles: Cooperative institutional research program, University of California at Los Angeles, 1987.

Astin, A. W. et al. *The American Freshman: National Norms for Fall 1994.* Los Angeles: Higher Education Research Institute at UCLA, 1994.

Barber, B. and R. Battistoni. *A Season of Service: Introducing Service Learning Into the Liberal Arts Curriculum,* pp. 235-240, 1993.

Bellah, R., R. Madsen, W. Sullivan, A. Swindler, & S. Tipton. *Habits of the Heart: Individualism and Commitment in American Life.* Los Angeles: University of California Press, 1985.

Bellah, R., R. Madsen, W. Sullivan, A. Swindler, and S. Tipton. *The Good Society.* New York: Alfred Knopf, 1991.

Boss, J. "The Effect of Community Service Work on the Moral Development of College Ethics Students." *Journal of Moral Education,* 23(2), 183-198, 1994.

Boyer, E. *Scholarship Reconsidered: Priorities of the Professoriate.* Princeton, N.J.: The Carnegie Foundation For The Advancement of Teaching, 1990.

Boyer, E. "Creating the New American College." *The Chronicle of Higher Education* (March 9, 1994): A48.

Bransford, J., S. Goldman, and N. Vye. "Making a Difference in People's Ability to Think: Reflections on a Decade of Work and Some Hopes for the Future." In *Influences on the Development of Children's Thinking,* edited by L. Okagaki & R. J. Sternberg, Directors of Development. Hillsdale, N.J.: Erlbaum, 1992.

Burkholder, J. L. "The Idea of Service in International Education." In *The Role of Service Learning in International Education,* edited by S. Showalter, 25-34. Goshen, In.: Goshen College, 1989.

Cohen, J., and D. Kinsey. "'Doing Good' and Scholarship: A Service-Learning Study." *Journalism Educator,* Winter 1994: 4-14.

Cohen, S., and C. Sovet. "Human Service Education, Experiential Learning and Student Development." *College Student Journal,* 23(2) (1989): 117-122.

Coles, R. Doing and Learning, *The Call of Service: A Witness to Idealism* (pp. 145-173). New York: Houghton Mifflin Company, 1993.

Coles, R. "Putting Head and Heart on the Line." *The Chronicle of Higher Education* (October 26, 1994): A64-A65.

Conrad, D., & Hedin, D. "The Impact of Experiential Education on Youth Development. In *Combining Service and Learning: A Resource Book for Community and Public Service* (Vol. I), edited by J. Kendall, 119-129. Raleigh, N.C.: National Society for Internships and Experiential Education, 1990.

Conrad, D., & Hedin, D. "School-based Community Service: What We Know from Research and Theory." *Phi Delta Kappan,* 72(10) (1991): 743-749.

Creighton, J. *Students Talk Politics.* Dayton, Ohio: Kettering Foundation, 1993.

Duley, J. "Continuum of Pedagogical Styles in Experiential Learning." In *Combining Service and Learning: A Resource Book for Community and Public Service,* edited by J. Kendall, 193. Raleigh, N.C.: National Society for Internships and Experiential Education, 1990.

Eyler, J. "Comparing the Impact of Two Internship Experiences on Student Learning." *Journal of Cooperative Education,* I (1993): 41-52.

Gardner, J. Presentation at the annual meeting of the Partnership for Service Learning at United Nations, New York, March 24-26, 1995.

Hammond, C. "Integrating Service and Academic Study: Faculty Motivation and Satisfaction in Michigan Higher Education." *Michigan Journal of Community Service Learning* 1(1) (1994): 21-28.

Hedin, D., & Conrad, D. Learning from Service Experience: Experience is the Best Teacher—Or Is It? In *Combining Service and Learning: A Resource Book for Community and Public Service* (Vol. I), edited by J. Kendall, 87-98. Raleigh, N.C.: National Society for Internships and Experiential Education, 1990.

Herzberg, B. "Community Service and Critical Teaching." *College Composition and Communication,* 45, 3 (October 1994): 307-319.

Hess, D. *The Whole World Guide to Cultural Learning.* Yarmouth, Maine: Intercultural Press Inc., 1994.

Jacoby, B. "Bringing Community Service into the Curriculum." *Chronicle of Higher Education* (Aug. 16, 1994).

Kendall, J. *Combining Service and Learning: A Resource Book for Community and Public Service* (Vol. II). Raleigh, N.C.: National Society for Internships and Experiential Education, 1990.

King, P., and K. S. Kitchener. *Developing Reflective Judgement: Understanding and Promoting Intellectual Growth and Critical Thinking in Adolescents and Adults.* San Francisco: Jossey-Bass, 1994.

Lackey, A. "The Process is Pedagogy: What Does Community Participation Teach?" *Community Development Journal,* 27(3) (1992): 220-234.

Lasch, C. *The Culture of Narcissism.* New York: Norton, 1978.

Markus, G. & Howard, J. "Integrating Community Service and Classroom Instruction Enhances Learning: Results from an Experiment." *Educational Evaluation and Policy Analysis* 15(4) (1993): 410-419.

Mintz, S., and G. Liu. "Service-Learning: An Overview" In *National and Community Service: A Resource Guide.* Washington, D.C.: The Corporation for National and Community Service. (1993).

Morton, K. "Potential and Practice for Combining Civic Education and Community Service." In *Rethinking Tradition: Integrating Service with Academic Study on College Campuses,* edited by T. Kupiec, 55-57. Providence, R.I.: Education Commission for the States, 1993.

Myers-Lipton, S. "The Effects of Service Learning on College Students' Attitudes Toward Civic Responsibility, International Understanding and Racial Prejudice." Unpublished Ph.D., University of Colorado. (1994).

Nofziger, L. *The Music Is With the River.* Goshen, In.: Pinchpenny Press, 1994.

Palmer, P. "Is Service Learning for Everyone? On the Identity and Integrity of the Teacher." In *Rethinking Tradition: Integrating Service with Academic Study on College Campuses,* edited by T. Kupiec, 17-18. Providence, R.I.: Education Commission of the States, 1993.

Sigmon, R. *Linking Service with Learning in the Liberal Arts Education.* Washington, D.C.: Council of Independent Colleges, 1994.

Weaver, F. S. *Promoting Inquiry in Undergraduate Learning* (Vol. 38). San Francisco: Jossey-Bass, 1990.

Weaver, H., N. Kauffman, and J. Martin. Educational Value of International Experience. In *The Role of Service-Learning in International Education: Proceedings of a Wingspread Conference,* edited by S. Showalter, 59-81. Goshen, In.: Goshen College, 1989.

CHAPTER 11

CONNECTING HEAD, HEART, AND HANDS

Developing Intercultural Service Competence

BY RICHARD SLIMBACH

Introduction

As we approach a new century, calls are sounding for experiential learning processes—and Service-Learning in particular—to help create a learning-centered, socially-responsible framework for higher education.[1] These expectations raise some probing questions: What is the purpose of a college education? Is it primarily to provide *instruction* or to *produce learning*? If the latter, what kinds of learnings is it to produce and how will its "productivity" be measured? And then, learning for what? Do universities have an ethical responsibility toward those outside the world of higher education?[2] If so, what is the relationship of public and community service to higher education? These questions form the backdrop for the following presentation of Service-Learning as the missing clinical component in the liberal arts and sciences for developing learner competence in pluralistic urban settings.

Developing Intercultural Service Competence:

What types of competence will constitute an educated person in pluralistic urban settings?

Many of our colleges are experiencing a shift in their sense of responsibility—from that of provid-

ing quality instruction to that of producing student learning. Among other effects, this shift begins to change our view of institutional "quality." Whereas the traditional benchmarks were *inputs* like the test scores of entering freshman, library holdings, and the number of faculty "stars," a focus on student learning urges us to judge our efforts by our ability to facilitate student achievement of particular competencies or *outcomes*. Not that the traditional gauges of academic quality are unimportant. It's merely to shift our focus from that of achieving visibility and recognition to that of enhancing the productivity of student learning. From a student development perspective, that is what we need to define and measure.

Service-Learning must link to our expectations for student learning. It might be helpful to begin with the end in view. "Mission statements" headline promotional literature for virtually any enterprise. They serve to articulate goal and direction and to provide a basis for setting priorities, planning programs, making decisions, and evaluating success. College mission statements often suggests goals for Service-Learning. If we are to pursue student learning as our ultimate end, we must creatively connect the institution's purpose and mission to statements of how students learn, and what and how much we are expecting students to learn while at our institution. In short, we must have a philosophy of student development at the center of our academic life. This philosophy will translate the school's mission into specific learning goals or outcomes—like critical thinking or communication skills—toward

Richard Slimbach is Chair of the Global Studies and Sociology Department at Azusa Pacific University, Azusa, California.

which student learning is directed. Assessment procedures will further serve as a means of judging how well students are progressing towards the achievement of those outcomes.

Working backwards from a vision of the desired end, our primary concern is to consider what competencies will be required for effective service in the 21st century, and how learners might develop those competencies most efficiently. For example, Azusa Pacific University (APU) is one of 30-odd colleges and universities in the Los Angeles area that together enroll almost half a million students. What *intercultural* awarenesses, knowledges, attitudes, values, character qualities, and skills should these institutions be designed to enhance if their broad mission is to prepare their students for personal and professional lives within this heterogeneous urban center? The emphasis on intercultural competencies is intentional. It suggests that the abilities once thought to be necessary only for those involved in international service assignments (e.g., with the Peace Corps, missionary societies, or in diplomatic service) are increasingly seen as having critical importance for virtually every profession in domestic settings as well, particularly in large urban areas.[3] Already in Los Angeles, dubbed "the capital of the Third World," public school children speak more than 135 languages. Social facts such as these are dramatic reminders of the major global forces that are intensifying the levels of contact between different cultural groups. By the turn of the century, one will be ill-prepared to serve as a public school teacher, health care worker, police officer, business person, social worker, religious minister, or service-level employee in urban America without some level of intercultural competence.

Gaining intercultural service competence is an infinitely complex process. Every student starts at a "lower" or "higher" position relative to the others and journeys on different paths at different paces in their development of competence. For that reason, we are hesitant to suggest a sequential model of stages and levels. Rather, we suggest that success in the world of work involves a clearly identifiable set of cognitions, attitudes, civic virtues, and interpersonal skills. Listed in the appendix at the end of this chapter are competencies in each of these domains. Although such an inventory could be produced at virtually any level (e.g., system-wide,

institutional, departmental, or single course), the list has been produced for use with the courses in the global studies department at APU. Not that every type or domain of competency presented is either self-evident or a matter of common agreement. They simply reflect one department's vision of a preferred future that its students and faculty are working to construct.

To realize this future, content knowledge and technical skills alone are insufficient. Research reported by Chickering and Reisser surveyed successful individuals in a variety of professional fields in order to determine the abilities that made them successful.[4] Their most consistent finding was that the amount of knowledge one acquires in a given area is generally unrelated to even acceptable performance in an occupation. What matters most is the individual's ability to process information well, to see multiple sides of complex issues, and to learn from one's experiences.

In addition to cognitive skills, effective service in the world involves various affective qualities, interpersonal (social) skills, and moral attributes as prerequisites for effective action. In reference to the often neglected dimension of character development, Dr. Martin Luther King, Jr. reminds us that:

> *the function of education…is to teach one to think intensively and to think critically. But education which stops with efficiency may prove the greatest menace to society. The most dangerous criminal may be the man gifted with reason but no morals. We must remember that intelligence is not enough. Intelligence plus character—that is the goal of true education. The complete education gives one not only power of concentration but worthy objectives upon which to concentrate.[5]*

The lists at the end of this chapter attempt to identify a broad range of competencies that connect head, heart, and hands in service within pluralistic settings. While presented as potential outcomes of Service-Learning processes, they are generic in nature. As such, they can be expected to transfer from college service experiences to most intercultural settings and professions.

The Social Imperative

What is the contribution of service-based learning to the development of intercultural service competence? Certainly few argue with the contention that higher education's chief product is learning. Or that learning consists primarily of *changes in people*—changes in their awareness of themselves, in their knowledge, their character, and their practical competence. But many hesitate in affirming higher education's direct responsibility for producing *changes in society*. While colleges and universities have always served the established interests of government, education, business, and medicine, they have tended to do so from cloistered positions "above the fray." Times are changing. Schools are increasingly looking to their communities to provide the context and process for engendering social responsibility and self-directed learning. As Edward Long has stated:

> *Higher education dares not become merely the avenue to success; it must be the gateway for responsibility. It should not be concerned with competence alone, but with commitment to civic responsibility. An academic degree should not be a hunting license only for self-advancement, but an indication of abilities to seek, cultivate, and sustain a richer commonweal. It is not enough to achieve cultural literacy; we must engender social concern.*[6]

Experiential learning processes like Service-Learning attempt a response to these questions by joining the intellectual disciplines of theoretical study and critical thought to the moral disciplines of compassionate action with real consequences. It challenges the assumption implicit in traditional liberal arts that students will not only acquire the understandings and skills necessary for effective professional service, but will inevitably apply that good knowledge in socially responsible ways. Students schooled under traditional methods will, no doubt, become more rational, more critical, more detached, and more adept at manipulating words and abstract concepts. But how will they learn to resist the cultural "pull" towards personal respectability and upward mobility (what Walter Bruggeman calls the "royal road") that pervades, not only the larger culture, but the very institutions in which they are being schooled? How will they develop the emotional, social, and moral competence necessary to empathize deeply, to initiate and maintain positive relationships, to motivate and influence, to trust feelings and intuitions, to value people above things, and to solve problems

in a self-directed way—all within intensely intercultural settings? In most cases the plain answer is, they won't.

> *At their best, Service-Learning experiences put abstract classroom concepts into concrete form and provide meaningful opportunities to test and refine theories while helping to meet basic community needs.*

A Response at Azusa Pacific University

Energized by a rich tradition of service within the Azusa Pacific community, the global studies department has designed service-based learning experiences aimed at nurturing a range of intercultural competencies. Our contention has been that, far from being a passing fad of suspect educational value, Service-Learning is a critical co-producer (along with academic learning) of good learning. Indeed, our experience would lead us to believe that responsible service-based learning provides students far more powerful learning environments than the traditional classroom for developing intercultural competencies in virtually every non-cognitive learning domain. In creative combination with academic learning (such as listening to lectures and reading), Service-Learning can also enhance cognitive learning better than either could do alone. Who hasn't experienced something read in a textbook or heard in a lecture suddenly come to life as the connection is made between the concept and its real-life application?

We have used the following description of Service-Learning to guide curriculum development in two courses within the global studies major:

A form of experiential education that expresses the values of care for others, community empowerment, and reciprocal learning by consciously connecting classroom learning with community service in ways that add value to both. At their best, Service-Learning experiences put abstract classroom concepts into concrete form and provide meaningful opportunities to test and refine theories while helping to meet basic community needs.

The first course involves learners in central, south central, and east Los Angeles through a one-week immersion-type field seminar followed by a 12-week placement within local service organizations. Students use the Kretzmann and McKnight text, *Building Communities From the Inside Out*, as a tool for basically self-directed (though campus-monitored) community involvement. With learning supervised by a faculty member and facilitated by local organizers, student teams design and then carry out community resource surveys in some of the most problem-stricken areas of the city. These field-based sources of input are blended with on-campus study, group reflection, and ongoing self-assessment.

This course is preparatory for the second course which is completed at specially arranged service sites throughout the world. In conjunction with their community service, students complete small-scale research projects on a problem or issue being addressed by the agency in which they are serving. As I write, Jessica and Alyson are caring for and conducting research on street children through one of Mother Teresa's orphanages in Calcutta, India. Two others, Jessica and Serena, are assisting in a village school outside of Valencia, Spain while they explore teacher-learner role relationships. Amarely is doing the same within a Swiss school that is trying to cope with the recent influx of school-age Yugoslavian refugees.

Common to both courses is the goal of providing students with structured opportunities not only to acquire important content knowledge (e.g., regarding various social problems), but also to see, think, and act with informed grace across national, ethnic, and linguistic borders. Their service placements are expected to fulfill the following criteria which define the kinds of learning environments in which progress toward competency development in multiple domains can be expected:

- it must be unpaid (voluntary);

- it must involve direct interaction with others, and can be performed with a student partner (community);

- it must involve students in a minimum of 40 hours of service within a single service organization (continuous);

- it must involve students in relationships across human differences, e.g., gender, race, age, economic status, national origin, faith, sexual preference, and/or educational attainment (multicultural);

- it must involve the accomplishment of specific tasks that address concrete human needs as identified by community members (social action-oriented);

- it must be motivated by a genuine concern to benefit the lives of others and not simply to gain power or personal gratification (sincere);

- it must provide a mutually-fulfilling arrangement where students and community members can each be learners and teachers, servers and served (reciprocal);

- it must include on-site supervision and off-the job support, reading, reflection, and self-assessment processes that promote conscious educational growth (instructional); and

- it must enable all those being served—students, staff workers, and clients—to be better able to serve and be served by their own actions (empowering).

Pedagogy With a Passion

What types of learning and assessment procedures will provide learners with opportunities to make progress toward the achievement of intercultural service competence in multiple domains?

At the beginning of one of my courses, I like to invite students to recall a learning experience that had a profound, even life-changing, effect upon their lives. I ask them to briefly describe that experience on paper, and also to note what in their thinking or behaving changed and how those changes were brought about. When all are finished, I ask them to indicate by raising their hands whether that dramatic learning experience occurred for any of them within a classroom environment. In the four years that I've done this, not one hand has been raised.

In our follow-up discussion, we reflect on the various elements that helped produce learning. The students consistently reiterate the insights of cognitive psychology on learning. They describe experiences where they were placed in direct relationship with a person or thing; where they were actively involved in getting something done; where that task required that they move beyond the known to the unknown, often at significant personal risk; and where there was a deep emotional impact, causing them to ponder the personal meaning of the experience for months afterwards. I invariably come away with a renewed appreciation for the pedagogical power of experiential learning.

In structuring opportunities for this kind of transformative learning to take place, one transitions from considering *what* is to be learned (the outcomes) to *how* one will learn them (the methods). For those engaged in Service-Learning projects, learning how to learn from one's service experience might be the primary educational goal. Various methods can compete freely with each other to produce this outcome. What matters most is to identify the actual practices—whether learning activities or assessment procedures—that will actually improve the quantity and quality of student learning. Our particular interest will be to know (a) how students may best *acquire* learning— derive various types of competence from their Service-Learning experiences, and (b) how students and faculty may best *assess* learning—know what competencies have been achieved in relation to prescribed standards as a result of their Service-Learning experiences. In actual practice, the line between acquiring and assessing learning becomes blurred. They should be seen as mutually reinforcing and virtually synonymous processes calculated to do one thing: produce the desired learning outcomes.

Because holistic competence is our goal, students are expected to learn not only to *know,* but also to

be and to *do.* Of course, no single assessment instrument or technique can hope to successfully investigate all possible outcomes of students' service experiences. We must also be careful to realistically establish what levels of competence can and should be expected. Our job in a nutshell will be to design a range of production tasks capable of eliciting realistic levels of student competence in various learning domains. At best, these tasks will employ a variety of performance modes such as surveys, group discussion, and self-reports. Even with these conditions met, the assessments make an meaningful though modest claim—that of providing formative (vs. summative) feedback to the learning process, focused on developing the individual (vs. the program or the institution). The following are some currently in use within our global studies program:

1. *Statement of Personal Learning Objectives.* Before their particular service project begins, students work from the catalogue of outcomes to specify the types and level (degree) of personal changes they hope to realize through their Service-Learning experiences. Stating their objectives at the outset serves to clarify the connection between these service experiences and anticipated learnings, while leaving room for the incidental, serendipitous learning that is bound to occur. For the primarily self-directed Service-Learning practicum completed abroad, precise learning objectives are developed in consultation with their faculty advisor and represented in an individualized learning contract.[7] The formulation of these statements provides feedback to both student and instructor on their ability to identify their own interests and goals, to correlate them with the goals of the host service agency, and to effectively communicate them (in writing and then orally).

2. *Community Research and Writing.* The Los Angeles-based course is designed to help students gain experience applying culture-learning and community development knowledge and skills. They do this by collecting and analyzing community data related to a specific issue/problem being addressed through their host service organization. Working either in pairs or individually, students design and carry out a small-scale survey project requiring a fairly high level of motivation/initiative, teamwork, and conceptual ability. The results are presented to

the staff of the service organization and in a final oral and written report.

3. Weekly Learning Log. Learning logs provide a method of reflecting on and recording learning experience. The logs not only provide a permanent record of learning experiences; they also help learners to identify the key elements of these experiences which produced learning. In our overseas program, for example, we ask students to complete eight learning logs that require them to make connections between what they read and what they experience in service. Most faculty are legitimately concerned that they impart and their students acquire general knowledge in a particular subject area. The readings serve this purpose by providing a framework for organizing and testing general principles related to the issues being addressed by their service organization. The logs do serve to increase the students' general knowledge of subject matter. But their primary aim is to provide them the opportunity to (re)examine their own faith perspectives, political beliefs, cultural values, and life commitments as they apply the theoretical knowledge within a broader community and professional context.

For each learning log, students write the date, service site, their service position, and the title of article or book chapter they will be referring to. Then they alternate between the following options:

Describe how this week's reading and service has helped you to better understand some aspect of your own life. Ask yourself: What was "said" (both in the **readings** and through my **experiences**) that helps you to better understand yourself and an authentically Christian perspective on service to others? What understanding (inspiration, strength, challenge) does your experience bring to your personal quest for meaning and significance? What "action plans" do these experiences inspire in you?

Describe how this week's reading and service has helped you to better understand the people in your host society or service organization? As yourself: What did you **read** that was valuable in guiding your experiences with members of the host society? What have you learned about those you serve (e.g., their beliefs, perceptions, attitudes, values, relationships, and practices) from your

experience with them? What aspects of the social life resemble similar aspects in your own community or personal life? In what ways are they different from your own? What means ("action plans") might you take to bridge the gap between your life and theirs?

Describe how this week's reading and service has suggested new ways for you to act. Ask yourself: What can you integrate into your personal faith and/or professional practice based on your **reading**, your community service **experience**, and your **reflection**? In what ways have you been able to apply abstract facts, concepts, or principles from the readings or classroom presentations in concrete service situations? How do your new understandings serve to equip you to struggle for changes in yourself and the social reality that surrounds you?

4. Continuous Self-Assessment. The purpose of student self-assessment is to provide students and their teachers continuous feedback on the quality of their learning. Particularly in reference to broad learning outcomes, it holds great potential for demonstrating the relative success of specific activities and assignments in producing different types of changes in different kinds of learners. It is something done *with* and *for* students, not done *to* them. As such, it suggests a deeper, more learning-centered view of assessment.

In both the Los Angeles-based and overseas programs, students use the competency list (see appendix) to rate their levels of development in each of the five outcome areas (awareness, affective, cognitive, character, and skills). They do this at pre-service, in-service, and post-service points. By so doing, we seek to gauge, however roughly, the relative growth in student competence as a result of their investment of time and energy in specific Service-Learning experiences. This is done primarily through student self-rating and self-reporting. Just as a singer might learn to assess her own development in the areas of voice quality, range, control, and originality, service-learners are guided in quantifying their development over time.

This is operationalized using a simple self-rating scale ("poor" to "outstanding") for use with each of the competencies in each learning domain. These self-ratings are then elaborated through self-reports in which learners describe in two or three sentences how they think their competence has changed in relation to each item. The pre-service assessment establishes a baseline level of competence against which to measure change in the midterm and final performance assessments (see below). It gives students an opportunity to envision specific areas for their growth during the term; it gives the faculty advisor a basis for suggesting acceptable performance standards for the course.

5. *Critical Reflection.* For our Los Angeles-based course, weekly two-hour meetings back on campus provide opportunities for further student training (learning how to learn from community experience), emotional support, problem-solving, reflection sharing, discussion of reading materials, and self-assessment. Group reflection lies at the center of the class session. Students take turns sharing their experiences while the others listen and then reflect back the information, feelings, and attitudes expressed. Out of the experience described, received by the group and reflected back, the class seeks to discover the main competencies operative within the experience or event. Out of these group "conversations," participants are enabled to (a) assess the service competencies they are successfully applying or are needing to develop and apply in order to enhance the quality of their service, (b) explore concepts (and thus build theory) that emerge out of their experience in order to better understand particular problems or issues, and (c) question and challenge each other toward a broader and more principled vision of public life.

6. *Weekly Time Diary.* The successful completion of both courses requires 30 to 40 hours of community service activity. One of the simplest means we've found for assessing student involvement is to have them keep a weekly time diary. Students indicate how much time per week they spend in various activities related to the course (e.g., reading, note-taking, team planning, travel, service, group discussion, and so forth). Each week the service supervisor can validate the service hours by "signing off" next to that activity. Because students receive course credit for the learning that takes place during the service term, and not for the service itself, a grade is not assigned to the diary as such. It simply provides a "quick and dirty" assessment of the time and energy students invest in Service-Learning activities.

7. *Service Organization Profile.* In the course of assuming myriad roles and functions within service organizations, students often wonder how they can better understand the social, economic, and managerial dynamics of the organization itself. To facilitate these learnings, each student participating in the overseas program is required to produce a three- to five-page profile of their service organization. The profile is generated from a series of informal interviews conducted with different agency constituents in an effort to "look behind" and "see through" the institutionally-sanctioned purpose(s) of social interaction. The interviews include questions related to the organization's local context, history, mission and goals, current constituents, management structure, funding sources, personal and social impacts, and future prospects.[8]

8. *Final Service Performance Evaluations.* Two final evaluations are completed and returned to the faculty advisor: one from the service site supervisor and one from the student. Using an instructor-prepared evaluation checklist, the service supervisor reports on the student's work habits, social skills, task performance, and general attitudes.[9] The students' performance evaluation is summative in nature, asking them to revisit the learning objectives and anticipated outcomes formulated at the beginning of the term and to evaluate the extent to which they achieved their goals. This self-evaluation is both a written product (which can take a variety of forms) and a process by which they work to make sense of what they have learned—to make critical connections between the world of ideas, the world of everyday experience, and the world within themselves.

Conclusion

Service-Learning is often perceived as just another Sixties fad, a passing fancy, or worse, an irresponsible use of student time and tuition. Many of these educators present serious philosophic and political reasons for not seeing more experiential- or service-based learning as essential elements of a liberal arts education. To a great extent, their hesitations express the larger conceptual tension that exists between the traditional teaching paradigm and the emerging learning paradigm of education. As long as our colleges and universities embrace what Alexander Astin calls the reputational or resources view of excellence—both of which focus on the *inputs* side of the learning equation—pedagogies which are explicitly directed toward developing and assessing the holistic competence of students will likely continue to be marginalized in the academy. Traditional faculty will not be won over with words alone. They will need to witness the pedagogical power of an outcome-based approach to Service-Learning—one that is able to demonstrate, however roughly, more diverse types and higher levels of student learning than they imagined. Much remains to be done in providing empirically-based evidence for the advantages of Service-Learning pedagogies. In so doing, we will have helped bridge the widening gap between the "head," "heart," and "hands" of higher education.

INVENTORY   **CHAPTER 11**

INTERCULTURAL SERVICE COMPETENCIES
Connecting Head, Heart, and Hands

Education enlightens the mind and inspires the heart so that the hands can serve.

—Richard E. Felix, President,
Azusa Pacific University

This inventory adapts the framework and many of the items developed by World Learning of Vermont and presented as "Competencies Required for Intercultural Competence." A Report Presented at the International Conference on Experiential Learning, Washington, D.C., November 1994.

HEAD

1. *Awareness Competencies* — The exhibition of conscious perception of and sensitivity to one's concept(s) of self and others, and approach to service context and experiences. Outcome measures include self-reports or reports by observers about how one's view of self and others has changed as a result of one's service experiences.

   1.1 Demonstrate an awareness of one's own reactions (e.g., fear, discomfort, judgment, disgust) to multicultural (linguistic, racial, cultural, ideological, social class) difference.

   1.2 Demonstrate an awareness of the manner in which community members and groups are viewed or perceived by oneself; the characteristics that are perceived.

   1.3 Demonstrate an awareness of how one is perceived (e.g., as an outsider) by members of the host community or culture.

   1.4 Demonstrate an awareness of, or sensitivity to, the sociocultural context (e.g., of the contact community or service site) as it affects perceptions, practices, and interactions.

   1.5 Demonstrate an awareness of oneself as a culturally conditioned human being with languages, perceptions, preferences, and habits formed out of one's life experiences.

   1.6 Demonstrate an awareness of responses to one's social identity within the context of the host community or culture (e.g., the moral- and cultural-superiority biases and assumptions we carry with us when involved with others who are different from us).

   1.7 Demonstrate an awareness of intracultural (e.g., regional, social class, ideological, age) differences *within* one's own culture and within the host culture(s) where service is performed.

1.8   Demonstrate an awareness of one's actual strengths and weaknesses in reference to the abilities required for effective service through the host organization.

1.9   Demonstrate an awareness of the strengths service organizations in marginalized communities bring to their local residents and to service-learners.

2.   *Cognitive Competencies* — Breadth of knowledge and understanding of facts and principles across broad and specialized areas of study. Includes an awareness of the discipline's history and various subfields, familiarity with its classic and current core questions and concepts, awareness of its available methods and techniques, and an analysis and synthesis of theories and frameworks. Outcome measures include student test scores or self-reports which reveal cognitive effects of one's service experience — e.g., knowledge and understanding of general terminology and facts; comprehension of general theories, processes and methods; increased ability to analyze, solve problems, and make inferences. The following are examples applying the field of intercultural communication to community service activities:

2.1   Describe the historical development of intercultural communication and its contribution to the community Service-Learning movement.

2.2   Develop basic working definitions of "culture" and "community service" as manifested in a multicultural urban setting.

2.3   Provide and compare basic information about one's own culture's history and community life and the history and community life of the host culture(s)/community.

2.4   Describe a limited set of field-based culture- and community-learning methods and techniques.

2.5   Demonstrate knowledge of the various

"themes" that will exhibit the dominant values, beliefs, customs, and behavioral norms of the host culture (e.g., work, leisure, time and space, language, family and work roles, relative importance of group and individual, rituals and superstitions, social hierarchies).

2.6   Articulate an understanding of those phenomena that one encounters in cross-cultural situations, regardless of the cultures involved: e.g., anxiety, disconfirming expectancies, in-group/out-group distinctions, ambiguity, confrontation with one's prejudices, learning styles, attributions.

2.7   Articulate an intellectual understanding of culture and the complexities of urban cultural systems using a limited number of relevant terms, principles, and concepts.

2.8   Provide and compare basic information about one's own cultural community (information about the history, local geography, sociology, education, family life, politics, religion, current events, etc.) and that of the host community.

2.9   Provide a detailed description of the "culture" of the host service organization (including its ideological, social, economic, and managerial characteristics) collating the perspectives of the organization's various constituents.

2.10 Describe and explain one's own behavior and the behavior of select group members of the host cultural community in terms of the cultural, social, economic, and political factors that shape it.

2.11 Describe and explain the main perceptions and/or opinions of oneself and select others residing in the host community concerning the causes and potential solutions to community issues (e.g., family, labor, health care, housing, urban education, gang violence, and race/ethnic relations).

2.12 Synthesize and describe relevant social and cultural information from oneself and from others in the host community that could be used to generate alternative ways of addressing issues or solving problems.

HEART

3. *Affective Competencies* — Patterns and directions of intercultural service competence typified by moral strength and emotion. Included are *attitudes* (predispositions to act in a certain way), *values* (a strong preference based on a conception of what is desirable, important, or worthy), and *commitments* (personal action based on principle or conviction). Outcome measures include self-reports on changes in one's attitudes, values, and commitments, and perhaps one's life philosophy, as a result of one's service experiences.

3.1 A demonstrated willingness to b*e with* community residents and organizational managers (e.g., does not always seek isolation or the company of classmates).

3.2 A demonstrated willingness to *empathically understand* the community—its people, processes, and problems—in both formal and informal contexts.

3.3 A demonstrated willingness to *deal with* one's emotional responses (e.g., fears, frustrations, and pleasures) to serving and learning in unfamiliar settings.

3.4 A demonstrated willingness to t*ake on* various roles as appropriate to both formal or informal contexts (e.g., as an observer-listener at a health clinic or as an informal interviewer on a street corner).

3.5 A demonstrated willingness to *reflect on* the impact of one's new experiences on the assumptions previously used to make sense out of the phenomena (e.g., poverty, unemployment, gang affiliation, etc.).

3.6 A demonstrated willingness to *try out* new ways of thinking, communicating, and interacting, and thereby grapple with alternative ways of perceiving, valuing, and practicing (e.g., a willingness to locate the problem of poverty in "structural" forces like the decline of industrial jobs and the persistence of decrepit inner city schools and inadequate health care, rather than in the character deficiencies of the poor).

3.7 A demonstrated willingness to *assess* the implications and thus the relative value of mul-

tiple beliefs, values, and practices.

3.8 A demonstrated willingness to reduce or eliminate conflicts or inequalities arising from a lack of responsibility taken by individuals, families, community groups, and government.

3.9 A demonstrated willingness to consistently put the interests of those being served ahead of one's own immediate (e.g., academic, egoistic) needs and concerns.

3.10 A demonstrated willingness to affirm the value, dignity, and importance of those being served, regardless of who they are or what they've done, by getting to know them on an individual basis.

3.11 A demonstrated willingness to accept the necessity of some mundane and repetitive tasks.

3.12 A demonstrated valuing of *community* as the spirit and values that will allow us to live with each other's deepest differences.

3.13 A demonstrated valuing of those served as *resources* to be developed rather than as problems to be managed.

3.14 A demonstrated valuing of *"downward mobility"* as a lifestyle of greater involvement with the people and problems in urban communities than seeking retreat and isolation from them.

3.15 A demonstrated commitment to serving within and through the neighborhoods, institutions, and social relationships of urban communities.

3.16 A demonstrated commitment to seeking personal meaning in giving oneself in service, rather than in material gain.

3.17 A demonstrated commitment to learning all the time through relevant, self-directed, and purposeful experiences set in right relationship to the larger society.

4. *Character Competencies* — Personal qualities and standards that sustain responsible involvement in public and community service within intercultural settings. Outcome measures include formative and summative reports by im-

partial observers (e.g., on changes in dependability and responsibility) and self-reports (e.g., on one's willingness to take chances).

4.1   Demonstrates a *sense of personal efficacy:* a strong sense of mission, purpose, and direction; the conviction that one can and will make a difference in the lives of those being served; the experience of a special delight in serving across human differences.

4.2   Demonstrates *respect of diverse others:* open with biases; open to honor cultural alternatives; able to accept others as unique expressions of specific character qualities in varying degrees of maturity; belief in intercultural experience for self and others.

4.3   Demonstrates *strong interpersonal relationships:* personal warmth; takes an interest in others; able to listen attentively and to respond with honesty and sensitivity; willing to disclose appropriately.

4.4   Demonstrates *inquisitiveness:* curious and experimental; stimulated and intrigued by uncertainty; preference for "stress-seeking" behavior; willing to take risks, to attempt new challenges, to follow that which motivates from deep within.

4.5   Demonstrates *initiative:* willing to initiate personal action or become personally involved; assumes responsibility for the well-being of others.

4.6   Demonstrates *flexibility:* able to adjust to new and changing situations and circumstances; patient with unanticipated sources of frustration (e.g., delays, logistical problems); willing to cheerfully change responsibilities and roles when unexpected conditions require it.

4.7   Demonstrates *cooperativeness:* learning the wishes and goals of those one is serving and adapting one's priorities to meet them; ability to mix with people easily.

4.8   Demonstrates *gentleness:* responds to others with kindness and love; knows what is appropriate to the emotional needs of others; serves without impatience or anger.

4.9   Demonstrates *humility:* carries a profound respect for the varied and complex nature of human experience; recognizes one's own limitations and imperfections; open to self-evaluation; able to receive and utilize criticism constructively.

4.10   Demonstrates *compassion:* able to be emotionally involved with the people one is learning with and from; willing to "suffer with" others and to do all that is possible to relieve their pain; able to use words and actions to bring comfort and healing.

4.11   Demonstrates *justice:* considers issues and circumstances through the eyes of each one involved in or affected by them; gathers facts before coming to conclusions; gives proper rewards to those who have helped them accomplish their goals.

4.12   Demonstrates *sincerity:* a genuine interest in those being served; an honest concern to benefit the lives of others and not simply for personal reward.

4.13   Demonstrates *joy:* sees value in circumstances that would normally discourage others; able to lift the spirit of those one serves; willing to not take oneself too seriously, to laugh at oneself; willing to play.

4.14   Demonstrates *creativity:* approaches new tasks with a sense of possibility and challenge; completes tasks with greater efficiency and quality.

4.15   Demonstrates *dependability:* reliable, trustworthy, and accountable for one's own behavior; lifts pressures from those one serves by applying energy and concentration to assigned tasks; arranges personal schedule around commitments made.

HANDS—The observable ability to *apply* "head" and "heart" competence within various planning, managing, social, service, and self-evaluation tasks. Outcome measures include self-ratings of interpersonal and leadership ability, faculty advisor ratings of oral and written communications, and supervisor ratings of service performance.

5. *Planning Skills*

5.1 Able to identify one's interests, skills, and life-goals in relation to community service opportunities

5.2 Able to formulate and fulfill personal learning objectives and goals in relation to the mission, function, and organization of the service agency

5.3 Able to identify one's preferred ways of learning

5.4 Able to relate specific learning activities to the accomplishment of objectives

5.5 Able to negotiate the interests and expectations of others (i.e., service supervisor, class partners, instructor)

6. *Managing Skills*

6.1 Able to understand and follow detailed instructions

6.2 Able to seek out and secure the necessary resources—material and human—to complete a project in a context alien to one's experience

6.3 Able to recruit other people (e.g., site supervisor, faculty advisor) to keep one "on-task" with the necessary emotional support

6.4 Able to manage time in order to complete assigned projects within agreed-upon time frames

6.5 Able to make independent decisions in the course of carrying out a project and take responsibility for the consequences of those decisions on other people

7. *Social Skills*

7.1 Able to express the full range of feelings (e.g., warmth and affection, frustration and anger) where appropriate and to assert one's own views and concerns without aggression or undue passivity

7.2 Able to work effectively with others of both sexes and of diverse ethnic, socio-economic, and religious backgrounds to accomplish cooperative goals

7.3 Able to relate effectively within service settings by *speaking* (conversing) with appropriate volume, timing, emotional tone, feedback, and self-disclosure, and *writing* with appropriate style, clarity of thought, and persuasiveness.

7.4 Able to develop friendships and trust relationships through communication, cooperation, and care

7.5 Able to help create opportunities for active participation, achievement, and accomplishment as defined by community members

7.6 Able to use strategies to effectively cope with moments of stress as a result of new circumstances and expectations (e.g., being the focus of attention)

7.7 Able to accept and follow one's "negative" feelings (e.g., impatience, frustration, anger, disappointment, defeat) as a means of working through differences

7.8 Able to interact with appropriate socio-cultural etiquette in both formal and informal contexts within the host community/service organization

8. *Service Skills*

8.1 Able to express oneself creatively through writing, painting, composing, singing, dance, drama, or playing instruments

8.2 Able to demonstrate competence in at least one service method (e.g., survey research, community organizing, counseling, legal advocacy, teaching)

8.3 Able to develop one's own computer-based information sources (e.g., through library databases or the Internet) instead of relying on those provided by an instructor or service supervisor.

8.4 Able to plan and execute independent research projects using a variety of strategies (e.g., systematic observation, active listening, informant interviewing, material collecting and reviewing, effective recording of field notes, and structured reflection) to collect and analyze information from the community or service setting

8.5 Able to apply particular ethical principles

to make value judgments in arriving at workable (compromise) solutions to problems

9. *Self-Evaluation Skills*

9.1 Able to decide what will count as a successful outcome of one's Service-Learning experiences

9.2 Able to set criteria by which one can judge the extent of success in achieving particular learning outcomes

9.3 Able to consciously and critically reflect on what one has learned in relation to the subject matter, and in relation to oneself, and in relation to the world outside oneself

9.4 Able to demonstrate what one has learned through written self-ratings and reportings which makes clear connections between one's service experience, academic learning, and competency development

9.5 Able to disseminate what is being learned through times of group reflection and discussion

REFERENCES

1 See Bruce Johnstone, "Learning Productivity: A New Imperative for American Higher Education," *Studies in Public Higher Education*, Number 3. Albany, N.Y.: Office of the Chancellor, State University of New York; Robert Barr and John Tagg, "From Teaching to Learning — A New Paradigm for Undergraduate Education," *Change* (November/December 1995); Peter Drucker, "The Age of Social Transformation" *The Atlantic Monthly*, (November 1994).

2 Boyer, Ernest. "Creating the New American College" *Chronicle of Higher Education* (March 9, 1994).

3 Demographic data indicate that, by the year 2000, African Americans will be the majority population in 53 major U.S. cities. By the same year, it is estimated that Asian American populations will increase by 22 percent, Hispanic Americans by 21 percent, African Americans by 12 percent, and European (white) Americans by 2 percent nationwide. If these predictions hold, traditional "minorities" will outnumber "majority" whites by the year 2050.

4 Chickering, Arthur, and Linda Reisser, *Education and Identity*, 2nd ed., 345. San Francisco: Jossey-Bass, 1993.

5 King, Dr. Martin Luther, Jr. *The Words Of Martin Luther King Jr.*, selected by Coretta Scott King. New York: Newmarket Press, 1983.

6 Long, Edward. *Higher Education As A Moral Enterprise*, 221. Washington, D.C.: Georgetown University Press, 1992.

7 These objectives will typically undergo some revision as the student-sojourners and their site supervisors become more familiar with each other's available resources and are able to plan service objectives and activities that are mutually beneficial.

8 This project is adapted from Barbara Hursh, "Learning Through Questioning in Field Programs" in Lenore Borzak. *Field Study*. Thousand Oaks, Calif.: Sage Publications, 1981.

9 A useful evaluation checklist is provided in Timothy Stanton, *The Experienced Hand*, 2nd ed., 76-79. Cranston, R.I.: Carroll Press, 1994.

CHAPTER 12

PHILOSOPHY 115: ETHICAL PRACTICE

Course Syllabus and Analysis

BY YORAM LUBLING

For faculty and administrators searching for a rationale for linking service and learning rooted in a philosophical tradition, this chapter offers a point of view for consideration. In this example, an independent liberal arts college has provided a context for academic change, an academic department has considered its overall role in this change, and one professor presents the story from the perspective of one course during one semester.

This chapter begins with excerpts from the introductory statement of the course given to students on day one, followed by Professor Lubling's analysis and assessment of the experience.

SECTION 1: SYLLABUS

Background

This year marks a serious and exciting change in the life of the academic community of Elon College. Last year the school challenged itself pedagogically and philosophically. The faculty embraced the challenge and produced a four-credit-hour system with a new General Studies Curriculum. The new curriculum better reflects contemporary needs in society and education by emphasizing a more multicultural approach to text and ideas, as well as a more experiential, practical,

imaginative, and creative educational engagement. Not only was the school, as a whole, charged with re-thinking itself, departments were also challenged to re-think their contribution to the learning process. The philosophy department, for one, took upon itself to re-examine the nature and function of its services to the college community. As a result, we have radically changed the nature of our teaching methods, text requirements, exams, and pedagogical goals. You are the first class to share our new ideas and we hope you will find them as liberating and constructive as we do.

Our intention as a department was two-fold: first, contribute to a "recovery" of philosophy by making its ideas and concerns more relevant to the lives of plain men and women. Second, to teach its wisdom through practice and active engagement, not through passive textual transmission alone. Regarding the first point, philosophy, as a profession and as the example par excellence of intelligence/ liberal thinking, becomes truly irrelevant when it only serves a small group of learned specialists. What will make philosophy relevant to our lives as teachers and students is if it concerns our everyday problems, and leads to constructive activity that can concretely bring about an improvement in the human condition. Indeed, the American philosopher John Dewey wrote over 80 years ago that, "Philosophy recovers itself when it ceases to be a device for dealing with the problems of philosophers and become a method, cultivated by philosophers, for dealing with the problems of men."

Yoram Lubling is assistant professor of philosophy at Elon College in North Carolina.

In this course, therefore, we will work as a group to make philosophical ideas relevant for our ordinary everyday experience. This brings us to the second point, that of practice and engagement. In order to make learning matter in your life, it is not sufficient to just make the subject matter apply to ordinary experience. We must also make knowledge and wisdom a tool to be used in practical, constructive, transformative, and physical ways. The wisdom of philosophical thoughts, from Plato to Woody Allen, is relevant only when it becomes part of ourselves through our habits and skills, i.e., as practice and as character. As R.W. Emerson correctly argues, "knowledge is in the muscles," it is not merely a cognitive matter good for contemplative joy alone. Genuine knowledge comes when it continuously, and successfully, transforms your life through learned skills and habits of cooperative citizenship and creativity.

Participatory Aspect of the Course

In this course we will emphasize relevancy and engagement. To this end we will reorganize the priorities involved in successfully completing a course in philosophy. Although I have assigned several books for this course, you will not be tested on whether or not you successfully memorized the important concepts. When it comes to questions of behavior in the context of a community, theoretical mastery becomes secondary in importance. How we practically act upon socially relevant situations is what we will consider of primary importance here. To accomplish this, the course will involve a substantial participatory component. The students will engage in work outside the classroom so as to provide a dimension of life and a general framework through which to introduce moral and social issues. Your participation in community affairs will be coordinated by our Volunteers Office. You will be expected to engage in community work for at least four hours a week. Your ability to integrate ideas introduced through the assigned readings into your everyday practice will constitute the primary portion of your grade in this class. You will be expected to present a weekly evaluation of your work and its relevancy to the assigned readings.

Structure of the Class

Our class meets three times a week. While we will keep this general structure we will use class time in a different way. Monday's class will be a lecture class where the relevant issues will be introduced. *All* the students in the class are to attend and follow the required readings for Monday's classes. The required texts in order of usage are:

1. Plato, *The Republic*

2. John Dewey, *Outline of a Critical Theory of Ethics*

3. ACLU's report on *Human Rights Violations in the United States*

4. Mike W. Martin, *Virtuous Giving*

5. Leroy Rouner, *On Community*

The class will then be divided into three groups. The groups will meet separately to discuss their community work and the problems that are associated with this engagement. The group will also be responsible for presenting the issues and ideas that are involved in a specific text that was assigned only to that group.

The small groups provide a better educational framework for cooperation.

Grade

There will be no "in-class" exams. This class will not test your ability to remember the correct answers. Fifty percent of the grade will be based on the way you perform your service. This means, the seriousness by which you handle the project, the way you engage the ideas you learn in class with their daily activity and class related service, and your own evaluation and the evaluations of your supervisors. The second 50 percent of the grade involves the readings, discussions, reports, and presentations. This 50 percent will be based largely upon your performance in the small group meetings.

Summary

These are very exciting times at Elon and in your lives as well. This new spirit of learning should be an opportunity for both of us to honestly engage in a constructive and enjoyable journey together. Our engagement here will succeed only to the degree to which we are willing to work for its accomplishment. As such, I cannot do it alone, your genuine involvement and willingness to learn are essential. I wish you the best of luck in this exciting journey.

SECTION 2: ANALYSIS

Implementation And Assessment

My first goal in teaching this course was to introduce philosophy as a practical engagement. Although an historically obvious notion, I had to work against a profession, as well as the academy in general, that considers the field of philosophy as primarily a mental and textual activity. Philosophy departments today attempt to attract undergraduate students with promises of "critical" skills that might assist them with admission to law schools. Philosophy, in the academy, views itself as merely a participant in a series of linguistic arguments grounded in rules of logic, with conclusions that are not subject to actual results in experience. Progress is judged by "objective" internal and formal standards, not by the actual push and pull of daily life. Rather than engagement endangering objectivity, as C.L. Stevenson has admonished, objectivity is actually sharpened, as John Dewey taught us, by continuing attention to exigent and moral realities.

Since this was a course on ethics as human conduct I faced a further difficulty in accomplishing my first goal. Traditional education in institutions of higher education inevitably involves a procedural distance between the thinker and the issue. The latter, we need to remember, is always a lived experience such as justice, equality, honesty, obligation, or duty. Such a duality between thinking and doing reinforces in the students, habits of indifference and disengagement. In order to contribute to the "recovery" of philosophy, I had to first engage in building a new philosophical and pedagogical paradigm, in which every detail was important. I literally had to execute a paradigm shift from a traditional dualistic conception of existence to a conception that is consistent with science and experience.

It was also essential to design a learning environment that would contribute to the construction of the new paradigm. I selected a large lounge, with moving and comfortable chairs, as a classroom. Students were allowed to move about and engage the professor or other students in a stress-free environment. The "theoretical" classes were primarily a discussion among adults who are part of a community of learners. As mentioned earlier, it is my belief that, if learning is to be continuous with the "reality" outside the college's walls, the classroom, as well as the issues, must resemble ordinary conduct.

To accomplish the first goal, that of thinking of philosophy as a practical engagement, I began the course with a discussion of Plato's *Republic*, following John Dewey's recommendation that,

> *Nothing could be more helpful to present philosophizing than a "back to Plato" movement; but it would have to be back to the dramatic, restless, cooperative, inquiring Plato of the dialogues; trying one mode of attack after another to see what might yield; back to the Plato whose highest flight of metaphysics always terminated with a social and practical turn, and not the artificial Plato constructed by unimaginative commentators who treat him as the original university professor.*[1]

My first goal in teaching this course was to introduce philosophy as a practical engagement.

Hence, the course began with the restless and cooperative Plato who attempts to construct the ideal state, i.e., the state in which an individual would know the meaning of his/her relations with others, and how to live a personal and flourishing life. The discussion of the *Republic* is helpful in putting the students into the framework of rethinking the structure of a community. With Plato we were able to engage in conceptual discussion regarding the "Just" state. Although Plato's division of labor in society, as well as the harsh treatment of artists, angered many students it allowed me to establish the notion that "state building" is a complex project that must be guided by practical reason; no matter who is lucky enough to extract him/herself from the cave's shadows. It was important, at this point, for the students to see that the process of education (as *philo-sophia*) carries with it social responsibilities. In the same way that the philosopher (lover of wisdom) is required to return to the cave and assist/educate others, philosophy, in its most genuine sense, is an activity of engagement that should be tested by concrete results. In other words, the value of philosophical activity must be measured by whether or not it assists in building a good community in which a good individual can live.[2]

In short, I wanted to use (not mention) Plato's *Republic* and its wisdom. It was important that students understand the relevance of Plato to everyday life and not simply focus on the *Republic* as a self-contained textual realm. I wanted to use the wisdom of Plato in order to bring the students into the context of community building. As such, whether or not Plato is "correct" in his conception regarding the structure of an ideal state is only secondary in importance. What is essential is that the students achieve an ongoing participation in a process where careful and consistent use of reason directs the very essence of our lives, i.e., the community.

At this point the class was ready to enter the community and find out the shape of its relationships. With the assistance of our Center for Service Learning each student was assigned 40 hours of community work within three categories of activities: relief (American Red Cross), education (ACC Literacy Program), and health and legal (Alamance Coalition on Adolescent Pregnancy). Logistically, the center assigned a student coordinator who was consistently available to the students.

The students were engaged for at least four hours a week in service in the community, which took many forms:

- training and tutoring younger students in the community with special needs
- training with the local Red Cross Chapter to became CPR instructors
- assisting as Blood Mobile volunteers
- performing office work
- providing child care for working mothers
- volunteering to build friendships with the elderly in the local retirement homes
- delivering meals for the county's community services
- connecting with the local churches to work at soup kitchens

An evaluation form was developed through which the various organizations' leaders could communicate with me about the students' work. This also provided a record for later evaluation of the students' final grades.

After the students had acquired some theoretical parameters to understand the philosophical work that is involved in forming a community, as well as actual engagement with their local community, we could move further. My next goal was to introduce the students to an historical discussion of ethics using John Dewey's *Outline of a Critical Theory of Ethics* as the primary text. My reason for choosing this text was twofold, 1) The class was conceptualized within the Dewey tradition and understanding of what it means to "do ethics," thus it provided the most appropriate intellectual framework for this class, and 2) Dewey's understanding of ethics provided the justification for Service-Learning since Dewey's insistence that ethics is a participatory and dramatic event involving habits and skills justifies the emphasis on "work."[3] Dewey ethics is best understood as the science of conduct, and conduct is understood as man's activity in its whole reach. Furthermore, conduct is that which is judged in its relation to the desired end, i.e., the *Summun bonum* (the "Supreme Good"). Conduct is generally judged by how it contributes to this end, and as such provides us with direction for activity (the ethical "ought") and social duties.

Next we engaged in an overview of the different conceptions of The Good introduced in our Western culture: the hedonistic theory, the utilitarian theory, and the Kantian theory.[4] I argue that the hedonistic theory is not an ethical theory at all; rather, that it provides the very essence of unethical behavior. There are many arguments that are available to make this point and Dewey's text provides them. However, the general point to make was that pleasure cannot be a common good since it fails to provide a "comprehensive end" for an individual's acts, as well as for various individuals' acts (a common good). As an ethical principle, pleasure fails to unify character and it forces an unreal division between conduct and character. Since individual pleasure is the ultimate yardstick, there can be no immoral acts at all. Everything must be directed to "serving pleasure."

We then considered Utilitarianism as an ethical account of the common good. Here pleasure is considered as a sum and quality of pleasures. Human activity is now being considered in terms of a collective standard, but as Dewey points out, there is no logically direct bridge from the hedonistic/privatistic notion of pleasure to the general and universalistic notion of pleasure. Finally, we considered Kantian ethics, or what Dewey refers to as formal ethics since all objects of desire have been excluded from it. Here the good is to be found in the will itself, irrespective of any end to be reached by the will. The motive for conduct is a universal principle derived from the will itself. Kant's failure can be identified in the emptiness of his universal principles.

However, both pleasure-oriented ethical theories and formalistic theories fail to recognize that the end of action (the common good) is neither pleasure nor an abstract law, rather,

> ...it is the satisfaction of desire according to law...The law is the law of the desires themselves. The harmony and adjustment of desires necessary to make them instruments in fulfilling the special destiny or business of the agent. The criterion is to be found neither in the consequences of our acts as pleasures, nor apart from pleasures. It is found in the complete consequences of our acts.[5]

By "complete" Dewey implies that the "yardstick" for ethical behavior must involve both the agent and society. The agent's interest in him/herself is as a member of society. The common good, then, must involve the will and interests of others. In the context of the students' work in the community, it is essential to show that individual and social goods are umbilically connected. Community work only makes sense when individuals can see that realizing their individuality must necessarily contain the realization of the community, and vice-versa. As Aristotle so beautifully argued in his discussion of friendship, it is in the consciousness of the existence of another that a person becomes truly conscious of him/herself.

After establishing, both ideationally and practically, the primacy and necessity of relations, I moved to enlarge my ethical framework by introducing the dialogical philosophy of Martin Buber.[6] In using Buber I was able to introduce the notion of choice and responsibility in forming relations with the world, i.e., "Love is the responsibility of an I for a Thou." Buber read correctly the Jewish view of the ethical person as the one who keeps relations of respect between individuals and between an individual and the place, i.e., creation in general. He also offers a view of ethics as an ameliorative activity, i.e., the more we try to form mutual, equal, and respectful relations with each other, the more we enhance the moral quality of life. The social metaphor in which I was working was that of a proletarian engagement in improving the human condition, while rejecting the traditional academic metaphor of the aristocratic "harm-chair" pedagogy.

Buber's dialogical system can be connected to service work by showing how perceptions of the world change when we enter into an I and Thou relationship with ordinary objects. Through Service-Learning the students came to see the homeless and disadvantaged individuals as fully human, not merely social objects. Such experiences, if persistent, can develop habits of respect in the students which is the central goal of this course. As a teacher in the Deweyean tradition, I am ultimately interested in making ethical virtues into habits and skills. By connecting the above philosophical conception with the actual experience of the students, I was able to provide a form of ethical training.[7]

Similarly, I continued to introduce (in both my main theoretical discussion and the small groups) theoretical ideas and values and then test them by connecting them to the students' experience. I have used the following recent texts on: philanthropy (*Virtues Giving* by Mike W. Martin); community (*On Community* edited by Leroy S. Rouner, *Care and Commitment* by Jeffrey Blustein, *Moral Responsibility and the Boundaries of Community* by Marion Smiley); Love and Friendship (*Friendship*, edited by Neera K. Badhwar, *The Pursuit of Love* by Irvin Singer); Responsibility (ACLU's Annual Report on Human Rights Violation in the U.S., *The Importance of What We Care About* by Harry G. Frankfurt).

Making the Connections

At this point in the course, with students engaged in their work and part of a larger discussion, it was relatively easy to make the connections between ideation and experience.

Philanthropy: The topic was a "natural" for such a course since "community service" is philanthropic. The only time that learning about giving to others can be genuinely examined is when it is practiced. Negative issues such as dependency and violation of person through public funds received a very dramatic framework. By engagement the student comes to truly understand that poverty and lack of opportunities are not the result of laziness, even though this is what some politician may want us to believe. At the start of the class, the more conservative-minded students tended to argue that it is inappropriate to require them to engage in giving to others. This conviction had to be tested later in the context of the students' work. As a result of Service-Learning, the students developed I and Thou relationships with the recipients of public giving. No longer were they seen as the demonic block of unidentified people, but instead they were seen as little children who needed help learning to write and read, or abused children with no place to go to escape the cycle of family violence. It is here that 19-year-old students with a $30,000 car and parental credit cards realize that not everyone is free to realize their "God given potential."

Community: Another "natural" for this course. The students' own involvement in the community was essential for them to begin an examination of different modalities of communities. It was in this context that the students had to show responsibility in making decisions that affect the welfare of others. They also encountered, for the first time, the frustration of seeing how countless lives are damaged in their interaction with the public system of education, the federal, state, and local health and human service agencies, the local, state and federal tax policies, the local police mentality of militant behavior that compromises our freedoms, etc. Again, in using their experiences, the students' questions about community now became "dramatic" since it matters how we act. In contrast, disengaged education

about theories of justice fail to incorporate into their pedagogical vision the overwhelming reality of our emotions, feelings, and concrete relations. Knowledge of the community, when taught as ideationally abstract and isolated, leads to ethical indifference even among the best "educated."

Responsibility: In conjunction with our discussion of the community I introduced the issue of individual responsibility and liberty. Drawing from the classical American tradition (Emerson, Royce and Dewey), I engaged the students in recognizing the inevitable tension that exists between individual and communal interests. The point to be made here is that such tension is the

> *Judging from final reflection essay required of each student, it appears that there is a new excitement about learning that is unusual in traditional philosophy classes.*

very essence of progress. This tension explains the paradigmatic changes that have taken place in the areas of human, animal, and environmental rights, etc. In fact, it is the common good that maintains a healthy balance between the needs of the individual and those of the community. Since both sets of needs are continuously changing, the shape of our relations with the surroundings changes and grows as well. The involvement with Service-Learning insures that the students, by assuming a position of responsibility in their community, will grow individually and socially.

Love and Friendship: My final goal in this course was to show that most of our ethical problems, as distinguishable from ethical puzzles, are resolvable by a genuine metaphysical shift in our understanding of ourselves and the world. My argument is that our conduct is largely motivated by bad metaphysics, i.e., dualistic and foundational. In contrast, I conceive ethical practice as involving the process of negotiation with the human and non-human environment. Ethical conflicts, furthermore, are those that arise between individuals or peoples with a different set of beliefs which are nothing other than "rules for action." Ethical conflicts take place in the very depth of emotions, feelings, and pre-reflective habits of thought and reason.

Such an ethical reality requires a metaphysical "map" that is consonant with ordinary experience in order to direct individual/environment relations and improve the human condition. My "metaphysical map" is a naturalistic and humanistic one, consistent with accrued wisdom and lessons learned. In this final part of the course I show how a non-dualistic reading of experience can result in the much-needed improvement in our dialogical relationships. While discussing different modalities of love I argue that they all lead to isolation and division since they are all "metaphysically private." In other words, love does not require that the object of love be real (philosophers will say that the actual reality of the object is neither sufficient nor necessary for love to dwell in the hearts of people). This reality is consistent with dualistic conceptions of reality and with ethical isolationism and indifference.

Friendship, on the other hand, requires the existence of the other in order to be formed. In the best tradition of Aristotle, I attempted to show that the act of friendship involves the recognition of the "other's" humanity and is primarily responsible for the formation of one's character, i.e., becoming a flourishing person. Through work at nursing homes, Red Cross, adolescent pregnancy programs, and literacy programs students formed relationships of friendship with other members of the community. Some students formed deep relationships with the people they assisted. In some cases they incorporated these relationships into their classwork by bringing to class a group of children or an elderly couple that they formed friendships with to discuss their experiences with the class.

By reading classical and contemporary texts about love and friendship, the students were able to continuously test these ideas through the different relationships they have both in and outside of class.[8] In essence, the class become a big labora-

tory in which classical and contemporary ideas were challenged in the face of concrete experience. I also used several movies to communicate ideas and to change the tension in the class, especially some of Woody Allen's films that show contemporary relational starvation.

Assessment

There are two central assessment questions. First, did the students learn better by testing and experiencing the ideas learned in class? Second, what did the student learn from such an engagement? With respect to the first question, over 50 percent of the students involved in the class exceeded their required 40 hours, and 30 percent remained in their Service-Learning positions after the class ended. Furthermore, judging from a final reflection essay required of each student, it appears that there is a new excitement about learning that is unusual in traditional philosophy classes. Through my classes alone (Critical Thinking; Philosophy of Love; and Ethical Practice), more than 3,000 hours of service were provided to the local community during an academic year.[9]

As to the second question, students learned about human conduct in all its aspects while being informed ideationally with the best in our tradition. While that alone may be sufficient for many philosophy programs, in this class they also learned the physical meaning of these ideas. From that alone I believe that the students learned substantially about giving, honesty, responsibility, friendship, cooperation, duty, community needs, selfishness, respect for others, etc. Although I required no exams and did not test my students' ability to memorize, I had no difficulty evaluating their understanding of philosophical wisdom by observing and discussing their work experience (the class had a total of 35 students). I observed them in their workplace and in our small group meetings. They were required to write several papers and were responsible for presentations and discussions in the small group meetings.

It is essential that this type of teaching have the strong support of the department and the school in which it occurs. In doing so, one must remember that it is not always easy to introduce education that requires one to get one's "hands dirtied" without being rejected by the traditionalists. In a posi-

tive context, the following members of the philosophy department at Elon College all participated in
this experiment in different and creative ways: professors John Sullivan, Anthony Weston, and Nim
Batchlor. Also, the deans and academic vice presidents assisted with our efforts by providing significant support and exposure to our Center for
Service Learning. I want to especially acknowledge
the support and assistance of my friend and colleague Eric Evans, for seemingly endless discussions about how to pedagogically connect
philosophical ideas with practice. Finally, I hope
the educators who read about our experience at
Elon College will be moved to acknowledge the insights of John Dewey who taught us that "education
is a process of living, not a preparation for future
living." This course attempted to march as close as
possible to this wisdom.

NOTES

1   Dewey, John. Cited in *Contemporary American Philosophy*,
    vol. II, edited by G.P. Adams and W.P. Montague, 21.

2   As a Jewish professor, I brought to bear on this discussion
    the Jewish conception of Tikkon Olam (amending the
    world). It can be helpful to show that historically there
    was much stronger emphasis on social/civil duties, and
    that the possession of knowledge was only conceived in
    terms of actual results in the welfare of the community.
    Whether by direct revelation or direct intellectual
    intuition, the having of knowledge is never for voyeuristic
    and aristocratic joy (notwithstanding Aristotle's position).

3   At this point the class only meets once a week for
    theoretical discussions. The other two meetings in the
    week are devoted to evaluation of their Service-Learning
    work. They need to make presentations relating ideas
    identified in class with activities in the "workplace." I also
    made sure to meet with small groups of students (12-15)
    to discuss other issues, text, and making connections
    between the ideas in class and their experience outside
    the class.

4   This in no way suggests that these are the only
    conceptions that matter. On the contrary, a multicultural
    discussion will be extremely helpful.

5   Dewey, John. "Outline of a Critical Theory of Ethics," in
    The Early Works, vol. III, p. 291.

6   I use the Scribner's edition of *I and Thou*.

7   By "ethical training" I am not suggesting any form of
    moral indoctrination. I take it without argument that
    habits of cooperation and respect are the ones that fulfills
    the social and individual end. This was not a graduate
    class in philosophy where the ultimate goal is to provide
    convincing arguments and reasons for every claim.
    Instead, this course is about "doing" ethics which involves
    social conscience and engagement. I consider these
    values to be of central social and civil importance. Indeed,
    these virtues are continuously challenged by my students,
    particularly the virtue of giving to others (philanthropy).
    Such challenges are the nuts and bolts of this course and I
    encourage discussions and presentations on such issues
    with references to the experience the students have in
    their service work.

8   The text examines theories of love and friendship from
    Plato and Aristotle to Stendhal, Ortega y Gasset, Simone
    de Beauvoir, Nietzsche, Emerson, Buber, Mead, to name a
    few.

9   This includes the hours provided by my distinguished
    colleague in the department, Dr. John Sullivan, who
    required twenty hours in his Ethical Practice courses, as
    well as interactive exercises, to assist in the formation of
    ethical habits and skills.

CHAPTER 13

SERVICE-LEARNING AND CAREER DEVELOPMENT

Incorporating Service and Guided Career Exploration with Academics to Deliver on the University's Mission

BY MATTHEW R. BERNDT

This chapter presents St. Edward's University's successful implementation of a comprehensive integrated multi-stage program for career planning, and management; a round-table model for incorporating Service-Learning pedagogy to enhance teaching effectiveness and student learning via service-based direct experience and to strengthen the relationship between academic learning and student services; and a vision for direct experience, specifically including Service-Learning, in higher education, recently affirmed by a Southern Association of Colleges and Schools (SACS) Alternate Model for Institutional Self-Study reaccreditation consulting team.

ST. EDWARD'S UNIVERSITY AND ITS STUDENTS

St. Edward's was founded on the verge of a new city in a new state at the dawn of a new era of social development. Throughout its 110 years as an institution of higher learning, St. Edward's has constantly sought to retain and refashion its initial newness while remaining true to the Catholic and Holy Cross ideals of education upon which it was founded.

Formerly the Director of Career Resources at St. Edward's University, Matthew R. Berndt is currently the Manager of Student and Corporate Relations at the University of Southern California's Annenberg School for Communication.

Today St. Edward's conveys its traditions to a very diverse group of students. Statistically, its students represent the "new majority" in college with an average age of about 27. They are 43% male and 57% female. Their ethnicity anticipates the diversity that will soon characterize Texas and the nation: about 61% white; 25% Hispanic; 7.5% black, Asian-American and Native-American; and 5% international students. Many begin here as first-time freshmen. The vast majority work, often full-time. Most who enter the university as first-time college students do not graduate from St. Edward's; and most who graduate began their college careers elsewhere.

Finding new pathways for scholarship, learning and the development of a fully realized humanity in its students is an ongoing task made necessary not only by the changing nature of the St. Edward's student, but still more so by the rapidly changing world to which they and their university now belong. ("St. Edward's University and its Students" is taken from St. Edward's University 1995-1996 Strategic Self-Study Report, pp. 2-3.)

Since 1990, St. Edward's University has undertaken three major steps toward finding these "new pathways" in career development and experiential and Service-Learning: The development and implementation of a comprehensive and integrated Career Planning & Management Program; the coordination of service-based learning programs and integration of Service-Learning into the curriculum of each of our six schools; and the development through the Alternate Model of Institutional Self-Study of a strategic vision for the role of direct experience in higher education, which builds upon and integrates lessons learned from SEU's previous and current success.

CAREER PLANNING & MANAGEMENT PROGRAM

In 1990, St. Edward's University received a two-year Vision Grant from the 3M Corporation to explore methods for "enhancing students' career awareness and increase their ability to use their college experience to effectively prepare for the world of work." The grant project involved students, faculty, staff and members of the Austin business and professional community, and was the catalyst for the Spring 1993 creation of a "School-to-Work" committee, assembled to research and make recommendations regarding how SEU could, on an institution-wide basis, most effectively support our students in making the transition from their undergraduate college career to their graduate and/or professional careers. Recommendations resulting from both of these exercises emphasized the invaluable nature of direct experience and applied learning and the necessity to integrate academically relevant direct experience more fully into the curricular and co-curricular activities of SEU students.

In September 1993, Career Resources Center (CRC) staff developed and implemented a comprehensive career exploration and development program that responded to the recommendations.

The Career Planning & Management (CP&M) Program is a four-stage career exploration and development program designed to provide undergraduate students a framework for career exploration while they are still in school. It assists students in identifying and selecting career paths best suited to their individual talents, skills, interests and professional and personal goals. Like an academic degree plan, it spans the students' college careers and helps them manage their time and activities. While a degree plan focuses on the academic coursework and testing each student must complete to receive a degree from St. Edward's, the Career Planning & Management

Program focuses on the co- and extra-curricular activities each student should complete throughout their college experience in order to match their academic studies with their personal and career goals. To earn a Certificate in Career Planning & Management from St. Edward's University, a student must complete all four stages of the CP&M Program.

To complete stage one, a student must complete all of the required activities in *Introduction to Career Planning & Management*. This course is designed as the cornerstone of the CP&M Program. Using a wide variety of exercises and assignments, it focuses on skill and interest identification, and on using this information about one's self as the basis for exploring academic and career options and opportunities. Emphasis in this course and stage is placed on developing the skills and information base necessary for ongoing career exploration, not on the specific act of identifying a major or career target, although these often occur.

The remaining three stages of the CP&M Program focus the career exploration and development into three primary unit areas: experience, personal development, and service.

Experience

The Experience Units are designed so that students can explore areas of career interest and acquire practical work experience in these areas. Students must complete three Experience Units (one each in Stages Two, Three, and Four) to be eligible for certification. These activities can include internships, part-time and full-time jobs, work-study jobs, experiential class projects (Service-Learning projects), and research or lab work.

Personal Development

The Personal Development Units are designed to help students develop their skills, interests, and aptitudes in ways that are unique to them. In addition, the Personal Development Units assist students in identifying and exploring their career options. Over the course of Stages Two, Three and Four, required Personal Development Unit activities include attending seminars or workshops sponsored by an on-campus academic or student services office or an outside agency, developing computer skills in word processing, spreadsheet or desktop publishing software applications, ongoing professional networking via student organizations and local chapters of professional associations, resume preparation, and, when appropriate, application to graduate school programs.

The Personal Development Units allow the individual student to match his/her skills and interests with classes and career options. They also assist students to develop a greater understanding of themselves and of the professions and career areas they are considering.

Service

Like the Experience Units, the Service Units provide students with valuable experience to include on their resume. The Service Units, however, are unique in that they provide students the opportunity to help others in substantial ways while gaining practical experience and helping themselves to develop personally and professionally. Students can earn a Service Unit by serving as a volunteer, a tutor or a mentor individually, through a club or service organization, or through a Service-Learning-based course offered at the University.

Students who have successfully met all requirements of the CP&M Program will have completed three applied learning experiences in areas of career interest, a series of personal development activities specifically tailored to meet their own career development needs, and three service-based applied learning experiences; all within a guided context of career exploration and development.

The CP&M Program is underpinned by a very simple philosophy:

Provide students the opportunity to develop a working awareness of their skills, interests and talents, help them use this information about themselves to guide their academic and career exploration and decision making, and they will be better prepared (a) to succeed in the worlds of work and/or graduate school and (b) to assume their role as citizens in the world community.

In this respect, the CP&M Program endeavors to fulfill the Mission Statement goal of helping students "understand themselves, clarify their personal values, and recognize their responsibility in the world community."

SERVICE-LEARNING: A ROUND TABLE APPROACH

The concept and application of Service-Learning are integral parts of St. Edward's University's mission, vision and strategic planning activities. As articulated in the SEU Mission Statement and cited in the preceding section:

" ...Students are helped to understand themselves, clarify their personal values, and recognize their responsibility to the world community." In addition, "The University gives the example of its own commitment to service.... St. Edward's expresses its Catholic identity by communicating the dignity of the human person as created in the image of God, by stressing the obligation of all people to pursue a more just world, and by providing opportunities for religious studies and participation in campus ministry...."

St. Edward's has a long history of service, concern and intervention in our community, almost to the extent of community activism. We have seen this commitment to service bear much fruit for the university, for our students and graduates, and for the greater community within which we work and live. SEU has a seven-year-old Community Mentor Program; a 20-plus-year-old College Assistance Migrant Program (CAMP); and a large number of student and University service initiatives and volunteer programs facilitated through the Career Resources Center, the Office of Student Financial Services, the Office of Student Activities and Campus Ministry. In addition, our Social Work curriculum, Cultural Foundations core curriculum and Capstone course combine with these other programs to inculcate both an ethic and practice of service which enhances the learning experience, the marketability of our graduates to employers and graduate schools, and the lives of our students and the individuals in the Austin community with whom they interact.

In general, St. Edward's recognizes that service is a way of acknowledging that people at every step along the journey (not just graduates, professionals, etc.) have something valuable to contribute. It helps individuals to recognize their own self-worth.

St. Edward's University's service-based and service-oriented programs fit well into the four quadrants in Robert Sigmon's four-part Service and Learning Typology (Sigmon, 1994).

With a service-oriented mission and a liberal arts core curriculum supporting more than 30 major areas of study, St. Edward's has many academic programs which fit the "service-LEARNING" definition, where learning goals are primary and service goals are secondary.

Further, certain academic and numerous co- and extra-curricular student clubs and organizations meet the "SERVICE-learning" criteria, where service outcomes and the service agenda are primary and learning objectives are a secondary, often unplanned, benefit.

St. Edward's, like many universities, has many classes, student activities, and organizations that pursue singular agendas of service or learning; the "Service-Learning" quadrant, where the learning and service goals are separate. There is no expectation that a service experience will be a part of or enhance learning or that learning will in any way provide a direct service. These three parts of the four-part typology are easy to identify, categorize and measure. They occur, generally, either in classes as structured parts of curriculum or as programming (both service- and non-service-focused) generated by student-driven organizations. The priorities are clear in virtually all of these instances.

Service-Learning has significantly enhanced student motivation for mastering course content.

The fourth part of the Service and Learning Typology, "SERVICE-LEARNING," where service and learning goals are given equal weight and enhance each other for all participants, is where these clearly defined lines of priority begin to blur and true Service-Learning takes place.

It is my assertion that a university must have the first three parts of this typology firmly in place be-

fore it can effectively move on to "SERVICE-LEARNING." St. Edward's University, with a long track record of success in these first three areas of Service-Learning, was prepared in 1994 to move into this fourth area. Council of Independent Colleges funding, combined with funding from the Corporation for National Service and SEU institutional funds, enabled us to take this logical next step and develop curricula to meet the criteria for SERVICE-LEARNING.

The Round-Table Model

St. Edward's University has multiple offices that are involved in coordinating community service, including the Career Resources Center, the Community Mentor Program, the Office of Student Financial Aid, the Office of Student Activities, Campus Ministry, and each of the six schools within the university. To ensure that true integration across the university could be achieved, a cross-functional, interdependent team of faculty and administrators was formed to oversee the development of these integrated, student-focused SERVICE-LEARNING curriculum models.

Service-Learning Coordinators were identified and trained in each of the six schools to serve as the primary Service-Learning consultants to their respective faculty. The director of career resources, the primary external relations participant; the director of the Community Mentor Program, the initiator of St. Edward's first forays into Service-Learning; the director of the Center for Teaching Excellence, the primary link to faculty continuing education and development; and the school-specific Service-Learning coordinators formed the core of this cross-disciplinary Service-Learning council and worked together to guide the curricular integration of Service-Learning at St. Edward's.

This integration process has been conducted in three phases of implementation: In Phase I of the SERVICE-LEARNING initiative, curricular integration of Service-Learning was focused within three University programs: the schools of humanities and education, traditional undergraduate programs; and the New College, a non-traditional undergraduate program for working adults.

Phase I began in March 1994 and continued through December 1994. In Phase II of St. Edward's University's SERVICE-LEARNING initiative, the remaining three academic schools (business, behavioral and social sciences, and natural sciences) were included in the curricular integration project. Phase II began in February 1995 and continued through Fall 1995 semester.

Service-Learning has heightened faculty enthusiasm for redesigning courses and updating curricular content.

Phase III of SEU's initiative is allowing us to continue to offer Service-Learning curriculum development stipends to faculty in all six SEU schools from 1996-2001. All of these stipends come from a combined resource pool which includes private grant funding, state, and federal grant funding, institutional funding, and funding from our community partners.

In terms of project assessment, formal evaluation of Service-Learning curriculum development projects is conducted at the end of each phase of integration. In these assessments, outcomes for the community-based partner and the university and impacts in the larger community are examined. As part of this assessment, each faculty member works on a multi-part assessment report that recounts how—and how well—Service-Learning was integrated within each course. Further, student and community partner input is incorporated into the overall assessment.

Principal questions in addition to the integration aspect address expectations of students' efforts and meeting the needs of the community partner. Each faculty member describes how goals were met, and obtains feedback from the community partner and from students involved. As more faculty members become involved with the Service-Learning efforts across the campus, additional comparisons will be made of the overall effects of Service-Learning on students' appraisal of courses. Follow-up efforts continue with community partners to determine the lasting effects and longer-term relationships with their campus collaborators.

In terms of the benefits of Service-Learning, we have identified eight general lessons. Service-Learning:

(1) has significantly enhanced student motivation for mastering course content;

(2) has heightened faculty enthusiasm for redesigning courses and updating curricular content;

(3) helps both faculty and students maintain a strong focus on course objectives throughout the semester;

(4) has increased our knowledge of our community partners' needs and our community partners' appreciation for the resources offered by St. Edward's University;

(5) has facilitated the development of effective structures for setting up, monitoring, assessing, and improving internships and other field-based experiential learning that were already in place;

(6) has increased the effectiveness of student learning;

(7) has enhanced procedures for assessing student learning; and

(8) has significantly increased students' ability and propensity toward self-assessment.

We have identified four primary lessons in terms of challenges that must be overcome to achieve success with Service-Learning. Service-Learning:

(1) requires a significantly greater amount of faculty time for course planning, development, implementation, and assessment;

(2) requires a significant increase in the amount of time students must devote to a course;

(3) is most effective when carefully structured and monitored by the faculty; student responsibility must be carefully regulated with specific procedures, activities, timelines, and opportunities for reflection; and

(4) input from community partners must be rigorously sought with procedures and instruments

requiring a minimal amount of time commitment.

Success Factors

The success St. Edward's University has experienced with Service-Learning can, in large part, be attributed to four key factors in our implementation model: institutional commitment, faculty involvement & development, strength of external relationships, and cross-disciplinary project management.

Institutional Commitment

Without institutional commitment ranging from the Office of the President to the offices of individual faculty and staff members, Service-Learning cannot effectively occur. This commitment involves not only a philosophical commitment on the part of the university, but a financial commitment as well. At St. Edward's, conscious efforts have been made to decrease our level of dependence on grant funding, increase participation by community partners in terms of both human and financial resources, and formally incorporate institutional human and financial resources in support of our Service-Learning initiatives.

Faculty Involvement & Development

Faculty buy-in is another critical element for achieving successful Service-Learning. Key to our success in getting faculty involved were our recruiting efforts, our efforts to promote and offer Service-Learning as an alternate pedagogy, and the participation and endorsement of the Center for Teaching Excellence.

The faculty members recruited to participate in the first two phases of the St. Edward's implementation process were targeted because of their reputation on campus as educational innovators, their demonstrated commitment to service, and their willingness to "go the extra mile." With the guidance of their Service-Learning Coordinators and the leadership within the faculty peer group of the Director of the Center for Teaching Excellence, these faculty turned into the campus cheerleaders for Service-Learning as a pedagogical option. It is important to note that Service-Learning at St. Edward's was from the outset promoted to faculty as an optional pedagogy that could find applica-

tion in most curricula, not as the new pedagogy to be incorporated into all curricula.

Lastly, "Redesigning Curricula to Include Service-Learning/Experiential Learning" is now an established part of SEU's portfolio of faculty development programs, and the faculty who have revised course curricula to include Service-Learning remain cheerleaders for the program. As a result, the number of integrated Service-Learning courses at St. Edward's University has increased from 13 at the start of this initiative to more than 25 at the present time, and only 18 of these courses were developed as a result of faculty receiving curriculum development stipends.

Strength of External Relationships

St. Edward's University has a long track record of success in working with community partners. The Austin community has come to expect a high level of quality from St. Edward's, its programs, and its people. The opportunity to partner with St. Edward's in Service-Learning was presented to a very supportive audience that was eager to work with SEU faculty, staff, and students. **A structured program of Service-Learning requires this kind of substantial, established commitment from external partners.**

Cross-Disciplinary Project Management

Effective Service-Learning involves having faculty, staff, students, and community partners participate in program development, implementation and management. In St. Edward's case, the director of the Community Mentor Program (an external university program based in the Academic Services part of SEU), the director of the Career Resources Center (an internal/external program based in the Enrollment and Student Services part of SEU), and the director of the Center for Teaching Excellence (an internal program based also in Academic Services) teamed with the faculty Service-Learning coordinators in each school (the internal faculty champions) to lead the university's side of this round table initiative. External relationships developed by every member of this team, and led by the Community Mentor Program and Career Resources Directors, brought community partners to the table.

Key Questions to Guide Service-Learning Project Development

St. Edward's decentralized round table approach to Service-Learning is successful for St. Edward's because of SEU's mission, organizational dynamic, and institutional culture. In short, this type of model made sense at St. Edward's University. It may not, however, be the model of choice for all institutions. In determining the type of Service-Learning program model that will be most successful in your institution, you must address issues in three key areas: strategic issues, operational issues, and financial issues.

Strategic Issues What are your institution's priorities for Service-Learning? What is your mission and where does Service-Learning fit? What does your institution's portfolio of service-related programs look like in terms of the four-part Sigmon typology? What do you want this portfolio to look like? How will you know when you have succeeded?

Operational Issues Who are your key players among faculty, staff, students, and community partners? Who needs to be and/or logically should be involved in the project? What level of support exists within the senior administration? What is the receptivity level of students, faculty, staff, and community partners? What will you use to assess your efforts?

Financial Issues What are your top two to three financial considerations? How is the initiative going to be funded? What roles will grant, institutional, community partner, and other funding play in your planning? What types of funding does your program depend upon to function? What will happen if that funding source disappears? What level of institutional financial commitment exists for the program? What grant partners might support this endeavor?

A VISION FOR DIRECT EXPERIENCE, INCLUDING SERVICE-LEARNING

Over the course of the past three years, the St. Edward's University community has been crafting a vision for the future through an "alternate" Self-Study for 1995-1996 reaccreditation process. This reaccreditation process concluded successfully in Fall 1995 when the reaccreditation visiting consulting team wholeheartedly affirmed St. Edward's vision for the future of the university.

The following excerpts from the Self Study Report provide the general scope of this vision and more specific information on the role of direct experience, including Service-Learning, within its context:

Today, in both public perception and, all too often in fact, higher education finds itself on the sidelines. Moreover, too many of its graduates remain on the sidelines when they leave the campus, failing to live in their personal lives what their alma maters have failed to embody in their institutional practice.

These conditions challenge St. Edward's to more fully and effectively incorporate several varieties of "direct experience" into the teaching-learning process and the life of the community and to provide more authentic, useful, and valid documentation of our graduates' competence. In teaching and learning, they challenge us to provide students with far more opportunity to apply, and thus extend, knowledge, skill, method, and motivation to the creative solution of problems, both the interpretive, analytic, and research problems of the disciplines and the collective problems of their society and world. The latter problems need to be addressed not only in the context of formal studies, but also actively in the context of the communities in which they exist. Current conditions thus challenge St. Edward's to give fuller life to our foundational ideal of service and greater promise to our commitment to instill such an ideal in our students. They challenge us to better prepare our students for careers and further study by ensuring that their competence for and understanding of the practical requirements for advancement are enriched in the ways best provided by experiential learning in applied settings. In assessment, they challenge us to replace the devalued currency of grades with documentation of achievement that students find more useful and external publics regard as more credible (pp. 6-8).

At St. Edward's, fulfilling the mission for our students now and in the future will require the effective, relevant, and rigorous incorporation of direct experience in many forms, including internships, practicums, and experiential class projects, to name a few. Service-Learning allows St. Edward's the opportunity to achieve these goals for direct experience in ways uniquely consistent with our mission for students. For this reason and for many of the other reasons cited throughout this chapter, St. Edward's will continue to develop our portfolio of "service learning, service-LEARNING, SERVICE-learning, and SERVICE-LEARNING" to the betterment of our community, our students, our faculty and staff, and our institution.

REFERENCES

Cappelli, Peter. "College, Students, and the Workplace." *Change* 25 (November/December 1992): 54-61.

Cappelli, Peter and Maria Iannozzi. "Rethinking the Skills Gap: Is It Craft or Character?" *EQW Issues* 9: 195. Philadelphia: National Center on the Educational Quality of the Workforce.

Crooks, Lois. "Personal Factors Related to the Career of MBAs." *Findings* 4 No. 1. Princeton, NJ: Educational Testing Service, 1977.

Dunn, William H. *St. Edward's University: A Centennial History.* Austin, Texas: Nortex Press, 1986.

Edgerton, Russell. "The Engaged Campus: Organizing to Serve Society's Needs." *AAHE Bulletin* 47 (November 1994): 3-4.

Hersh, Richard. Interview. *AAHE Bulletin* 47 November (1994): 8-10.

Livingston, J. Sterling. "The Myth of the Well-Educated Manager." *Harvard Business Review* 49 (January-February 1971): 79-89.

Marshall, Ray and Marc Tucker. *Thinking for a Living.* New York: Basic Books, 1992.

Pascarella, Ernest T. and Patrick T. Terenzini. *How College Affects Students: Findings and Insights from Twenty Years of Research.* San Francisco: Jossey-Bass, 1991.

Sigmon, Robert. *Linking Service with Learning.* Washington, D.C.: Council of Independent Colleges, 1994.

St. Edward's University 1995-1996 Strategic Self-Study Report to the Southern Association of Colleges and Schools: Redesigning the University. 1995.

CHAPTER 14

EVALUATING A NEW SERVICE-LEARNING PROGRAM

BY SISTER GRACE ANN WITTE, NANCY HEMESATH, AND
ROBERT L. SIGMON

Introduction

This locally crafted Service-Learning program evaluation design is included here as an example of what a small liberal arts college can conceive and carry out with limited resources. The College of Saint Mary (CSM) is a Catholic college for women in Omaha, Nebraska. The enrollment is 1,200 with 600 full-time students and 200 living on campus. About one-half of the students are of a non-traditional student age.

Since 1990, the spirit of service which animated the founders, the Sisters of Mercy, has been rekindled among the students through the Campus Ministry program. This led to founding the Mertz Outreach Center, a student-run office which promotes and facilitates volunteerism among CSM students.

A further enabling step toward a comprehensive Service-Learning program was made possible by a small grant from the Council of Independent Colleges in 1994. At that time the educational element of reflection was often missing from the volunteer activities. What was desired was a way of mainstreaming service into the curriculum so that more students would benefit from its educational value and more services would be rendered to the

Sister Grace Ann Witte teaches sociology at Briar Cliff College. Nancy Hemesath is Campus Minister and Coordinator of Service-Learning at the College of Saint Mary. Robert Sigmon is President of Learning Design Initiatives.

community. Some of the faculty members were willing to try Service-Learning but none felt they had the necessary expertise to make it work. The CIC grant provided for an intensive summer workshop for 14 faculty members, representing all divisions of the college, who wanted to employ Service-Learning effectively. Following the workshop, these faculty all implemented Service-Learning in one or more of their fall and spring classes.

To document the benefits and/or deficiencies of this Service-Learning project, an outside evaluator, Sister Grace Ann Witte, Ph.D., a professor of sociology at Briar Cliff College, was contracted to conduct an assessment of the faculty, students, and community agencies involved in the project. No control groups were involved. The primary purpose of the assessment was to trace changes in attitudes and identify the learning outcomes in the participating faculty and students. Dr. Witte reviewed the faculty and student applications, evaluation forms, and course syllabi; administered pre- and post-tests to participating faculty and students; conducted focus groups with students; and interviewed agency representatives. What follows are excerpts summarized by Nancy Hemesath, Project Director, and Robert Sigmon from a huge set of data from the Summary and Recommendations Section of Dr. Witte's report to the CSM faculty. The sentences in bold type represent 12 specific recommendations she made to the CSM faculty and staff for future Service-Learning programs.

SUMMARY AND RECOMMENDATIONS TO THE FACULTY: EXCERPTS

The Design

This evaluation summary is based on four faculty components, the student participants' pre- and post-test questionnaire responses and their focus group comments, and interviews with participating community agency representatives.... Since the evaluation design could not include equivalent control groups, it cannot be asserted that the re- ported outcomes for students and faculty are the direct result of the Service-Learning project and not any other factors.

This study focuses on 15 courses which were taught with a Service-Learning component, with one faculty member teaching two sections of a course and one teaching two different courses. Nine classes were taught in the fall semester and six in the spring, with a total of 301 students taking the pre-test and 274 taking the post-test in these classes. The courses were spread across the class levels, with most at the intermediate level: there were six courses at the 200 level and five at the 300 level. Three were at the 100 level and one was at the 400 level. Based on the number of students tak- ing the post-test, the size of the Service-Learning classes ranged from six students to 59 students. The average number of students was 18.27. Two classes had 39 and 59, with seven having between 10 and 17 students.

Questionnaires were administered to students by the instructor at the beginning and end of the Ser- vice-Learning course and were completed anony- mously by students.

In both semesters the composition of the pre- and post-test groups was very comparable so attri- tion is not a problem in comparing pre- and post-test responses. Self-selection is not a concern for the first semester since students generally regis- tered for their fall classes before the Service-Learn- ing courses were formally identified. It may have been a factor in the second semester if informal student awareness of the Service-Learning courses was widespread by the time students registered for the spring. This may have functioned as a "reality check" since student expectations were lower for

the second semester. However, these diminished expectations did not interfere with the accomplish- ment of the desired outcomes. The percentage of spring semester students who reported actually ex- periencing the listed outcomes is higher in every case....

The Faculty

The faculty chosen to participate were already committed to the service aspect of the Mission of CSM, personally involved in community service work, and highly motivated, as evidenced by their applications. Their workshop participation re- vealed a high level of receptivity to new ideas and very high aspirations for the Service-Learning project. The workshop met both their need for so- cial support and for information about specific tasks associated with Service-Learning. They found the collegial interaction stimulating, especially the shared reflection session and the sharing of syllabi. At the end of the workshop there was still some de- sire for further help with syllabi details and evalua- tion methods, and some hesitation about making effective community placements, but the general attitude was very positive.

Similarly, the faculty pre-test revealed that the participants' thinking was already in line with the Wingspread "Principles of Good Practice for Com- bining Service and Learning." After the Service- Learning course experience, faculty participants' responses were even more strongly aligned with the Wingspread principles, especially those related to the idea that college student community service can be significant and meaningful, that it helps the college fulfill its mission, that it should respect the goals of those being serviced, and that it should provide opportunities for students to interact with diverse people. Clearly, the idea of Service-Learn- ing was endorsed by the faculty participants at the beginning of the project, and their experience with it did not lessen this endorsement.

...If these faculty are to continue their commit- ment to Service-Learning with the same level of en- thusiasm, it would seem advisable to **provide opportunities for the same type of supportive shar- ing that characterized the preparatory workshop.**

...If the goal is expansion of Service-Learning in the curriculum, then **attention should be paid to** the under-representation of male faculty and faculty from the business and science areas.

It would be presumptuous to assume that new faculty would bring the same levels of receptivity, experience, and enthusiasm as was found in these initial applicants, so **if new faculty become involved in Service-Learning courses, orientation and preparatory sessions should take this into account.** Furthermore, syllabi sharing and the sharing of "inside" information about what worked and what did not work in community placements should provide invaluable assistance to new faculty without the expense of outside consultants.

…A definite advantage from an educational standpoint was the variability in the syllabi of the set of 15 courses in the study. They were far from uniform in their way of including Service-Learning, and thus the differences among the courses should provide a pool of varied experiences for sharing and future planning….

It is not possible to look carefully for associations between student outcomes and any of the four dimensions used in the analysis of course syllabi. An informal assessment of such relationships did not show any clear patterns between the type and level of student outcomes and the centrality, integration, structure, and accountability dimensions of Service-Learning in the syllabi. **Faculty, through on-going sharing of their syllabi and their experiences, may discover what combinations work best with particular levels of students and types of courses.**

Student Responses

In terms of student-reported outcomes, the Service-Learning project at CSM must be viewed as a successful educational innovation. It produced positive outcomes in the broad intellectual and affective domains which are targeted by the college's mission statement…. Comments in the focus group conversations confirm these outcomes. There was an emotional as well as cognitive awareness that they had learned through the service experience, and that what they had learned was important for life. The proposal that Service-Learning be incorporated into the college's general education requirements testifies to the fact that they recognized its broad and generic impact. **After some additional experience with Service-**

Learning, the college might give this proposal some consideration.

The effects of the Service-Learning courses, as measured by the post-tests, are generally across-the-board effects, and not a function of the students' age, year in college, campus residence, or GPA, nor of the courses' size, level, or curriculum division. Service-Learning, based on these findings, would be appropriate for broad-based utilization throughout the curriculum.

There was an emotional as well as cognitive awareness that they had learned through the service experience, and that what they had learned was important for life.

An obstacle which Service-Learning faces is the typical student's need for structure. More than half of the students coming into the Service-Learning courses reported that they felt most comfortable in classes with a high degree of structure; about a fourth wanted some choice of assignments and responsibilities. After the Service-Learning courses there was some small shift toward the "choice" option, the increase coming about equally from the high-structure option and the two very loosely structured options. However, the need to know what to do and how to handle situations, though lower than in the pre-test, was still reported by 40 percent of the participants in the post-test.

In the focus groups, it was clear that a major source of stress for the students was the responsibility of locating their own service placements. In addition, an underlying theme in their comments about the need for explicit integration of the service component into the course was their uncomfortableness with relatively "open" or unstructured service components. Courses with more closely integrated and highly structured service components were definitely preferred by the students. They also appreciated having their agency supervisors informed about course expectations and structures. **Those faculty planning Service-Learning courses should be especially sensitive to what may be a heightened need for structure in innovative Service-Learning components of their courses.**

In the participants' written comments, the most frequently listed "best aspect" of Service-Learning was the "real life" quality of the experience. In their oral comments, a major theme was the depth and quality of the classroom reflection and discussion sessions. **The positive response of students to class discussion of their service experience should give faculty pause before they rule it out of their Service-Learning course syllabi.**

Those students who agreed after the experience that the "idea of Service-Learning can be scary" may have been referring to the same factors that some focus group members described as "dangerous" aspects of community service; e.g., the location of their service site and nighttime service work. **This concern for dangerous aspects should be further specified and addressed in future planning.**

Concerns about finding the right type of placement and handling the extra work actually rose, being reported by over half of the participants on the post-test. Grading concerns declined, but were still reported by about 30 percent of the students. All student concerns cannot, and probably should not, be eliminated, but **concerns which seem unique to Service-Learning courses should be monitored.**

The major concern expressed in the focus groups was the issue of time....Some of it was the sense that Service-Learning requirements were added without commensurate reductions in other course requirements...**special efforts should be made to keep the course requirements as fair and comparable as possible in order to avoid the creation of any general negative student reaction to this educational innovation.**

Community Sites

Based on interviews with seven of the 30 agency representatives involved, they also viewed the Service-Learning project of the CSM as a success. Their evaluation of the students was very positive, they were grateful for the students' service, and they would like to see the program continued.

There was some ambiguity on their part about how Service-Learning differed from simple volunteering. **Placement site contact persons would benefit from some simple, straightforward description of what Service-Learning means at the CSM, its goals, and its general guidelines.**

Agencies also offered to clarify for potential student workers the service opportunities which they could provide, along with guidelines and requirements, to facilitate mutually effective and satisfying student placements. **The Mertz Outreach Center might be the logical place to locate responsibility for collecting this information from cooperating community agencies and organizations.**

Some agencies reported that they would prefer a more formalized relationship with the Service-Learning course instructor or with CSM. Since students found it more comfortable to have the instructor in contact with their placement supervisors, **faculty members should consider developing some type of relationship with the agencies and organizations where their students serve.**

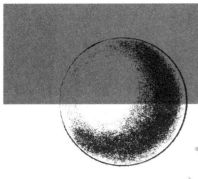

TASKS ASSOCIATED WITH INTRODUCING SERVICE-LEARNING

Data shown here are from one of the charts produced by Sister Witte which shows (1) how a consultant's set of guidelines for faculty were used as a pre- and post-test measure of faculty comfort with key tasks involved in Service-Learning; and 2) the results as reported by the faculty, showing increased comfort at all 10 levels within one year.

Listed below are the 10 tasks derived from the principles of Jeffrey Howard which formed the second part of the questionnaire. Faculty indicated their comfort level from five (high) to one (low). The responses have been "averaged" and are shown from both the pre- and post-test in rank order based on the post-test. The higher the score, the more comfortable the respondent feels about the task; the lower the score, the more uncomfortable.

		PRE-TEST	POST-TEST
1.	Adjusting other course requirements to "make room" for the community service assignment.	3.818	4.50
2.	Building Service-Learning into my grading system for the course.	3.364	4.10
3.	Adapting my regular classroom procedures to "fit" the new learner-role that community service demands of students.	3.273	4.10
4.	Preparing students for their service experience so that they know what they are expected to learn from it.	3.000	3.90
5.	Setting clear learning goals for the community service component.	3.182	3.80
6.	Selecting the right type of community service for my course.	3.455	3.80
7.	Providing the appropriate opportunities and experiences for reflection by the students on their community service.	2.727	3.80
8.	Re-thinking my own instructional role in the light of the students' new way of learning.	2.727	3.80
9.	Developing ways to make classroom learning a more communal experience so that social responsibility isn't associated only with community service.	2.909	3.50
10.	Handling the unevenness in student experiences that can arise from community service experiences that vary a great deal.	2.636	3.00

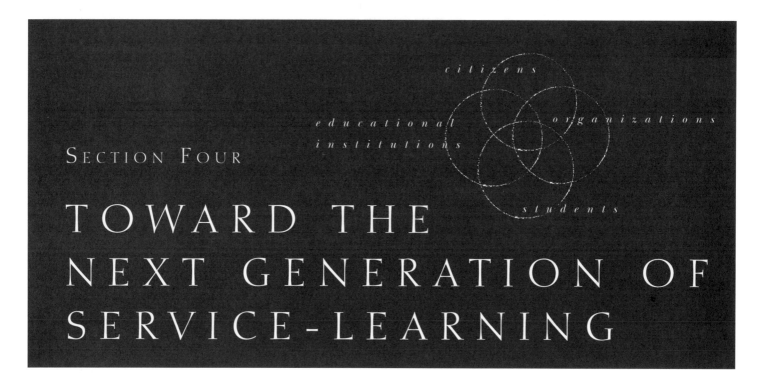

SECTION FOUR

TOWARD THE NEXT GENERATION OF SERVICE-LEARNING

INTRODUCTION:

As Allen Splete writes in his preface, this book has dual purposes: "We want to both capture ideas emerging from recent work and set a continuing agenda." This section considers the latter purpose, proposing ideas about directions for the future of Service-Learning. As Dr. Splete states, our rhetoric about the "next generation" of Service-Learning reflects ambitious goals. We also know that in many cases institutions and people have yet to fully explore the possibilities of their current work in Service-Learning, let alone think about next steps. Still, as a way to push the dialogue along, and to give practitioners further food for thought, we propose in this section several directions in which we may want to advance the practice of Service-Learning.

Journal Entry 7

"In the Hands of Developing Imaginations"

I n the hands of developing imaginations" is an appropriate headline for this final section of *Journey To Service-Learning*. While rummaging through dusty attic files this past winter, I found in my 1970-71 journal some notes from a formative conversation with a wise community organizer/educator. Excerpts from these notes introduce the entries that follow, for our purpose is to show several perspectives on Next Generation Service-Learning Programs. Earlier essays in this book, including Matthew Berndt's essay and the one by Plaut, Landis, and Trevor, eloquently describe processes that *over time* had set the stage for the next iteration of Service-Learning activity in their communities and on their campuses. This set of notes, now more than 25 years old, is another example of the over-time theme in the Journey to Service-Learning. The next generation depends on the coming together of many hearts and minds and bodies over time deciding individually and collectively how to continue contributing and learning.

In a conversation more than 25 years ago, a friend had this to say:

1. In order to make an experience-based learning program work, there have to be "adult" organizations, businesses, public agencies, levels of government, and institutions (church, hospital, mental, rehabilitation, etc.) as well as schools (junior, high, and post-high schools), willing to commit themselves and be involved.

2. This requires that we look back in history and learn from the examples of guild apprenticeships, church novitiates, ships' cabin boys, apprenticeships in the arts (e.g., Michelangelo apprenticed to a stonemason, then as a student housed in the Medici palace); and we have to evaluate present on-the-job, pre-apprenticeship, apprenticeship and journey-man, and institutional training; we have to evaluate present internship programs; and we have to listen to what students say.

3. We also have to examine the attitudes of the community to education now and education in the past. We'll have to face the fact that a community once felt responsible for the education of its young, whereas now it feels that

Journal Entry 7

educational institutions are responsible.

4. If each adult segment of society assumed that it had a role in the process, then the tie between education and the outside world would develop and strengthen. The educational process would be two-way, with adult organizations learning to change as well as young people learning through experience and beginning to put down roots in something outside what they now consider prisons.

5. Real learning comes when interest is aroused by involvement. It's a pretty well established fact that if a student who is doing poor work becomes stimulated and does well in one subject, his performance in others often improves. It's also a pretty well established fact physiologically that increasing stimuli and varying them increases the physical capability to handle and respond to even more stimuli (although there is, of course, a point of "information overload"). The reverse is also true. Rats deprived of visual stimuli, or raised in an absolutely bare, white, box-like cage, during the first few weeks of their lives can never learn later to adapt to a patterned life. Their behavior is always warped by the initial deprivation. In the same way that inadequate protein in the very young child permanently prevents full maturing of the brain, the lack of varying and adequate stimuli for the student's imagination stunts his mental and creative and social growth. Schools are better if they only stunt; more often, like prisons, they teach skills like the ability to avoid, to get by, to scheme, to hate, to scorn, to lie, and to cheat. The main positive social skill they teach is a cohesive friendship among differing kids in opposition to the faculty, rules, and often even to learning.

After our conversation, my friend sent me this note: "The concept of education for all, tried only by the United States on such a broad scale, is crumbling not because all people can't be educated, but because the public school system often attempts to give the same education to all, and the same world view. Education is, by definition, the development of potential; the encouragement of variety, of growth, of change; new visions of old knowledge, and the examination of old visions by new knowers. Money for helping to save and change our educational system will go as far as the bounds of the imaginations of those who control it. Is the leadership, business and governmental, willing to let some of that control rest in the hands of developing imaginations?"

Upon revisiting this conversation and correspondence, I noted in my current journal that the phrase "in the hands of developing imaginations" has been a mantra of mine for 25 years now. How deeply I have longed to see "developing imaginations" have a chance to create conditions for teaching, learning and serving consistent with the Service-Learning practices I have seen work so well.

CHAPTER 15
SUGGESTIONS FROM PRACTITIONERS

*I*n addition to focusing on current practices in Service-Learning, CIC has throughout its project been
interested in the future of the practice—the "next
generation" of Service-Learning. Accordingly, during the
spring of 1995, we asked college-based colleagues involved
in the CIC National Institute on Learning and Service
for their thoughts about the future of Service-Learning.
Excerpts from their responses follow.

Letter 1. We are hearing more often from the
community, "what have you done for us lately?

Among many of my faculty colleagues, there is
an intuitive sense that we have a responsibility to
the "community." As a result, I hear now more support for promoting successful collaborative partnerships that promote faculty teaching and
research interests while meeting community needs.
I hear less and less of the current hot button of integrating a little touch of community service into a
bunch of academic courses.

Some of us are meeting regularly around the
question: "How can Service-Learning introduce
the campus to larger community/global initiatives
outside the traditional boundaries of higher education." The conversation is rich.

Letter 2. Meaningful integration of Service-Learning into the academic program throughout the
campus will be necessary for Service-Learning to
survive in a next-generation form. If it remains a
sidecar or novelty, it will not survive the next novelty or sidecar "hot" idea to come along.

Why is such integration a good idea? It can serve

as a launching pad for a campus's greater, more
structured and formal involvement with its community; an involvement which involves faculty,
staff, administration, students—the WHOLE campus involved with (not directing) the community.

I do not believe we can force-feed an ethic of service on a campus or in a community. There can be
"too much of a good thing." People will choose to
incorporate service into their personal/profes-
sional lives in different ways and to different ex-
tents. We must respect the difference. Still, an
environment must be present within which each
student and faculty member and community citizen can explore and identify the role service will
play in their lives. Above all things, I feel this crite-
rion is essential in next-generation Service-Learning programs.

Letter 3. Before we can fully imagine the next
generation of Service-Learning, we need to examine the nature of service in this generation within a
broader cultural context. I think this generation of
service is seen largely from the Eurocentric world
view which dichotomizes, separates, and makes hierarchies out of differences. The Eurocentric
world view, its language, its basic values and beliefs,
and thus the thoughts of its people emphasize
selves versus others. In this view it is not easy to
think about choices that connect, that mutually enrich. Past generations of service, seen as charity,
with their noblesse oblige foundation, were and
are a peculiar combination of self-righteous service, mostly to others. When service is conceptualized within the Eurocentric world view, self and
others become alienated from one another.

TO/FOR OTHERS	FOR ME	WITH OTHERS
duty to others	duty to myself	building connections
responsibility for others	feel better about myself	mutual understanding
I give so others can receive	makes me a better person	joint benefits
to meet the needs of others	meeting my own needs	shared/linked destiny
haves helping the have-nots	personal enrichment	common goals
helping those in need	personal inspiration	mutual growth
understanding others	personal blessing	exchange of views

I think we can avoid this dilemma of alienation and separation as we move toward the next generation of Service-Learning if we conceptualize service somewhat differently. I suggest that we begin conceptualizing service in ways that borrow from other world views that emphasize the reciprocal relations between selves and others, rather than the selves and the others. To this end, what is included in the chart above are several sets of phrases that might be used to assess why people engage in Service-Learning. The first two columns express the dichotomies in the Eurocentric approach, and the right-hand column states motivations in more non-Eurocentric terms, the next generation of Service-Learning perhaps?

Non-Eurocentric world views emphasize the relationships between selves and others. The whole is enriched by balancing (with emphasis on an on-going process) the differences, the perspectives, the strengths, the substances.

Letter 4. Get with it, man! The next generation of Service-Learning? Have we really had a first generation yet? The future of Service-Learning depends on who is willing to pay for it. At our college, most of us teach at least four courses, some five. We have too many advisees, serve on too many committees, have spouse and children at home, like to see our neighbors sometimes and are writing the book of all books. To work with students out there in service-based experiential learning requires time for planning and relationship building that I do not have, skills I do not possess, and asks me to change my way of teaching. Yes, I know the feds and states are giving up on the safety net. Let the churches pick up the slack. There is a major flaw here. The churches are not run anymore with squads of women who make this their unpaid "Lord's work," because they are out working for money somewhere. And besides, there are children at home and no adequate daycare, especially beyond the few prescribed hours. So, wow, let's turn to the college gang to fill the gap. Do you think, for a minute, a bunch of 19- to 21-year olds and the 20-30 crowd coming back to college can serve a few hours a week and meet the needs being unattended? Who is going to provide the dollars for the faculty release time, the coordination support, the rigorous planning required for this next generation of Service-Learning programs? I am ready when the money is there. Let me know.

Letter 5. I look for two things in the next generation of Service-Learning programs. One is a set of common goals that all of us should be striving for. The other is the need for a team of experienced Service-Learning and community-connected practitioners to be available for visits to campuses to evaluate existing programs and structures, and offer suggestions on next-generation directions.

Journal Entry 8

Stopping Out to Serve
*Service-Learning for Students Who Need Time Out
from Academic Pacing*

In November 1995, a friend called for help. She was trying to assist the first-year liberal arts students coming to her Learning Lab with so-called "learning disabilities." Focus groups with these students had revealed that many were not ready for a lock-step academic discipline routine, were burned out from overactivity in high school endeavors, felt the burden of high tuition fees, and did not see any reasonable alternative. Many were very bright and questioned the way the college structured and controlled their lives. Several years earlier, I had spent a day on this campus interviewing students about their interest in a service and adventure year. My friend wanted to talk about a proposal for funds to try out a service and adventure year. What follows is the quick note I sent by fax that afternoon.

Dear Sue:

...We were thinking about an idea for one year that would offer 50 first-year students an option to plunging immediately into a liberal arts curriculum. Each student would be offered deferred admission for the following year. A special program would create a structured and self-directing set of experiences (work, service, travel, and learning) for these students. Guidance from competent staff would be available. On-campus housing would be an option. The structure would include the following:

August	One-week planning and organizing period with students in residence.
September–December	Students involved with paying jobs or volunteer activities in either public or private settings. Special training for their adult mentors.

- One or two evenings a week—group reflection seminars

- Other self-organizing activities by the group itself

- Throughout the four-month period, students offered planning tools for thinking about what they

Journal Entry 8

would like to pursue when enrolled in college—and beyond

- Students could audit one class, with no academic credits

- Students would plan their January-August next year's agenda.

January-May Teams of students would take on a "service" related project of their own choosing, but "invitational" from a community. Students could have part-time jobs for pay as well. (If the college would guarantee a steady, dependable flow of students on the terms a community organization would want them, then a long term relationship can be developed.)

Pairs and trios would be encouraged to travel in the United States and abroad—travel in ways that fit with the planning they did in the fall. On return, they formally share with their colleagues their learning.

More class audits or selective browsing would be in order. Encourage participation in extracurricular intellectual events.

More time for one-on-one planning for the next year available.

In May, a five-day debriefing and celebration would be organized for the students, those they had worked with, and staff involved. Part of this debriefing would be a revising of the program for future groups.

Students would be expected to pay a fee for the services rendered by the college staff (or contract staff) and any costs associated with room and board. If students did some of the work for pay they can cover the costs, save some money for future tuition bills, and gain some sense of self-respect and autonomy. The initial financial objective would be for the college to break even on this arrangement.

The college obligation would be to offer a framework for the experience (e.g., the one-week planning session, the reflection events, the one-on-one planning time, minimal help with job opportunities, assistance with finding the creative "service" projects, some counseling about auditing courses, and the final debriefing and celebration). Someone would want to do a solid data gathering/research effort on the experiment.

I suggest you take this or some other outline of the possibilities and check it out with your students. Run it by the college attorney to see what the legal issues might be. Run some numbers of costs and see what they suggest.

Journal Entry 8

The bottom line, in my view, is that if you made this structure available and granted deferred admissions, you would have a huge leg up on a lot of colleges for recruiting bright students. And the college would learn a lot about learning that is self-initiating and not controlled exclusively by curricular demands.

An additional note. When I talked with juniors and seniors there several years ago, the surprising response was that the seniors were the ones ready for a program like this. They said that they were drained from the academic grind and wanted a break before they hit full-time jobs or graduate school. So a companion program for graduates might also be something to explore.

CHAPTER 16

COLLEGE/WORKPLACE SERVICE-LEARNING CONNECTIONS

BY ROBERT L. SIGMON

In his fine work *Teacher as Servant,* Robert Greenleaf offers several suggestions for building relationships between business leaders and the growth and development of students in service-based learning arrangements.[1] Over the years I have been talking with business leaders about this connection. The following are notes I've made about these conversations. Included is an outline I have been suggesting to business, governmental and non-profit leaders.

1. School to work transitions are a major concern to employers. On the one hand employers sense that many students come out of liberal arts colleges with limited awareness or capacity to be productive. As a result, training and start-up curves are expensive, but necessary for businesses as they take on young liberal arts graduates.

On the other hand, with the nature of work changing so rapidly, the limited number of high quality (i.e., high paying) jobs is creating a pool of underutilized employees. Another concern of employers is that the relatively unskilled jobs that exist are low paying jobs, particularly many in the "service" sector of the economy. In any of these situations, employers tell me that it is rare to find self-starters, self-directing learners and doers.

2. Employers are aware that many of the larger corporations are "buying" into the research universities, creating partnerships for the purposes of primary research as well as product development. They are concerned about how the line is being drawn between serving the public good and serving private gain. For the smaller companies and entrepreneurs, there is a sense among them that they would like to link up with faculty with specialties in their areas to explore common research interests. They wonder why the small liberal arts colleges are not coming out to talk with them about this. When I ask these business folk what they might have to teach the young and the faculty, they often light up and talk about what they wish they had been able to do when they were in school (e.g., have experiences in business that were real while being a part of school) and then talk about specifics of what they could teach college students. The most vocal and passionate business folk who talk this way are fathers and mothers with high school and college age children. When I talk with college faculty and administrators now, I promote how business interests can be partners in the education of students as well as partners in the research and service efforts of interest to each.

3. Two moral concerns crop up in almost every conversation with business people which have some relationship to the practice of Service-Learning.

a) Many employers have experimented with teams or quality circles or other practices which create more autonomy and responsibility at the level of the actual work being done. This is done primarily to increase yields and profits, but I increasingly hear employers talking about their long-term hopes that "team" processes in the workplace will carry over into families, neighborhoods, and other associations that workers engage in beyond work lives. That is, they express a hope that more participation, more involvement in public decisions will emerge. Sounds very close to the "citizenship" voices speaking in much of the Service-Learning circles these days.

A few suggest that "social capital" creation will eventually become as important as "economic capital." By this they are suggesting that if their workers are coming to work from dislocated, conflictual, non-community orientations in family, neighborhood, church, club, and community then their work productivity will be limited somewhat and worker satisfaction indexes will be low. So they see a self-interest in being attentive to playing a role in citizenship development, in supporting neighborhoods, in assisting their employees to gain competence and confidence in their abilities to be creative forces in their own families and neighborhoods.

b) My conversations sometimes touched on a concern of some business folk that a general consumer mentality will lead us too far toward the production of luxury and unnecessary goods and services in place of a primary focus on necessary goods and services. They are concerned about the societal implications of the growing gap between the well off and those not well off. They worry about using up the earth's limited resources. They sense that the connections among us all are important. Several have asked me whether I believe the younger generation will be able to help us reach a point where we create goods and services that make it possible for all citizens of the globe to be free, healthy, able to work and learn, and capable of caring for themselves and others. They nod affirmatively when I come back with a response that says, "would you like to have a chance to talk with college professors and administrators about this?"

4. Business leaders are increasingly aware of their educational role with the customers they serve, their employees, and their suppliers. These three major parties in their business relationships receive priority attention. When I suggest that they could include the young, from middle school to graduate school, to their list of priorities, they are wary to a degree. But many do hire summer replacements for vacationing employees. Many do hire young people for part-time, periodic work. Many do have exposure tours and career day expositions. Others have longstanding cooperative education and internship agreements in certain area. Some have days when employees are encouraged to bring their children to work to see what Mom and Dad do all day long. Many have extensive on-the-job training programs, staff development and training offices and a wide range of offerings, fitness programs, tuition assistance programs for employees to take academic courses at colleges, and other "learning organization" type programs. Yet, they have trouble identifying themselves as "learning" places. This lack of openness to seeing themselves as "learning organizations" always surprises me since so much learning is going on in their workplace everyday. And much of it is experiential learning in a service setting.

Business workplaces throughout the country are worthy of private liberal arts college engagement in conversations about mutual interests. It seems to me that the first level for this conversation is among the trustees of private liberal arts colleges, which are often comprised of business leaders. As trustees, administrators, and faculty struggle to create the conditions which will make it possible for all to contribute and learn in the next century, it is my strong sense that the business community will be a primary player in reshaping the educational enterprises we so much need to be alive and thriving in the future. In my experience, the building blocks for a creative partnership already exist for liberal arts institutions to explore.

The scenario which follows is a one-page picture for a community of liberal arts educators and business leaders to examine and work toward in their journey to Service-Learning.

REFERENCES

1. Greenleaf, Robert. *Teacher as Servant.* New York: Paulist Press, 1979.

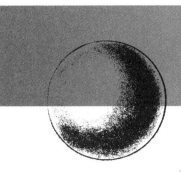

A POSSIBLE FUTURE RELATIONSHIP BETWEEN INDEPENDENT COLLEGES AND THE WORKPLACE

Every business, public agency, non-profit group, and community-based organization creates one full-time equivalent position for young people (middle school through college level) for every 50 full-time employees, or 100 members if a membership organization.

Each workplace establishes a Work/Service/Learning (WSL) Office staffed by a dually employed practitioner, with salary and supervision provided equally by the employer and the educational institutions.

Five-year basic agreements are negotiated, spelling out the goals and conditions for working together. One-year operating agreements (including budgets) are worked out within this framework for stating workplace roles and the number of students and faculty who will be involved in the workplace, what they will do and when they will do it.

Results from these partnerships include:

1. Workers and students become contributors and contributed to, teachers and learners.

2. The educational faces of workplaces become more prominent.

3. Both workplaces and educational institutions become more self-conscious moral agents in society as a result of the partnerships.

4. Leadership ceases to be of the heroic, Lone-Ranger type when all citizens develop capacities to serve and lead, be served and follow. And leaders emerge with broad interests and capacities to see the whole.

5. The culture moves slowly from being "out of community" to being "in community."

6. Experts are seen more as partners.

7. Experiential learning pedagogies grow in sophistication and practice, both in the workplace and in educational institutions.

8. An ethic of just relationships grows to a dominant position in workplaces and educational settings.

Journal Entry 9

An Earth Restoration Corps

A friend's monthly newsletter which came today proposed a national corps of workers to restore and expand ecologically damaged natural environments.

My friend argues that "the human species is a subsystem of Earth's life system, dependent on the health of the larger system." He reasons that the ability to work is our only ultimate resource, and that we grossly misapply work through our degradation of the Earth's surface, air, and once-abundant wildlife. By drawing on the successful outcomes of the National Recovery Act of the 1930s, he wants to see the formation of partnerships that would work toward cleaning up hazardous waste sites, creating cleaner air and water, restoring wetlands, revitalizing animal habitats, restoring wilderness, and other such projects. By engaging young, middle-aged, and elderly people in this Earth Restoration Corps, he believes that we will come to our senses and stop producing the junk we don't need and turn to producing necessities for health and well-being. "We, the people, must take charge of the application of human labor so that it is matched to authentic need....Matching work to real need involves finding where work is needed, and putting it there is a priority that makes the best sense for the continuing functioning of the Earth system and for us."

With major national government and foundation incentives, local areas through the leadership of local private colleges have an immense opportunity at this level for linking service and learning. Can you imagine a more interesting way for college students to work with others at the turn of the century than to work toward creating conditions for their own children and grandchildren to inherit an Earth restored partially to its beauty and natural wonder? As Thomas Berry keeps saying to us: "The human community and the Earth community form the single sacred community. We go together into the future as the single sacred community or we both perish on the way."

The journey to Service-Learning clearly has a challenge to help with the restoration of the Earth and create work that is well applied and refusing to produce junk and its remains. The potential for learning about science, natural systems, and community are enormous in this idea. Who will take the lead? Which private college is positioned and ready? How can we all encourage that college to get on with it and show us a way?

Thanks to James F. Berry, author of Circular #172, *Establishing an Earth Restoration Corps*, Published by James F. Berry, Director of The Center for Reflection on the Second Law, Raleigh, N.C.

CHAPTER 17

CONTINUING THE JOURNEY TO SERVICE-LEARNING: A FABLE

BY ROBERT L. SIGMON

As a concluding chapter for this Journey to Service-Learning, I thought it would be fun and interesting to look forward a few years. Accordingly, I wrote the following piece as a newspaper article I hope to see 10 years from now. Written, as I imagined it, by a team of reporters from The New York Times, the story tells about a 10-year sustained effort, begun in 1996-97, in which five independent liberal arts colleges work with businesses, public agencies, non-profits, and community-based organizations to develop the capacity to engage all young people (elementary school through undergraduate education), young workers in the work force, experienced workers in the work force, and all other citizens in linking service and learning. What follows are excerpts from one of the five front-page stories reporting and reflecting on the processes and outcomes of the 10-year effort. This was my way of brainstorming about a next generation of Service-Learning. I encourage you to do the same. Let your imagination flow. The journey to Service-Learning is before you.

EARTH, 2007—The effort began with individuals in a dozen small-town and rural regions of the country who came to realize that "none of us is smarter than all of us." In several areas, groups representing the interests of citizens looked around for leadership, personal and institutional, to create a forum for open communication about how to deal with keeping a region alive and well. These regions wanted to deal openly with the problematic situations (e.g., poverty, violence, uneven economic opportunities) that persisted year in and year out; with creating opportunities to serve and learn for all citizens; for evolving systems that work well for all citizens; and for creating conditions that honestly seek to listen and respond to all the voices of a community.

Each of the communities independently discovered that faculty and administrators from its local private liberal arts college were the most likely initial leadership group. This determination was based on the observations that faculty and students through existing and expanding Service-Learning experiences were engaged already with most of the organizations and issues that were active in the region. Field studies, internships, cooperative education, practice teaching, health profession practicums, voluntary action efforts, and particularly the service-based learning activities connected to academic disciplines and community requests for assistance were operating to some degree in each area.

The Council of Independent Colleges, in listening to what independent liberal arts campuses were being asked to do in their community, discovered that a dozen locales around the country were asking a local independent college to take the leadership initiative in creating a major collaborative effort in a region to look systematically at current realities and future possibilities. CIC began talking with major funding sources. An invitation from three sources came back to put forth proposals to respond to the community calls for assistance in concert with the colleges.

A design team representing voices from these communities along with Service-Learning consultants and CIC staff crafted a plan that had the following features:

1. The design set as primary criteria the existence of two parallel movements for involvement in the proposed 10-year process: a) business, public agency, non-profit, and community-based organizations had to be actively seeking to form a partnership capacity in creating work, service and learning opportunities for young people enrolled in schools, for citizens who had deferred continuing their formal education, for experienced employees, and all others and; b) these same entities, along with the educational leadership (public and private K-12 and higher education), were actively engaged in creating the conditions for more collaborative partnerships among all the institutional elements of a region for promoting the public good.

2. Requests for Proposals were circulated throughout the country based on the locations of independent liberal arts colleges. Twenty planning grants were available for communities to link their collaboration planning with the liberal arts colleges' commitment to more active service and learning engagements within the total community. Technical Assistance via a team of seasoned collaboration facilitators was available to each of the 20 grantees. Each community receiving the planning funds had 18 months to design a eight-year process with clearly articulated outcomes/benchmarks for specific individuals, organizations, institutions and systems of relationships in the area. The principles of reciprocity and movement toward just relationships in the activities of linking serving with learning for all participants to be involved in the process were given as major underlying guidelines for the planning.

From the 20 planning teams interested in pursuing a public-good-oriented collaboration rooted in Service-Learning, five areas were granted financial support for the next eight years, with expectations that another six months would be given over to systematic review of the overall experience for sharing with wider populations. Throughout the eight-year experience, a network of resource team members, including an assessment team, were available to the five areas. However, the expectation was that the five long-term-supported communities and the 15 that planned (but were not granted long-term

funding through this particular grant), would be the primary technical advisors to one another. Three-day gatherings of teams from the 20 sites were held each year to reflect upon what was going on in both the funded and unfunded areas.

Following this introduction, the newspaper story highlighted the plan and outcomes from one of the areas. The area and college chose to focus on three priorities, each for two years at a time, leaving open the priority for the fourth two-year period to emerge from the experiences gained in the first six years.

For the first two years, with few exceptions, all the participating organizations and institutions in the region agreed that the initial building block of the process was to be designed to support the proposition that each person in the region has the right to knowledge, skills, and culture. Each person should be able to write, compute, analyze his/her own situation, critique that situation and act on it so as to be able to have high self-respect, competence, and a sense of belonging to a community of caring persons.

The outcome goal stated the following:

"Ninety percent of the citizens in this region will be able to read and understand printed materials; will be able to express opinions openly about public issues in public spaces created for this purpose; will demonstrate ways of contributing to the common good as well as learning about self and others in the process of becoming literally literate; and 10 new business operations will be created based on opportunities and learnings gleaned from the carrying out of this goal."

To work toward this goal, college students provided 10 percent of their time to designing and implementing programs consistent with this goal in neighborhoods. Employers granted up to 25 percent of their work force two hours per week to assist in invitational literacy and civic education programs in their own workplaces and in the community. Elderly citizens challenged themselves and became involved. The local liberal arts college provided a range of literacy methods training, connected about one-half of all their academic courses to the effort in creative ways, and designed and implemented a thorough yet unobtrusive evaluation process of the two-year effort. By focusing on literacy in two realms—actually learning to read printed material and becoming literate as a person within a public situation—the learning-to-read folk became teachers to their tutors at the same time the tutors were their teachers. Many of the tutors had limited, if any, knowledge and awareness of the conditions in which the literacy learners lived. By the 18th month of the first two- year period, clear evidence was presented that the goals had been achieved. But remarkably, many other learnings and public-spirited activities and relationships had emerged beyond the original goal.

As interest evolved in these first 18 months, careful planning for the second two-year focus was taking place. New voices were added to the planning team from the capable persons identified in the first stage. Stage two plans were centered in the realization that a literate population which does not eat nutritious foods and have quality physical exercise is not going to be healthy and able to take advantage of their capacities as learners and contributors.

Accordingly, goal two was stated as follows:

"Ninety percent of the citizens will have access to information about nutritious foods; 75 percent will be within 10 percent of their optimum weight; 60 percent will have designed and stayed with a regular exercise routine appropriate for their situation; and 50 new entrepreneurial businesses will have begun based on learnings from this process."

With the adult-led organizations, particularly sustainable agricultural interests, taking the lead, young people invented, designed ,and established with local communities ways of growing, selling, buying, and preparing nutritious foods. Likewise, hundreds of exercise classes in informal settings were designed and operated, mostly by young people. Sustainable agricultural practices were introduced and by the end of the second year of this plan, food imports into the region had been reduced by 25 percent and exports of food staples increased by 20 percent. Projections by the area chamber of commerce groups showed annual increases in these figures of 10-15 percent for the

next 10 years. By the end of the two-year designated period, 60 new entrepreneurial businesses were operating successfully; nutrition awareness was noted as being very high in 75 percent of the population; 64 percent of a random sample were within 10 percent of the desired body weight; and 70 percent reported at least 45 minutes of exercise three times a week. The evaluation report noted the extraordinary involvement of the local college in creating the conditions for this goal to be reached. At one point, all students and faculty were noted to have been involved either as participants in growing food, teaching about diet or exercise, or creating a new business enterprise related to this healthy-living goal.

During this second stage, the wisdom of the original planning group was noted. The assumption the original planners stated, which was born out in the first four years of the process, was that a literate, well-nourished population would begin demanding living spaces that were affordable, energy efficient, and offered an appropriate mix of privacy and community contact.

Therefore, goal three for the fifth and sixth years was established:

"Ninety percent of the citizens will be housed in safe and adequate housing; 35 new businesses would be created in the building of appropriate housing; and the crime rate would be reduced by one-half."

Literacy, nutrition, and exercise activities were continued and very much in evidence in the planning for housing. As the need for childcare expanded, childcare centers were established in workplaces, adjacent to retirement communities, on the college campus, but more often in planned co-housing and other innovative housing enclaves consistent with the desires of the citizens and the goal. Passive solar housing designs emerged with a wide range of building materials created and manufactured from area resources. Electric power generation from streams, lakes, and windmills met 30 percent of the area's local electricity demand. Food production through community gardens flourished. Landscapes in the new and remodeled housing all contained active gardens. Students from the college were active in all levels of planning, designing, innovating, and construction—as were faculty. The linking of community engagement activities with formal learning began to take on a more polished and deeply rooted pedagogical stance. Faculty were being recognized around the country for creative teaching and learning designs as they worked hard to connect their own academic strengths to the desires and hopes of the communities around them and to the high expectations of the students who were enrolling in the college. In fact, the college decided, with the community and students, that students should live in the community with area residents since about one-half of the formal learning curriculum was taking place in the community now. Older buildings once used for dormitories were converted into studios in anticipation of the stage IV plan. Seventy new business operations were initiated by the end of the two years. The crime rate by the end of year six was so low that the jails were filled with contract inmates from other parts of the country, the police-force engaged in many proactive community building enterprises rather than exclusively working on traffic control and criminal investigations.

Recognizing that progress had been made toward several goals—literacy, better nourishment, physical fitness, improved housing—along with other material enhancements in the communities around the college, the Partnership Council (now overseeing the process) concluded that an intangible element they referred to as the "human spirit" was the next challenge to face. The original planning design had left open the final two years, guessing that the process would produce the focus for the seventh and eighth years. Artists in the community had been actively involved in the first three phases, but at this point in the process, it was clear to most that if each citizen had access to expressing himself/herself through an artistic medium, the spirit of the human community in the area would be further enhanced.

Therefore, goal four reflected this desire:

"In two years 75 percent of all the citizens will have developed at least one active means of artistic expression; the economic growth in art supplies sales would triple; artists' sales would triple; and the creative process from learning to express oneself would be measurable in workplaces and community life."

The old dorms of the college were transformed into studios, theaters, rehearsal rooms, and galleries. Workplaces created space for workers to learn under the tutelage of artists. Drama and music productions increased. Natural spaces were designed and landscaped to provide areas for food production as well as aesthetic charm. Via the arts, the original goal of civic literacy and personal self-expression reached a new plateau, as citizens found another voice to express their hopes, fears, and thanks. The production of art supplies and artists' creations more than tripled in the two years. Worker satisfaction indexes were the highest they had ever been. Workplace aesthetics were noticeably improved, with work performance records routinely improved over previous studies. In the study of art, the college faculty were overwhelmed with requests to teach the history of art, to help citizens understand the cultural and historical conditions of various periods of artistic development, to study Shakespeare, to help citizens connect their own life with the intellectual and emotional understanding of the development of human consciousness over time, and many other science and humanities topics the faculty were most able and willing to share.

At the end of the eight years of this community focus on individual and public capacity building, the final six months of the original 10-year process has focused on "so what?"

As reporters who have been in and out of these areas since the process began, we can summarize our own point of view by indicating that we have observed data in the research reports that clearly show that the collaboration process with an intentional focus for each two-year period has transformed an entire region into a sustainable economic order with minimal extractive and polluting by-products; has shown what a 'learning community' can mean as a strategy for creating value for citizens as they come to know themselves, care for others, develop capacities to contribute and learn, and discover creative ways to be in community without fierce competition and daily attention to difference and fear; and has fostered a sensitivity to others which does not evangelize, but accepts invitations from others when asked for assistance.

A former college president who was a supportive enabler of the early part of the process, most often behind the scenes, sees the picture this way:

"When we first began to realize that we did not live in isolation and detachment from the community as a result of our students engaging in well-planned Service-Learning activities, we knew we were on a journey that would lead us to a future that none of us could see at the time. But we knew we had to make the journey with our colleagues in the business, public agency, non-profit, and community-based-organization world. The central principles of reciprocity, of mutual service and learning, and of movement toward just relationships have been the bedrock of the developments here. It has been exciting for me, an old, hard rock professor in the sciences, to be a part of and observer of the transformation of this college I love so much into an integral part of this fabric of communities here. Over half of our professors now spend more time teaching and researching in community settings than they do at the college. In fact, the whole area has become an engaged learning environment in which multiple teachers and mentors work at many levels with children, young people, working adults, and senior citizens. It all started with the formulation of Service-Learning that early on transformed our voluntary action, internships, career development, and leadership development programs into more self-conscious interfaces with the world around us and into new (actually old) styles of learning and doing."

The final 10-year project report concluded with this paragraph:

"Through the hands of developing imaginations working in partnership with one another, these communities have created a framework for individual excellence to flourish, for public affairs excellence to thrive, and for a variety of serving and learning opportunities for all citizens to grow. A literate, healthy, well-housed, and expressive population with well-honed service and learning capacities will continue to focus regularly on the questions of 'what is worth doing?' and 'what do we need to learn in order to do it well?'"

The Partnership Council continues to operate. With the advances in communication technology, 70 percent of the population has access to the Internet and Web connections at home, and the other 30 percent has access through public libraries, schools, workplaces, and businesses. Programs are operating in the region for a regular check-in about matching interests and problems with resources. Public spaces for airing interpretations of experience are readily available to all.

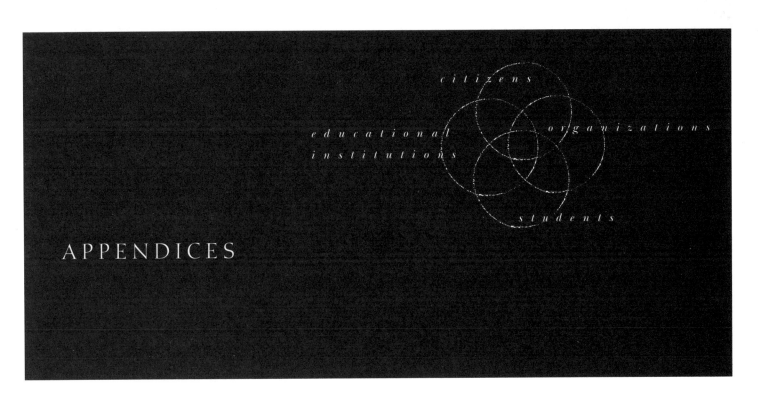

APPENDICES

INTRODUCTION:

We wanted to share with our readers three additional pieces that did not quite fit with the rest of the book. The first entry here is Robert Sigmon's distinctive Service-Learning Timeline, which highlights milestones in the organizational development of Service-Learning. Second, Russell Garth summarizes experiences and lessons learned from CIC's project *Serving to Learn, Learning to Serve*. The third appendix offers a brief compendium of resources in Service-Learning.

APPENDIX A

A SERVICE-LEARNING TIMELINE

BY ROBERT L. SIGMON
APRIL, 1996

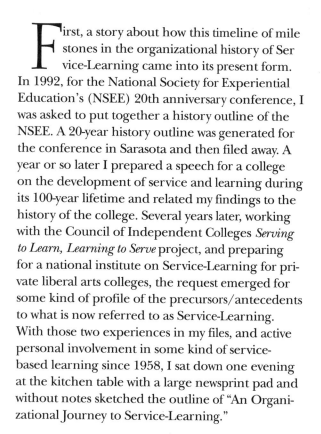

First, a story about how this timeline of mile stones in the organizational history of Service-Learning came into its present form. In 1992, for the National Society for Experiential Education's (NSEE) 20th anniversary conference, I was asked to put together a history outline of the NSEE. A 20-year history outline was generated for the conference in Sarasota and then filed away. A year or so later I prepared a speech for a college on the development of service and learning during its 100-year lifetime and related my findings to the history of the college. Several years later, working with the Council of Independent Colleges *Serving to Learn, Learning to Serve* project, and preparing for a national institute on Service-Learning for private liberal arts colleges, the request emerged for some kind of profile of the precursors/antecedents to what is now referred to as Service-Learning. With those two experiences in my files, and active personal involvement in some kind of service-based learning since 1958, I sat down one evening at the kitchen table with a large newsprint pad and without notes sketched the outline of "An Organizational Journey to Service-Learning."

This outline was typed and sent to a dozen colleagues around the country asking them to add, delete, edit. These reviewers compiled and also suggested I talk with others, so phone calls were in order and more material was located with specific dates and names. A final typed version was produced in May 1995 and the creative folks at CIC formatted the timeline in its current form. Each participant at the CIC's 1995 Institute on Service-

Learning received the timeline in a rolled up scroll and was invited to write their own history with Service-Learning in the blank spaces and to suggest additions for future use. Readers of this book are encouraged to write a personal history and add to this work in progress.

Now the timeline appears in this publication. We have decided to leave it in its original cast (with editorial corrections and a slightly different layout to fit the format of the book.) This original version echoes a conceptual phenomenon that has haunted many of us who have stayed with the evolution of service-based learning over the past four decades. That echo in the timeline is the glaring omission of multiple references to community-based and grassroots organizing groups that have actively been engaged with educational institutions in creating service and learning programs. Too often, in my observation and experience with service-based learning activities rooted in educational settings, the agenda of the educational institution has been dominant and the agendas of the people and groups hosting students and faculty undervalued. I was conscious of the omission when the timeline was completed, making a judgment that it was difficult to identify the national bodies involved, since most of the community and grassroots activities were local and discrete in character. So, I ask readers to forgive us for this omission and ask you to add that line from your own experience to your own journey profile in your local situation. At some point, I hope that someone will be able to generate a thorough history of the community-based and grassroots movements that have been inspirations to and collaborators with educational groups in promoting and sustaining service-based learning.

For me, and I hope for you, the message in what is here is that the practice of linking service with learning is not new. The timeline can be extended back in history many centuries, and I look forward to others writing more about this. At this current moment, a strong "Outreach" movement is taking place in public and private higher education circles with partnerships with communities a primary strategy. So linking service with learning is taking on a fresh coloration here at the end of the 20th century.

Two recent publications add much more depth to the timeline. Seth Pollack at Stanford prepared a major paper for a December 1995 Wingspread conference, entitled "Higher Education's Contested Service Role: A Framework for Analysis and Historical Survey." Using four case histories—the Land Grant College movement, the Settlement House Movement, the CCC Work Camps, and the Citizenship Education Schools of the Civil Rights Movement—Seth offers a refreshing perspective on higher education's response to social problems. He suggests that efforts "to link service and learning must negotiate the interplay between three contested terms: democracy, education, and service. As each of these terms have different meanings to different people in different sectors of society, Service-Learning programs, like other attempts to link learning and society, must somehow negotiate this highly contested terrain."

Goodwin Liu, now at Yale Law School and former federal policy maker promoting campus-based community service, has written a paper on "Origins, Evolution, and Progress: Reflections on the Community Service Movement in American Higher Education, 1985-1995" under the auspices of the Providence College Feinstein Institute for Public Service. His focus is on the 1985-95, 10-year period of rapid growth in this field of linking service with learning. Three overlapping stages—student leadership, institutional support, and Service-Learning—are lifted up to "be a conceptual history of our approaches to and understand-

ings of campus-based community service, a history that critically examines the forces that have and have not shaped the movement's evolution." Both papers are available in "To Strengthen Service-Learning Policy and Practice: Stories From The Field" (interim report from a Service-Learning history project, 1996, Haas Center for Public Service, Stanford University).

The timeline, "An Organizational Journey to Service-Learning," is still a work-in-progress and our hope is that readers will generate their own histories and critiques of their journeys to Service-Learning.

The timeline follows...

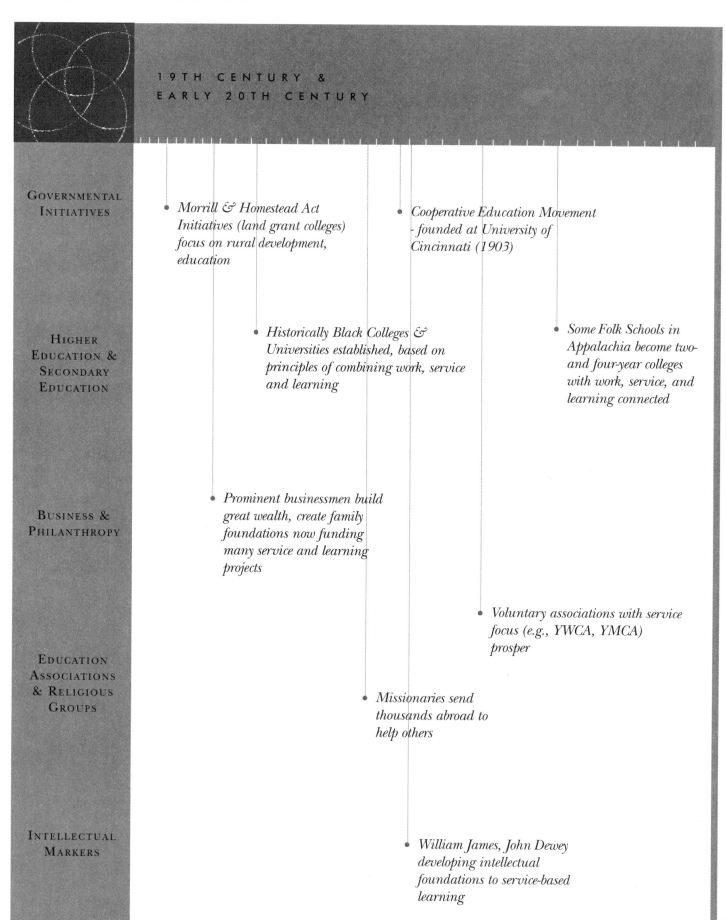

19TH CENTURY & EARLY 20TH CENTURY

GOVERNMENTAL INITIATIVES

- *Morrill & Homestead Act Initiatives (land grant colleges) focus on rural development, education*

- *Cooperative Education Movement - founded at University of Cincinnati (1903)*

HIGHER EDUCATION & SECONDARY EDUCATION

- *Historically Black Colleges & Universities established, based on principles of combining work, service and learning*

- *Some Folk Schools in Appalachia become two- and four-year colleges with work, service, and learning connected*

BUSINESS & PHILANTHROPY

- *Prominent businessmen build great wealth, create family foundations now funding many service and learning projects*

EDUCATION ASSOCIATIONS & RELIGIOUS GROUPS

- *Voluntary associations with service focus (e.g., YWCA, YMCA) prosper*

- *Missionaries send thousands abroad to help others*

INTELLECTUAL MARKERS

- *William James, John Dewey developing intellectual foundations to service-based learning*

1930S, 1940S, 1950S

- *Civilian Conservation Corps —required 10 hours learning per week*

- *Work Projects Administration (needed public work for people who needed jobs)*

- *National Youth Administration*

- *GI Bill*

GOVERNMENTAL INITIATIVES

HIGHER EDUCATION & SECONDARY EDUCATION

- *Lisle Fellowships (early 1930s)*

- *Experiment in International Living (1932)*

BUSINESS & PHILANTHROPY

- *American Friends service committee (work camps in U.S. & other countries)*

- *Religious denominations begin youth service programs in United States and abroad (post WWII)*

EDUCATION ASSOCIATIONS & RELIGIOUS GROUPS

- *Dewey continues writing about linking experience and education*

INTELLECTUAL MARKERS

1960S

GOVERNMENTAL
INITIATIVES

- Peace Corps
  - VISTA

- College Work-Study
  (1965)
  - White House Fellows
    initiated

HIGHER
EDUCATION &
SECONDARY
EDUCATION

- Experimental colleges
  emerge

  - Political Science
    Departments
    sponsor legislative
    and public service
    programs

- Community Colleges on the scene
  with experimental learning &
  connections to practice settings

BUSINESS &
PHILANTHROPY

- Ford Foundation
  support for National
  Urban Fellows and
  Urban Corps

EDUCATION
ASSOCIATIONS
& RELIGIOUS
GROUPS

- School for International
  Training (1964)—
  founded by Experiment
  in International Living

- National Service
  Secretariat Conference on
  National Service (1968)
  in Washington, D.C.

INTELLECTUAL
MARKERS

- James Coleman—exponent of
  alternating experience with
  schooling; Harrison and Hopkins
  article (1967); Phillips Roupp, The
  Educational Use of the World, Peace
  Corps Pub.

1960S

• *Urban Corps emerged, funded with federal work-study dollars (1966)*

• *State government internship programs in New Jersey, North Carolina, Georgia and Massachusetts*

GOVERNMENTAL INITIATIVES

• *1966-67—"Service-Learning" phrase used to describe a TVA-funded project in East Tennessee with Oak Ridge Associated Universities—linking students and faculty with tributary area development organizations*

• *January terms popular, with many experiments linking learning and service*

• *Professional clinical training involved in linking learning with service*

HIGHER EDUCATION & SECONDARY EDUCATION

BUSINESS & PHILANTHROPY

• *Atlanta Service Learning Conference (1969)—sponsors included Southern Regional Education Board, U.S. Dept. HEW, City of Atlanta, Atlanta Urban Corps, Peace Corps and VISTA*

EDUCATION ASSOCIATIONS & RELIGIOUS GROUPS

• *Civil Rights Movement strong; Vietnam War & protests*

INTELLECTUAL MARKERS

1970S

GOVERNMENTAL INITIATIVES

• *Action Agency formed (1971)*

• *1971 White House Conference on Youth report full of calls for linking service and learning*

• *Funding for Area Health Ed Centers extends health manpower training into rural/community settings so students could serve and learn (started 1972)*

• *National Student Volunteer Program (became National Center for Service-Learning in 1979) Published Synergist, a journal promoting linking service and learning*

HIGHER EDUCATION & SECONDARY EDUCATION

• *Urban Semester Programs emerge*

• *University Year of Action (year-long service tied to academic performance)*

• *Private colleges create specialized service-learning programs*

BUSINESS & PHILANTHROPY

• *Kettering Foundation published 3 vol. Service for Development Study by Irene Pinkau, comprehensive review of study-service outside the U.S. (1979)*

EDUCATION ASSOCIATIONS & RELIGIOUS GROUPS

• *Associations begin:*

National Center for Public Service Internships *(1971)*

Society for Field Experience Education *(1971) (these two merged in 1978 as National Society for Internships and Experiential Education)*

Association for Experiential Education *(1972) (initial conference in North Carolina in 1968, incorporated in 1972)*

• *AEE publishes Experiential Education journal; Jossey-Bass series published on New Directions in Experiential Education; NSIEE newsletter grows and carries more articles*

• *"Three Principles of Service-Learning" published in Synergist in 1979*

INTELLECTUAL MARKERS

Cooperative Assessment of Experiential Learning *(CAEL) founded in 1974. Name changes in 1977 to Council for the Advancement of Experiential Learning and in 1984 to Council for Adult and Experiential Learning*

• *David Kolb work on Experiential Learning Theory evolving*

• *Conrad and Hedin research on value added to learning when service involved*

1980S

▶

• *NCSL phased out (very little governmental attention at federal and state levels)*

• *Campus Compact formed by college presidents (1985)*

• *Points of Light Foundation honors service providers*

• *Spring and fall breaks create many service opportunities, some with learning*

• *National Youth Leadership Council (1982) — preparing future leaders*

• *Colleges and high schools continue programs & affiliations initiated earlier. Primary meeting places are NSIEE, AEE, CAEL and COOP ED conferences*

• *Carnegie Unit on Service created (1987)*

• *SCALE — student initiated literacy program (nationwide) in 1989*

• *Secondary School Service and Learning programs gain in numbers*

• *National Center for Service-Learning for Early Adolescents (1982)*

• *American Youth Foundation begins linking programs which connect service and learning in 1988*

• *Wingspread Principles of Good Practice in Service-Learning (1989) — 70+ organizations collaborate to produce ten principles*

• *Partnership for Service-Learning (1982) — International opportunities*

• *Campus Outreach Opportunity League (1984) — student-led service advocacy*

• *Youth Service America (1986) — promotes service for youth*

• *John McKnight writing on dangers in service work. Donald Schon on reflective practitioners, how professionals are trained and then work*

GOVERNMENTAL INITIATIVES

HIGHER EDUCATION & SECONDARY EDUCATION

BUSINESS & PHILANTHROPY

EDUCATION ASSOCIATIONS & RELIGIOUS GROUPS

INTELLECTUAL MARKERS

1990S

GOVERNMENTAL
INITIATIVES

● *National and Community Service Act of 1990 passed*

● *National Service Bill passed in 1993 — AmeriCorps and other programs linking service with learning*

HIGHER
EDUCATION &
SECONDARY
EDUCATION

● *Campus Compact expands: (state organizations, 3 national institutes, publications, more Presidents join)*

● *NSEE develops five-year High School Service Learning Initiative (1991)*

● *Stanford Service-Learning Institute (1994)*

BUSINESS &
PHILANTHROPY

● *20 Bonner Scholars Programs (19 private, 1 public) initiated, honoring high school students who have served (or are expected to serve) four years of service and learning experience as condition of scholarship funds*

● *Dozens of state, regional, and national conferences/workshops on linking service and learning organized by many organizations and institutions*

EDUCATION
ASSOCIATIONS
& RELIGIOUS
GROUPS

● *Association of Supervision and Curriculum Development endorse importance of linking service with learning (1993)*

● *Publications: 3 vol. Combining Service and Learning published by NSEE, 1990; R. Coles, The Call of Service; Praxis I and II; Campus Compact publications; COOL publications; Michigan Journal for Community Service Learning, Vol. 1, 1994); and many more*

INTELLECTUAL
MARKERS

● *Strong emergence of civic arts, citizenship education focus in higher education (Barber, Battastoni, Lappé, et al.)*

1990S

167

GOVERNMENTAL
INITIATIVES

- *Service-Learning network on Internet, via University of Colorado Peace Studies Center*

HIGHER
EDUCATION &
SECONDARY
EDUCATION

- *CIC Serving to Learn, Learning to Serve project includes National Institute on Learning and Service in Chicago, 1995*

- *Ford Foundation/United Negro College Fund Community Service Partnership Project—10-college program linking direct service and learning begun (1994)*

BUSINESS &
PHILANTHROPY

- *AAHE Annual Conference March 1995, on linking of service with learning*

EDUCATION
ASSOCIATIONS
& RELIGIOUS
GROUPS

INTELLECTUAL
MARKERS

APPENDIX B

CIC'S JOURNEY TO SERVICE-LEARNING

A Summary of the Council of Independent Colleges' Project
Serving to Learn, Learning to Serve

BY RUSSELL GARTH

Colleges have long been infused with a purposeful mix of service in the context of learning. As part of an overall orientation toward values-rich education, CIC institutions have been extraordinarily active in engaging students, as well as other members of the campus, in community service and outreach. It follows quite naturally, then, that CIC as an organization would decide to pursue a project agenda designed to explore the connections between service and learning.

Our thinking on this subject evolved over a period of several years. The issues of community service and learning were first highlighted as possible follow-up activities to CIC's National Institute on Values and Education in 1991.

Our early research coalesced in a major project, titled *Serving to Learn, Learning to Serve*, begun in September 1993. The project sought to improve the capacities of independent colleges and universities to connect service activities with educational programs. This agenda has encompassed using service experiences to enhance learning—serving to learn—as well as helping students recognize, nurture, and refine an ethic of service—learning to serve.

The funded project was announced as a part of CIC's fifth annual Conversation between College

Russell Garth is Executive Vice President of the Council of Independent Colleges, where he helps direct the organization's Service-Learning activities.

Presidents and Corporate/Foundation Officials, held in Washington, DC, on September 24, 1993, which focused that year on the theme of Service-Learning. The Conversation was attended by some 70 college and university presidents and corporate or foundation representatives.

One central goal of the project was to foster significant progress on the Service-Learning agenda at selected institutions, and to learn about both substance and process of those improvements so that they might be shared more broadly. A second goal was to involve a considerably larger number of institutions than those selected institutions in making Service-Learning a higher priority on their campus. Accordingly, several different types of activities were undertaken to communicate these issues to a wider audience.

PROJECT ACTIVITIES

The project consisted of several related components:

Learning and Service Alliance. Thirty colleges and universities were selected, from 155 applicants, to receive either $50,000 grants (5 institutions) or $22,000 grants (25 institutions) that enabled them to improve service-based learning activities at their institution and to work cooperatively, in three project meetings, to develop and share ideas with other private colleges and universities. In pursuing this overall agenda, participating colleges and universities have employed three types of strategies—building a campus infrastructure for Service-Learning, engaging faculty more fully in these activities, and learning to conduct campus and community conversations that develop deeper understandings of Service-Learning.

National Institute on Learning and Service. This national conference for campus teams attracted 745 individuals from 171 institutions, making this CIC's largest meeting ever. Grant dollars were used both for general meeting expenses and to provide travel scholarships to teams from 118 institutions.

Inventory. As part of its research, CIC designed and administered a survey instrument that sought information on current Service-Learning practices.

Publications and products

- "Linking Service with Learning," an essay by Robert Sigmon, was mailed to member colleges in fall 1994.

- Four different articles were prepared for CIC's newsletter, "The Independent," from October 1994 to October 1995.

- A Resource Notebook, comprised of both newly written as well as reprinted materials, was distributed at the National Institute.

- A "Organizational Journey to Service-Learning" Timeline, sketching the history of community service activities within higher education, was distributed at the National Institute.

- This book, *Journey to Service-Learning.*

Greater detail about these activities follows below.

Learning and Service Alliance

A group of 30 colleges and universities, selected competitively, constituted the Learning and Service Alliance. Through the review process to select the 30 colleges and by working with these institutions in the Alliance, CIC was able to develop a much richer understanding of the needs, interests, capacities, and potential of private colleges as they connect service and learning. The content of the National Institute and the publications was shaped by this knowledge (though we had also moved ahead on both of those fronts before the Alliance institutions had completed the individual projects on which they had been working). Moreover, the

Alliance institutions made presentations at the National Institute and contributed materials for this book, *Journey to Service Learning.*

Selection. Following the 1993 Conversation between College Presidents and Corporate/Foundation Officials, CIC staff sought advice from a variety of individuals and organizations active in this area.

These conversations helped us to understand further the considerable work—on CIC campuses and elsewhere—already underway in combining service and learning, and confirmed our earlier strategic preference to seek preponderant, though not exclusive, initial participation from colleges and universities that had already had at least some experience in Service-Learning. The fact of an already-established experience base, coupled with indications of considerable interest in this topic, encouraged us to work towards what we labeled a "next generation" of Service-Learning.

Institutional activities. One central project insight is that, under a fairly wide-open applications process, independent colleges would overwhelmingly choose to work on two types of problems, both addressing issues of capacity and infrastructure:

- Engaging faculty and integrating service with the curriculum—conducting faculty workshops, providing course development mini-grants, preparing handbooks.

- Enhanced coordination and visibility—hiring staff coordinators, starting campus-wide offices, developing newsletters, building databases of service opportunities.

Alliance Meetings. In addition to improving their individual capacities for Service-Learning, the 30 institutions were also expected to send two representatives to each of three meetings of Alliance institutions. The purpose of these meetings was, first, to offer technical assistance to the participating institutions as they pursued their individual objectives and, second, to find ways to coalesce and share what they were learning with others through publications and the National Institute.

Inventory

A key goal of the overall project has been to understand, both broadly and in depth, the state of Service-Learning on independent college campuses. Therefore, to augment what we have been learning via the 154 Alliance applications and by working with the 30-college Alliance, CIC also surveyed all member institutions as well as other similar private institutions.

CIC received completed questionnaires from over 400 faculty and staff at more than 100 institutions (the analysis was based on the 372 faculty and staff at 99 institutions). Robert Serow, professor of education at North Carolina State University, assisted Robert Sigmon in analyzing and reporting on the data.

In general, the conclusions from this inventory are consistent with what we have been discovering in other aspects of the project—that a growing number of faculty members are interested in integrating service activities into educational programs, that those faculty need support from colleges in doing this, that Service-Learning coordinators are a key form of such support, and that considerable dialogue on these issues is still required.

National Institute on Learning and Service

CIC holds national institutes for campus teams once every four or five years, on a topic of broad interest to administrators and faculty. Indeed, as we noted earlier, the kernel of the idea leading to the Serving to Learn project came out of the previous national institute.

The National Institute on Learning and Service, held on May 31 - June 3, 1995, at the Arthur Andersen Professional Development Center in St. Charles, Illinois, attracted 745 individuals from 171 colleges and universities, typically in three- to five-person teams. Cosponsors of the Institute included the Bonner Scholars Program, Campus Compact, COOL, Ford/UNCF Community Service Partnership Project, National Society for Experiential Education, and The Partnership for Service-Learning.

Teams. Designed for campus teams, national institutes depart from the more typical pattern of annual CIC institutes or workshops, where presidents, deans, and faculty each meet separately. In general, we expect that teams increase the chances that plans developed at the Institute will actually be implemented, and the Institute design allowed op-

portunities for teams to work on their own issues as well as meet with other teams. Thus the Institute was very much a working meeting.

Planning guide. To encourage institutional teams to begin their collaborative work before arriving at the Institute, CIC mailed a "Pre-Institute Guide for Campus Teams" that suggested what kinds of information teams should gather and what conversations they should have prior to the Institute. In addition, each team had been asked to bring 20 copies of their preliminary planning worksheet (two pages maximum) to share with other teams with whom they would be meeting.

Community or student participants and travel scholarships. To ensure that the Institute reflected the broad partnerships necessary for success in this area, CIC offered travel scholarships to encourage institutions to include students and representatives of community organizations as members of their teams. CIC received applications for travel grants from 143 colleges, and awarded $1,500 grants to 33 institutions and $1,000 to another 77. In addition, CIC received $35,000 from the Arthur Vining Davis Foundations to provide travel scholarships to 18 private, historically black colleges.

Program. The program was a blend of several elements—presentations by national experts, sharing by campuses (including most Alliance institutions) of model programs, break-out meetings by campus or community role, opportunities for campus teams to work on their own agendas, and consultations between campus teams.

Major speakers included: Frances Moore Lappé and Paul Martin DuBois, authors of *The Quickening of America: Rebuilding Our Nation, Remaking Our Lives* and heads of the Center for Living Democracy; consumer advocate Ralph Nader; Tim Stanton and Nadinne Cruz from the Haas Center for Public Service at Stanford University; Janet Eyler, Associate Professor of human biology at Peabody College of Vanderbilt University; Gary Hesser, Professor of Sociology and Director of Experiential Learning at Augsburg College; Robert Sigmon, CIC Senior Associate; Jane Vella, author of *Learning to Listen, Learning to Teach*; Victor Stoltzfus, then president of Goshen College; and many other experienced Service-Learning practitioners from academe, community groups, and elsewhere.

The Institute drew enthusiastically positive ratings from participants. More to the point, the experience of teams at the program sparked exciting plans for campus work.

Publications

Publications and the National Institute were the two key means of involving a broader range of CIC institutions in the project. The literature on Service-Learning has become quite extensive (with more on the way). Accordingly, we were selective about printed materials and other products, seeking to develop a few high-quality items that could push the project along and perhaps simultaneously advance the larger movement (see discussion below under "Ideas" in the "Results and Impact" section).

The first publication, "Linking Service with Learning" by Robert Sigmon, was mailed to CIC member institution presidents, chief academic officers, chief student affairs officers, and Service-Learning contacts, along with the initial announcement of the National Institute in October 1994. This brief report was well received. Some long-time thinkers and writers in the field of Service-Learning consider the "Service-Learning" typology a significant contribution. Several institutions, large universities as well as a number of CIC colleges, requested multiple copies.

Two items were prepared specifically for the National Institute—the timeline and a resource notebook.

The "Organizational Journey to Service-Learning" Timeline, arrayed in a 5.5" x 37" format, sketches the development of Service-Learning over the last century in several contexts: governmental initiatives, higher and secondary education, business and philanthropy, education associations and religious groups, and intellectual markers (the timeline is reprinted in this book).

The loose-leaf Resource Notebook consists of already published writings that we pulled together—as well as a few pieces that we developed—that provide background and can assist colleges in understanding the issues and framing the conversations that must occur as they move forward in this area. The Notebook also provided several bibliographies of key materials, tailored for individuals in differ-

ent stages of development. It also contained names and addresses of all Institute participants and information about the other co-sponsoring organizations working on Service-Learning.

The project's final publication is this book, *Journey to Service-Learning*, by Robert Sigmon and colleagues.

RESULTS AND IMPACTS

Institutional improvement

Each of the 30 Alliance institutions conducted local activities to improve the connections between service and learning. Taken together, the 30 Alliance institutions employed three broad strategies to increase their capacity to offer Service-Learning—creating conversations, building infrastructure, and engaging faculty. In general, the individual campus projects showed significant progress in those directions. The promise of institution-wide effect seems to be playing out in practice.

Conversations. An important lesson of this project was the importance of conversations about various aspects of Service-Learning—the nature of service in today's world, what and who constitute community, the substance of a Service-Learning pedagogy, and definitions of Service-Learning. The importance of this topic was not apparent from simply reading the initial Alliance proposals. Discussions at Alliance meetings, as well as the written reports from the colleges, however, indicated the importance of this strategy. Ultimately, the art of conversation among faculty, between faculty and students, between college and community, and among colleges themselves about these issues of Service-Learning has been a singular—though difficult to capture—highlight of this project. Indeed, in those instances where academic and community interests achieve a desirable reciprocity, conversation is often a key pathway toward that balance.

> *"We assembled a group of 20 faculty and academic support staff as a task force to examine Service-Learning on campus...with a series of questions: what is service? what is community? what do we mean by giving service?...." (Alverno College)*

> *"To be able to serve the community for the long haul, sustainable community partnerships will be*

designed. More dialogue with local government planners will be sought...discussions are being held...." (Seton Hill College)

"Our students spend night and day talking with people, playing games, sharing perspectives, working with people and finally caring for the people they stay with and missing them very much when they leave. The intensity goes both ways.... The service which can be justified, I think, is our presence....(Warren Wilson College)

"We sponsored our first Community Service Partnership Project Community Forum attended by 52 persons....to allow community input and to focus on themes identified by the Advisory Council.....housing and home ownership; economic development; and employment...." (Stillman College)

Building infrastructure. In order to move from conversation to plan to action to assessment in finding ways to link service with learning for the several purposes noted in the original RFP, participating institutions gave primary attention to structural and staffing considerations. The approaches listed below (each mentioned by several institutions) illustrate this infrastructure development:

"The Service-Learning Committee, now a standing faculty committee..."

"The faculty voted to make the Service-Learning Committee a standing committee."

"A Service-Learning Advisory Committee is providing leadership...."

"The part-time Service-Learning coordinator's position is now full-time."

"Service-Learning, by its nature, is a collaborative exercise....In this spirit, Wartburg College became a founding member of the Network for Iowa Service-Learning...."

designing and publishing manuals and handbooks for all the parties involved

curriculum redesign, from one course to a discipline to whole core including Service-Learning in strategic planning for the college

creation of innovative, experimental projects for "learning by doing"

sophisticated data gathering to understand better the nature of the activities

A search for sustainability and comprehensiveness in linking service with learning, particularly with the community, also undergirded many of these infrastructure developments:

"Currently the college is focusing its efforts in the one-to two-mile radius of the college, exploring ways to sustain our commitments to the wider community in ways that are mutually beneficial to the college, our students and the community." (Augsburg College)

"LeMoyne-Owen College seeks to combine two primary objectives, the concentrated effort to enhance the life of residents of the LeMoyne Gardens Public Housing Development...and the implementation of an academically strong Service-Learning curriculum for all students." (LeMoyne-Owen College)

"Over 35 agencies have received student assistance...." (Spalding University)

"Partly because of the input from the community, most courses in the second semester were designed collaboratively between the professors, the community agencies, and the Service-Learning coordinator...." (Sacred Heart University)

Engaging faculty. Since the inception of the Serving to Learn project, CIC has specifically stressed the importance of greater faculty involvement in promoting Service-Learning activities; and indeed, working with faculty has been the dominant program initiative noted in the reports from the colleges in the Alliance.

For example, almost all institutions conducted at least one major workshop for faculty, enabling faculty to learn from each other and to develop greater appreciation and understanding of the philosophy and practice of Service-Learning. Many campuses used CIC funds to create mini-grants to faculty for the purpose of redesigning an existing course to include a Service-Learning component or create a new course with Service-Learning at its base. In addition, a number of campuses created dialogue groups among like-minded faculty for ongoing conversation about Service-Learning and their own concrete experiences with it. Finally, about half the schools used consultants to add perspective, offer technical assistance, and challenge and inspire deeper exploration into the philosophy and practice of Service-Learning.

"It is heartening that the number of faculty members interested in Service-Learning has increased over the last year from a core of five...to 19." (Central College)

"Twenty-five faculty have been active in reviewing progress to date and continuing their learning in linking service with learning at Elon." (Elon College)

"The grant funded a day-long workshop for faculty interested in learning how to incorporate Service-Learning into their courses. Twenty places were budgeted and 21 faculty attended." (Nazareth College of Rochester)

"The primary focus of our program is on faculty....In May 1995, Dr. Sharon Rubin led a faculty workshop...the workshop concluded with a tour of Service-Learning sites, which led to the question, 'where to go from here?' That question led to a draft of an interdisciplinary course proposal, 'Values Education Through Community Service'" (Presbyterian College)

"Based on an earlier model of 'working' visits to El Salvador, 13 faculty and administration members spent a September 1995 weekend in nearby Bridgeport to work and learn firsthand about the problems of the urban neighborhoods and the possibilities for increased Service-Learning for the university in the city." (Sacred Heart University)

Working together. An initial premise of the Alliance was that institutional improvement would be furthered not only by grant dollars but by the ideas, energy, and support provided by similar institutions tackling similar problems. The 30 Alliance institutions offered to one another encouragement, technical assistance, new ideas, critiques and good times. While doing so, they also contributed from their experience to the design and implementation of the successful National Institute. Moreover, at least five of the colleges have been explicitly involved in leadership and networking with other colleges at state, regional, and national levels, and new papers are coming out of these colleges for the larger Service-Learning community.

"The Alliance meetings provided time for conversations with faculty from West Virginia

Wesleyan which have led to nine students from there coming to Pittsburgh during the January 1996 interim to participate in a variety of urban service experiences. The students will be housed at Chatham College....An upcoming program is planned for Chatham College students to visit the Wesleyan community for an alternative break program...." (Chatham College)

"In response to Alliance meetings, a serving and learning 'partnership' has been formed with the school district...." (Seton Hill College)

"As a result of grant funding and the Alliance influence, the philosophy and processes of Service-Learning are becoming well developed at Central. Continued funding will be required. Continued opportunities for conferencing, networking, and support will also be helpful...." (Central College)

Assessment. Assessing outcomes of Service-Learning activities is still in early stages, mentioned in approximately 20 percent of the college reports. These colleges have shared their designs and are beginning to share their outcomes with others. As institutions begin to examine these issues more fully, a general pattern of evolution has emerged:

"West Virginia Wesleyan has moved from volunteer programs to Service-Learning contracts, and now to courses with Service-Learning components. The next stage might be finding and funding new initiatives that draw on Service-Learning courses from several disciplines to address a set of related social problems. Such a course of action would give greater focus to the college's curriculum and create an expanded partnership with the community." (West Virginia Wesleyan College)

Lessons learned. Particularly from reading the reports from the Alliance institutions, but also supported by discussions at the National Institute, five cautionary themes have surfaced—time pressures, student preparation, past college/community relationships, lack of mutuality, and the limitations of existing assumptions.

First, time pressure on faculty, community mentors, and students was reported as a major dilemma. The overly busy, overly programmed nature of much of campus and community life tends to restrict imagination and energy to engage in a process of linking service with learning that demands extensive relationship building and maintenance, challenges old ways of doing things, and has a limited track record in the academic and community primary currencies.

"The greatest obstacle faced by students and faculty is that of time constraints." (Saint Mary College)

Second, some institutions discovered that students were unprepared for the level of responsibility for their own learning and performing real tasks with real people required in much community service, and thus had to redesign their programs to do more preparation and provide more structure. Other schools were amazed at what their students could do when granted appropriate amounts of freedom to learn and serve in situations beyond the classroom. The predicament is finding appropriate ways to live within the tensions inherently rooted in Service-Learning programs.

"In general, schools and agencies were pleased, except for the one-day projects....The long-term projects are almost all extremely successful...."
(Sacred Heart University)

"The goals changed as we became aware of what our students needed in terms of preparation for the project. Initially, students were required to do community research, identify a need, and complete a hypothetical action plan. We found many students unprepared for this level of sophistication. The goals changed to focus on the relationship of self to society...." (Tusculum College)

Third, the past legacies of community-school 'unrelationships' have haunted some of the colleges as they began to reach beyond the campus. Either the decades of indifference from the college or a perceived one-way approach has left many community leaders and residents very cautious when the college comes seeking to help or is asking for help in educating its students.

So the task of creating and sustaining partnerships of mutuality and trust are made more difficult as a result of these past histories.

"In Madison County, N.C., suspicion of outsiders is both strong and in many cases, well founded...."
(Mars Hill College)

Fourth, students believing that service means "what I have been blessed with needs to be shared with those who have not been as blessed" have difficulty seeing the ways that they are also served by the exchange. Even more difficult is understanding that mutuality and searching for reciprocal, just relationships is a way of relating and learning. For some colleges, this is a tougher issue than for others.

"It takes a great deal of reflection to move from an orientation of 'service to the less fortunate' to one of 'service-learning' in which there is more mutuality. Encouraging that transformation is difficult, but it is perhaps uniquely a function the college can provide...." (Mars Hill College)

Finally, since service and learning activities deeply challenge many traditional ways both of offering service in communities and of teaching in classrooms, Service-Learning advocates face barriers in these traditions and approaches. Acknowledging that all the parties to a Service-Learning arrangement can be teachers and learners as well as served and servers is a challenge which calls for change in habits and ways of being and doing, teaching and learning, serving and being served.

Wider influence

A number of project activities were explicitly designed to promote Service-Learning beyond the 30 Alliance members—the inventory, National Institute, and publications. Among independent colleges and universities not in the Alliance, 240 participated in the project in some way, either by applying for the Alliance grants, completing the inventory, or attending the National Institute. Indeed, 19 institutions did all three and 54 did two. Several colleges have asked for consultant help and for permission to reprint Robert Sigmon's "Linking..." essay or a newsletter piece. Moreover, we have some intriguing anecdotal reports of publications finding audiences beyond CIC institutions.

These capacity-building efforts also point toward this project's particular potential for contribution to the larger Service-Learning movement with higher education—institution-wide as opposed to purely course or departmental initiatives.

Through the *Serving to Learn, Learning to Serve* project, CIC has found important connections with ongoing CIC programs, as well as opportunities to connect with other meetings and organizations.

These connections have twin functions of disseminating information about CIC's project and gaining greater knowledge of related initiatives.

CIC conferences. In addition to the two regular CIC meetings that have been completely devoted to Service-Learning—1993 Conversation between College Presidents and Foundation Officials and 1995 National Institute—CIC's two principal annual meetings, for presidents and deans, offered sessions on this topic.

Other organizations and meetings. Because of CIC's work in this area, CIC staff have been asked to participate in a number of other activities addressing issues in learning and service.

Ideas for the Service-Learning movement

In reviewing the set of activities comprising this project, we have been encouraged by several ways in which our efforts have appeared to contribute to the larger national movement toward the integration of service and learning.

Institution as a whole. Perhaps the most important contribution that CIC's project has made is in showing the ways in which entire institutions, in contrast to specific individual faculty members, departments, or schools, can construct a capacity to promote Service-Learning. In addition, as we extend our work in this area into a greater focus on the community, we may be able to demonstrate some institutional approaches to establishing reciprocal community relationships.

Service-Learning conceptual typology. Several individuals have told us that the four-part typology presented in "Linking Service with Learning" by Robert Sigmon and also used in the Inventory (service-LEARNING, SERVICE-learning, service learning, and SERVICE-LEARNING) has conceptual utility for both longtime promoters of Service-Learning and those newer to the field.

Timeline. CIC's entire project has been predicated on the observation that a great deal of service-based activity—and writing about it—was already underway, and thus our efforts could intentionally both build on that work and seek to envision new horizons. The "Organizational Journey to Service-Learning" Timeline was an explicit way to

recognize this considerable body of work. Recently, this timeline was used—graphically enlarged from its small scroll-like size to take up an entire wall—at a Wingspread conference on the history of Service-Learning.

Next steps and the "Next Generation" of Service-Learning

The Serving to Learn, Learning to Serve project—via the Alliance, publications, and Institute—created a significant foundation for the larger group of independent colleges. From the beginning of this project, we raised the explicit possibility of moving to a "next generation" of linking service and learning. Most colleges are not yet there, but through our work with the Alliance institutions, as representatives of this larger universe of institutions, we can see that their journeys enable them to envision a next generation. For the foreseeable future, CIC is committed to helping colleges refine and expand their Service-Learning activities.

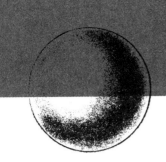

SELECT RESOURCES FOR SERVICE-LEARNING

Practitioners in Service-Learning have an abundance of resources on which to draw for inspiration and information. This appendix includes some of those resources, including sections on books, organizations, and relevant sites on the World Wide Web. Our list is by no means exhaustive, and there are many valuable references available that are not included here. Our appendix is intended as a guide for those who wish to compile their own list of references.

PART 1—BOOKS

Just a few of the many valuable books on Service-Learning are listed here. We have tried to identify texts that we have found to be seminal.

Section 1: **For the desk or bookshelf of a faculty member or administrator getting started in connecting service with learning on a liberal arts campus.**

Kendall, Jane C. *Combining Service and Learning: A Resource Book for Community and Public Service.* Three volumes. Raleigh, N.C.: National Society for Experiential Education, 1990. [NSEE: 3509 Haworth Dr., Raleigh, N.C. 27609.]

Three volumes of the best of the literature about combining service and learning until 1990. Introductory chapter provides a succinct recent history and rationale for combining service and learning in secondary and higher education. Resources for this work came from 91 collaborating organizations. Vol. I focuses on rationales, policies and major issues. Vol. II provides examples of how policies look in practice. Vol. III is a bibliog-

raphy, now somewhat dated, but still is an excellent pre-1990s summary.

National Society for Experiential Education. *Strengthening Experiential Education Within Your Institution.* Raleigh, N.C.: NSEE, 1986.

Advice and models that have worked to integrate experiential education into institutional missions, campus values, curricula, faculty roles, financial and administrative structures, and evaluation systems. Very practical.

Kupiec, Tamar Y. Editor. *Rethinking Tradition: Integrating Service With Academic Study on College Campuses.* Providence, R. I. : Campus Compact, 1993.

Lessons from experience of campus teams after participating in workshops designed to develop campus action plans for integrating service with academic study. Useful essays on service-based learning pedagogy and on institutional development strategies. Appendix outlines 13 exemplary syllabi highly applicable to private liberal arts colleges.

Kolb, David A. *Experiential Learning.* Englewood Cliffs, N.J.: Prentice-Hall, 1984.

Outlines basic experiential learning theory model. Many other articles and interpretations of this model in print. Look them up. Also, the Learning Style Inventory, developed out of this theory, is available through McBer and Co. Training Resources Group, 116 Huntington Ave., Boston, Massachusetts 02116.

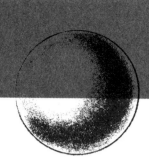

Vella, Jane. *Learning to Listen, Learning to Teach. The Power of Dialogue in Educating Adults.* San Francisco: Jossey-Bass, 1994.

Twelve illuminating stories that begin with the concrete daily life situations of people in community and show us 12 principles growing out the stories for learning and teaching. Written for adult learner practitioners, but faculty and students in private liberal arts colleges will find this easy-to-read and insightful book a very valuable asset in developing and sustaining service-based learning programs with communities.

Delve, Cecilia J.; Mintz, Suzanné; & Stewart, Greig. *Community Service as Values Education.* New Directions for Student Services, #50, Summer 1990. San Francisco: Jossey-Bass, 1990.

Makes compelling case for increased involvement by student-affairs practitioners in public and community service and learning initiatives. The author's introductory chapter suggests a thoughtful five-phase Service-Learning model which sets the stage for the remainder of the book. Excellent resource for looking at the developmental strategies for student learning outcomes.

McKnight, John. *The Careless Society: Community and its Counterfeits.* New York: Basic Books, 1995. See also, McKnight, John and John P. Kretzman. *Building Communities from the Inside Out: A Path Toward Finding and Mobilizing a Community's Assets.* Chicago: ACTA Publications, 1993.

In various writings, John McKnight challenges us to consider the disabling aspects of service and the enabling aspects of capacity-building when we serve and learn in commu-

nity service. Look also for articles by McKnight.

Wingspread Special Report. *Principles of Good Practice for Combining Service and Learning.* Racine, Wisc.: The Johnson Foundation, 1989.

Ten principles outlined, with examples that illustrate the principles. Widely-used resource in service-based learning field.

Section 2: **For the desk or bookshelf of faculty and administrators who are well into conceptualizing service-based learning programs:**

Albert, Gail, and staff of the Center for Service-Learning, University of Vermont. *Service-Learning Reader; Reflections and Perspectives on Service.*

Offers a collection of articles used in a Field Studies Program evolved over past 25 years at the University of Vermont. Program wants to "insure that students would do more than simply go to work each day, do their job, learn some new skills and return home." Readings offer a structure for reflection on experience, particularly on the meaning of service and the institutional impacts on a person's view of service. Intended not as the definitive word, but as a catalyst for further action. *Available now through NSEE, 3509 Haworth Dr., Raleigh, N.C. 27609-7229.*

Coles, Robert. *The Call of Service: A Witness to Idealism.* Boston: Houghton Mifflin Co., 1993.

A highly personal account of what inspires and sustains service, how it is expressed and why it is necessary for all of us to serve. Chap-

ter on "Doing and Learning" helpful for faculty and students in private liberal arts settings.

Schon, Donald. *The Reflective Practitioner: How Professionals Think in Action*, New York: BasicBooks, New York, New York, 1983; and *Educating the Reflective Practitioner*, San Francisco: Jossey-Bass, 1987.

Eloquent treatment of how practitioners learn from experience once they have completed their formal educational requirements and begin practicing their craft. Understanding the processes delineated by Schon's research will enhance the connections between academic learning and service-based learning. Critically important for graduate faculty involved in preparing professionals for service fields.

Howard, Jeff, Editor. *Praxis I: A Faculty Casebook on Community Service Learning* and *Praxis II: Service-Learning Resources for University Students, Staff, and Faculty*. Ann Arbor: OCSL Press (2205 Michigan Union, Ann Arbor, MI 48109), 1993.

University of Michigan faculty stories and reflections on their extensive experience arranging and evaluating service connected to academic courses for students. Lessons learned relate to linking academic disciplines to explicit community situations, lessons not unlike what private liberal arts college faculty face every day when they link service and learning. Two volumes packed with impressions and ideas based on working faculty in numerous disciplines who have thought deeply about the meaning and power of service-based learning.

Kraft, Richard J. and Swadener, Marc, editors. *Building Community: Service-Learning in the Academic Disciplines*. Denver, Colorado: Colorado Campus Compact (1391 N. Speer Blvd., Suite 200, Room A, Denver, Colo. 80204), 1994.

Faculty, primarily from Colorado institutions, share their philosophies; syllabi; bibliographies, and personal dilemmas in initiating and sustaining service linkages with academic courses. Very useful and extensive current bibliography concludes the book on pp. 247-276. In this and the University of Michigan books, the primary voices are those of faculty who have included service activities in their courses.

Hutchings, Pat and Wutzdorf, Allen, editors. *Knowing and Doing: Learning Through Experience*. San Francisco: Jossey-Bass, 1988.

Alverno College faculty articulate their understandings of experiential learning in this very readable book.

Care, Norman S. *On Sharing Fate*. Philadelphia, Temple University Press, 1987.

A philosophy professor introduces a notion of "shared-fate individualism" in light of a world crippled by destitution, gross inequalities in opportunity, and the meager attempts to address the destitution and inequality. Proposes a value that "other-responsibility" comes before "self-responsibility." As students, faculty, and community members face these dilemmas, this book offers a way to talk together about the meanings of "shared-fate individualism" for each of us.

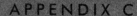

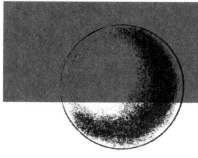

Hyde, Lewis, *The Gift*. New York: Vintage Books, 1979.

"What is good is given back." This phrase introduces this rather ponderous book about how different cultures interpret the giving and receiving of gifts, or in our language, services. In much service-based learning, the concept of reciprocity is used. This book offers a fascinating view of reciprocity, plus more food for thought as to why we engage in common acts of work and compassion.

Orr, David W. *Ecological Literacy: Education and the Transition to a Postmodern World*. Albany, N.Y.: State University of New York Press, 1992.

This book asks us to think institutionally and educationally about what we should be doing and learning given the limits of the Earth. As students and faculty engage community residents in common problem solving and learning, the reminders of the limited resources available for us all become increasingly important conversation topics. Reading this book will force conversations about the nature of education and the appropriateness of linking academic learning with the community through student service-based learning.

Schorr, Lisbeth B. *Within Our Reach: Breaking the Cycle of Disadvantage*. New York: Doubleday, 1988.

Presents case after case, experience after experience, where intention and action have been linked to create increased opportunity for citizens who previously had almost no opportunity to grow and develop. Look at these stories and see how your institution and students view these same realities of marginalized people and your own role in being alongside them as you both learn and serve.

Ignatieff, Michael. *The Needs Of Strangers: An Essay On Privacy, Solidarity, And The Politics Of Being Human*. New York; Penguin Books (Elisabeth Sifton Books), 1984.

Documents the breakdown of human solidarity and shows how it might be recreated. Here is a philosopher thinking out loud and potentially helping us come to terms with why service-based learning may be an urgent matter for our survival.

Stanton, Timothy K.. *Integrating Public Service with Academic Study: The Faculty Role: A Report of Campus Compact: The Project for Public and Community Service*. Providence, R.I.: Campus Compact (Brown University, Box 1975, Providence, R.I. 02912).

Title indicates the substance of this very useful report.

Section 3: **An older reference that still has something to say.**

Batchelder, Donald and Warner, Elizabeth, editors. *Beyond Experience: The Experiential Approach to Cross-Cultural Education*. Brattleboro, Vt.: The Experiment Press, 1977.

Rooted in the years of preparing and debriefing people learning in other cultures, this Experiment in International Living book outlines a sophisticated set of concepts and methodologies in cross-cultural education and training which can be useful to service-based learning programs in private liberal arts colleges. The book moves from concepts to practice to assessment, all based on practical experience rather than library research.

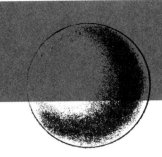

Section 4: **New Entries. As this book went to press in October 1996, we have learned of these additional resources:**

Kraft, Richard J. *Learning by Serving and Doing.* Special issue (vol. 28, no.2) of the journal *Education and Urban Society.* Thousand Oaks, Calif.: Sage Publications, February, 1996.

> A valuable contribution to the literature.

Jacoby, Barbara. *Service-Learning in Higher Education: Concepts and Practices.* San Francisco: Jossey-Bass Publishers, 1996.

> Combining theory, practice, and examples, this book is a comprehensive guide to developing high quality Service-Learning experiences both in the curriculum and through student affairs programs.

Stanton, Timothy, with Nadinne Cruz and Dwight E. Giles, Jr. *To Strengthen Service-Learning: Policy and Practice, Stories from the Field.* Palo Alto, Calif.: Stanford University, Haas Center for Public Service, 1996.

> A new resource from some of today's most thoughtful Service-Learning practitioners.

Zlotkowski, Edward. "Linking Service-Learning and the Academy: A New Voice at the Table?" in *Change* Magazine, January-February, 1996.

> A provocative magazine article.

Ray, David, editor. *Service-Learning: Listening to Different Voices.* Fairfax, Va.: The College Fund/ United Negro College Fund, 1995.

> Reports on experiences in Service-Learning at private historically black colleges and universities and the Ford Foundation/UNCF Community Service Partnership Project.

PART 2—ORGANIZATIONS

Contact these groups directly for information about current programs, books and other printed materials, and additional resources for Service-Learning.

The Bonner Scholars Program

A Model For AmeriCorps, Work-Study, And Community Service Scholarships

> Bonner Foundation, PO Box 712, Princeton, NJ 08542
> (609) 924-6663 office, (609) 683-4626 fax

The Bonner Scholar Program is one model for how colleges and universities can create their own community service scholarship program using AmeriCorps, Federal Work-Study, and/or private scholarship funds. Because of limited funds, the Bonner Scholar Program is not able to fund additional colleges and universities. However, the Foundation is eager to work with institutions as they replicate its model.

Campus Compact

> Campus Compact, c/o Brown University, Box 1975
> Providence, Rhode Island, 02912
> phone: (401) 863-1119
> fax: (401) 863-3779
> e-mail: campus@compact.org

Campus Compact: The Project for Public and Community Service is a coalition of more than 500 college and university presidents who believe that institutions of higher education have a primary responsibility to foster students' sense of civic respon-

sibility and to contribute to the welfare of their communities. The Compact works on the national level to cultivate public discourse and support for public and community service; develop resource materials, grant programs, workshops and institutes; and support a network of state compacts and two specialized offices, the Center for Community Colleges, based in Phoenix, and the Historically Black Colleges and Universities Network, based in Atlanta.

Campus Outreach Opportunity League (COOL)

1511 K Street, Suite 307, Washington, D.C. 20005
phone: (202) 637-7004; fax: (202) 637-7021

The Campus Outreach Opportunity League (COOL) is a national non-profit that works with college students to start, strengthen, and expand community service programs. Founded in 1984 and directed by recent college graduates, its mission is to educate and empower college students to strengthen our nation through community service.

Corporation for National Service

1201 New York Avenue, N.W.
Washington, D.C. 20525
(202) 606-5000
http://www.cns.gov

Created by Congress in 1993, the Corporation for National Service offers Americans of all ages and backgrounds opportunities to strengthen their communities through service. CNS programs include AmeriCorps, Learn and Serve America, and Senior Corps.

The Council of Independent Colleges

One Dupont Circle, Suite 320
Washington, D.C. 20036
(202) 466-7230
fax: (202) 466-7238
e-mail: cic@cic.nche.edu

Founded in 1956, the Council of Independent Colleges (CIC) is an international association of more than 400 independent liberal arts colleges and universities. CIC works with college presidents, academic deans, other administrators, and faculty to help its member institutions enhance educational programs, improve their administrative and financial performance, and increase their institutional visibility. The Council is known as both a source of practical advice for college leaders and as a resource of ideas for educational reform. A recent CIC project, *Learning to Serve, Serving to Learn,* was a $1.25 million effort to encourage a more institutionalized approach to student service. One product of that project is the book, *Journey to Service-Learning,* by Robert Sigmon and colleagues. CIC was also the chief sponsor of the 1995 National Institute on Learning and Service.

Ford/UNCF Community Service Partnership Project

c/o United Negro College Fund, Inc.
8260 Will Oaks Corporate Drive
Fairfax, VA 22031-4511
phone: (703) 205-3400; fax: (703) 205-3550

The Ford/UNCF Community Service Partnership Project, a project of the United Negro College Fund with funding from the Ford Foundation, is designed to promote productive partnerships among colleges, universities, and their surround-

ing communities, and to strengthen the role of community service in the academic curriculum.

National Society for Experiential Education

3509 Haworth Drive, Suite 207, Raleigh, N.C. 27609-7229
phone: (919) 787-3263; fax: (919) 787-3381
e-mail: info@nsee.datasolv.com
http://www.tripod.com/nsee/index.html

The National Society for Experiential Education is a membership organization and national resource center that supports the use of learning through experience for intellectual development, civic and social responsibility, career exploration, cross-cultural and global awareness, and ethical and leadership development. Among other services, NSEE publishes resources for Service-Learning, maintains a resource center, and offers consulting services.

The Partnership for Service-Learning

815 Second Ave., Suite 315, New York, N.Y. 10017-4594
phone: (212) 986-0989

Founded in 1982, the Partnership for Service-Learning is an incorporated, not-for-profit educational organization of colleges, universities, service agencies and related organizations united to foster and develop programs linking community service and academic study.

PART 3—INTERNET RESOURCES

From on-line discussion groups to relevant sites on the World Wide Web, the Internet is a rich source of information about Service-Learning. Since it would be impossible to list all the relevant sites, we chose three that have an abundance of links that should connect you to the information you seek.

SERVICE-LEARNING Home Page

http://csf.colorado.edu/sl

Rich resource, with connections to publications, articles, bibliographies, model programs and many other links to relevant Web sites.

National Service-Learning Cooperative Clearinghouse

http://www.nicsl.coled.umn.edu

Something of a K-12 focus, but many links to higher education sites, too.

Rutgers University Citizen and Service Education (CASE) Program

http://www.scils.rutgers.edu/case/case.html

Describes Rutgers' program. Has links to other Service-Learning sites, including many at colleges and universities.